On the Lookout

Other books by C.H. Sisson include

POETRY
The London Zoo
Numbers
Metamorphoses
In the Trojan Ditch
Anchises
Exactions
Collected Poems
Selected Poems
God Bless Karl Marx

FICTION
An Asiatic Romance
Christopher Homm

ESSAYS
The Spirit of British Administration
Art and Action
The Case of Walter Bagehot
English Poetry 1900–1950
David Hume
The Avoidance of Literature
Anglican Essays

TRANSLATIONS
Versions and Perversions of Heine
The Poetry of Catullus
Horace: The Poetic Art
Lucretius: The Poem on Nature
Some Tales of La Fontaine
The Song of Roland
Dante: The Divine Comedy
Du Bellay: The Regrets
Racine: Three Plays
Virgil: The Aeneid

ON THE LOOK-OUT

A PARTIAL AUTOBIOGRAPHY

C. H. Sisson

CARCANET

First published in 1989 by
Carcanet Press Limited
208-212 Corn Exchange Buildings
Manchester M4 3BQ

British Library Cataloguing in Publication Data

Sisson, C.H. (Charles Hubert), *1914-*
   On the lookout.
   1. Poetry in English, 1945-. Biographies
   I. Title
   821'.914'09

ISBN 0-85635-758-8

The Publisher acknowledges the financial support of
the Arts Council of Great Britain.

Typeset in 10pt Bembo by Bryan Williamson, Manchester
Printed in England by SRP Ltd, Exeter

Contents

The larks flew up like jack-in-the-boxes
From my moors, and the fields were edged with fox-gloves.

The farm lay neatly within the hollow
The gables climbing, the barn beside the doorway.

If I had climbed into the loft I should have found a boy
Forty years back, among the bales of hay.

He would have known certainly all that I know
Seeing it in the muck-strewn cobbles below.

(Under the dark rim of the near wood
The tears gathered as under an eye-lid.)

It would have surprised him to see a tall man
Who had travelled far, pretending to be him.

But that he should have been turning verses, half dumb
After half a life-time, would least have surprised him.

Preface

ONE DAY in February I found myself on the banks of the River Parrett, just below the windows of my house on Langport Hill. There was an icy wind, but I was not allowed to move out of it. I was awaiting the pleasure of a team of film makers who at that moment were haunting this corner of Somerset like the wild swans who are more commonly seen there. I was ultimately to appear for a few seconds before the camera, walking along the river bank, but in the meantime the team were stalking the swans in one of the pools still left in the frozen river. They were delayed by the reluctance of their prey to stage the spectacular take-off the director had in mind for them. I grew colder.

The bits of Somerset which interested the director included some which had made their way into my poems. Besides the immediate area of my present residence – a particular oak tree, a few acres of the levels which I know well – there was the area about Burrington Combe, which is not only the point of reference for a late sequence of poems, but the explicit subject of a poem, "Ellick Farm", written after a fleeting visit to the periphery of that house some thirty years ago, when I was working in London. Under the aegis of the film-makers – a more prestigious class than poets – I was allowed to mooch around the old stone-work and even to climb into the loft I had known as a child.

In real life, the scene-shifting has been more complicated. I tried to evoke some scraps of it, years ago, in two manuscripts which have remained unpublished. The earlier was the first piece of continuous writing I undertook after my release from the army in 1945. It deals with the two and a half years I had spent in India. What happened to me there reflects no military glory. My account of these events does, however, give fleeting pictures, if not of India – herself too multifarious to be seen – at least of a world which could have been seen only by a British Other Rank in the closing years of the Raj. The later manuscript dates from a time when I worked in a room in St James's Square. It was an account of the first fifty years of my life, including, rather summarily, my time in India. It could have been called a straightforward piece of autobiography, but for the fact that, as in my then still unpublished novel, the story was told backwards. It began in 1964 and ended in 1914. As I had arrived nowhere, I could not decently end with the later date. It could hardly be denied, however, that something of significance had happened to me in 1914; I had been born.

It seemed to me that both narratives were worth bringing to the light of day, for the sake of the past scenes they represented if not for the sake of the author. It was a small matter to excise the sections of the 1964 manuscript which cannibalized the Indian story, but that left a gap which spoiled the sequence. The Indian interlude was short, but it had an importance beyond what the time-scale suggested. It had taken me beyond Europe for the first time; it was also the first time that I wrote poems since I had given up that folly at the age of twenty. I decided that the best way to account for the period would be to insert in its chronological place in the autobiography what I had written in 1946-7. So in Part II of this volume time moves forward instead of backward; the perspectives are different; the narrative is told in the third person, as if by this sleight-of-hand I could distance myself from the incommunicable dream I had lived through. But with *One Eye on India* the story of my life would have its true middle in the war which for me, as in one way or another for most people of my generation, is the Great Divide.

So that is how it is. *On the Lookout* is the story of a man who, after some resistance had to admit to being a poet. The scenes and reflections here displayed – whether from St James's Square, from a commuter train, from a sergeants' mess, from among the Storm Troopers of Hitler's Germany or from a Bristol elementary school in the 1920s – all have their part, sometimes overt but more often covert, in the *Collected Poems 1943-83* (1984) or in *God Bless Karl Marx* (1987). This explains the title of the book, and it is with a view to illustrating the connections that I have interleaved the chapters of Part II with poems written at the time it relates to, and added at the end of each of the chapters of Parts I and III a line or two which might not have existed if I had not lived through the time in question.

I   Pretensions

I HAVE the greatest difficulty in believing in the existence of human personality, and I hardly know what sort of thing it would be, if it did exist. That there are people – men and women, conveniently classified as such – I can of course see as well as the next man. But it is evident that when people talk of themselves they are thinking of something quite different. If they are right I must have, or be, something of the same kind. I find it easier to believe in God than in the existence of personality. That puts some difficulties in the way of an autobiography.

I can at least describe to you the room in which I am writing. It looks out on tree-tops – a group of silver birches, a great ornamental pine, of a kind I cannot classify, in the background chestnuts. There is also one bit of roof and a chimney-pot. And blue sky, though you could not count on that. On one wall there is a drawing or two. There are a lot of books, including a complete set of Johnson's poets, though that is an accident; my brother happened to find them in a piece of furniture he bought at a sale. Yet I suppose that we are already beyond the reach of pure accident, for the effect of their being here was produced by the solid cause that I was known to be a willing recipient of that sort of thing. Most of the other books have come to me by the same sort of attraction – not as gifts, but they have stuck to me as to a fly-paper as I have perambulated through bookshops. By that I mean that they are almost all books to which I at one time or another adhered, not that I have taken any of them without payment. Indeed I have suffered some of my most noticeable moral agonies in bookshops, hesitating to spend on my passions money which could be conceived of as already appropriated by my duties. These anxieties have of late years been much abated. My duties have become so expensive that books seem cheap by comparison. You might notice the works of de Quincey, in fourteen volumes, which David Wright pointed out to me only a year or two ago at Beach's bookshop in Salisbury; the works of the Rev William Law, in nine volumes, found in London; Hooker, Berkeley, Blackstone's *Commentaries*; volumes of Kafka bought in Berlin, Munich or Freiburg in 1935; Proudhon as well as Maurras, mostly bought in Paris before the war. The English poets (apart from the specialist collection I have mentioned) are downstairs, outside my bedroom door. And on the ground floor you will find Wyndham Lewis, Ford Madox Ford, the *Diary* of Samuel Pepys. There is no rhyme or reason about this collection, nor much in the selection of the odd few I have chosen to name. In the hall there is also a small drawing by Henry Moore, and a bronze bird. There is also a brush drawing by Gaudier-Brzeska.

11

It is the periphery of London. As a *bourgeois* area *on ne peut plus*, I suppose. An unlimited number of house-agents grow rich on buying and selling houses for a changing population of commuters. The inhabitants grow rich, and move into farmhouses further out. Or they grow rich, and move into flats in town. Or their children grow up, and they move into smaller houses anywhere. Or they retire – the great object they spend forty years in pursuit of – and move to wherever their hopes are finally to be deceived. Meanwhile the *pères de famille* – almost all, I have noticed, men of remarkably reliable appearance – make for the station each morning and find each morning almost the same place on the same train. Any rearrangement of the coaches which results in a smoker being where a non-smoker should be, a first where a second should be, or an open coach where there should be compartments, understandably gives them cause for concern. Naturally I share these feelings. We are all very anxious not to notice life. Or, supposing we have personalities, we want to keep them wrapped up for use on some other occasion. I am not clear when it would be.

Of course while we are in London our wives and families dominate the town. I know very little about this world, except that the motor car plays an important part in it. One assumes that what is left, when the morning train moves out, is the society for the maintenance of which this daily voyage is undertaken. There is the war memorial, the public library – not a very good one –, the High Street with its shops, several churches. These things, one supposes, are there all day, though really one has no proof of it. There may even be some sort of society in the evenings, for those who get home early enough. I have seen posters and pictures in the local paper indicating that there have been amateur performances of Gilbert and Sullivan. Of all these things I know nothing. They set the tone, however.

My knowledge of the town would be better if I played golf. Come to think of it, the omission has been a basic error, but at fifty, and with my addiction to other pursuits, I can hardly put it right now. Once or twice on the golf course – which I occasionally cross carrying a jam-jar to catch tadpoles or, more often, merely on my way to visit the deer – my presence has been acknowledged by people quite unknown to me in their disguises but whom I take to be men I should say good morning to in the train.

Weekends are the time for religion, for the few who practise it. As it happens, my role has become that of a disturber of the peace, and if I have not disturbed it much that only shows how faint my impact on the town has been. I have sometimes walked out in the middle of

sermons, being unable to stomach any more. I have given the mem
bers of the Parochial Church Council the benefit of my opinion in
circular letters; I have even written to the local paper and to the parish
magazine, and it has been indicated to me that my contributions to
the latter are not welcome. With the help of someone much more
long-suffering than I, I even organized an address to the rector, signed
by people from each of the four parishes in the town, and making a
very modest and orthodox proposal. This document the rector refused
even to discuss with the signatories. It will be evident that I am not
very persuasive. The members of the P.C.C. are chosen for their
sectarian opinions, and for the simple parishioner the position is somewhat like that of a man who happens to belong to a trade union branch
which is run by Communists. The parish is one to make Papists laugh,
and Anglicans weep unless, like me, they expect comedy in the
Church Militant. So I go on among these straggling grotesques, who
come straight from the pages of *Hudibras*. I have always liked the bit
in the Puritan *Directory* about the Burial of the Dead. After a few tips
about how to get the body underground "without any ceremony...
kneeling down,...other such usages...reading, singing" without
anything, in fact, which would dignify the poor relic or remind those
present that they too have bodies, it is provided:

> That this shall not extend to deny any civil respects or differences
> at the burial, suitable to the rank and condition of the party deceased
> whilst he was living.

This parish church is rich; its income has gone up considerably over
the last few years; and the rector reads prayers under a tablet which
recalls that one of his predecessors was John Donne.

From one of the cages on the periphery

MY train journey ends at Charing Cross, and I walk across the north
side of Trafalgar Square. It was here that I was accosted, a few months
ago, by a French grandmother (not mine), completely spherical, who
had been launched out of a small Renault by an equally monolingual
youth. What she wanted to know, pointing at the top of the column
which graces the square, was this:
"C'est bien Napoléon là-haut?"
From Trafalgar Square I go along Pall Mall, up Lower Regent
Street, along Charles II Street, and so to St James's Square – when I
do not delay my arrival at the office by going up Charing Cross Road,

along the south side of Leicester Square, across Whitcombe village and finally into Jermyn and Duke of York Streets. It is the variety and comparative squalor, as well as the delay of this route which pleases me. It would be an extraordinary defection if I strayed further than that on the way to the office. The whole operation, from the moment of getting up, is less a series of choices than a process of being sucked by a vacuum cleaner which has the unusual capacity of drawing in circuitously the rubbish it picks up.

When I am deposited at my desk I become, as nearly as may be, purely functional. Outside the windows, which are spacious, there are trees, and an equestrian William III turned, it is said, towards the Boyne. More seductively, one can see the London Library in a corner of the Square. My eye never strays to these things for more than a second. Nor to the paintings by Patrick Swift which hang on the walls, though to one of those I have reverted, in a series of seconds spread over years which must make up quite a respectable time in total. My entry into the office is rather like that of a garment into a spin dryer. Until I am switched off the forces at play around me determine all my movements. I can remember, when I first went to work in an office, waiting for the end of the day. Now the day is no sooner begun than ended. It is certainly an efficient way of passing the time. This extraordinary phenomenon, in the like of which thousands spend their days in every great city in the world, has no literature of its own. People continue to write about love, as if that were the main occupation of our days, or even crime, as if the activities of those lunatics of sobriety who, like myself, for hours each day link themselves up to a system, counted for nothing. It may be because we, who do these things, are by definition already safe. The problem of the world is getting everything equally well organized. That the pockets of resistance are generally felt to be more interesting than the organized structures which, after all, are the characteristic achievements of the human race, shows how deep-seated the indiscipline is. Yet to all appearance the order of an organization like mine is satisfactory. Throughout the country twenty thousand people carry out each day the tasks appointed for them, or something bearing a close enough resemblance to those tasks for no one to notice. The crimes and defections of the participants are minimal, their persistence in their tasks astonishing. For the most part they are people who find no great difficulty in keeping regular hours, performing tasks assigned to them, sleeping regularly with the same partners. There are people who can do none of these things, but our kind of fun is not for them. We can rely on one another, we get our money regular; we make, one way and another, an infuriating phalanx to people who are without these really common gifts.

It is not to be supposed, however, that we have not the art of infuriating one another. The great organizations of our time, like the camps and courts of our ancestors, engage the passions profoundly. All kinds of victory have to be fought for, and you are unlikely to win unless you know your man as well as your subject. Of course knowing your man, and knowing your subject, mean in this context knowing how to operate them. No absolute understanding is required for the despatch of business. But the professor's understanding of his subject is likewise only what will impress, in his world. And the persistent amorist does not necessarily understand women better than others do; he is better at operating them, that is all. I draw this red herring across the page merely to reassure myself that time in the office is not all lost, that human life, whatever that may be, is played out there as well as in the scenes which make the subject of the television plays.

The social vices of sexual indiscipline, drunkenness, lying and thieving, are played down in these strange monasteries only to make room – it goes without saying – for ambition, love of power, mere inability to see the object of discourse. I have little sympathy with ambition, which except in the sturdiest characters distorts the perceptions as nothing else does, and leads to various forms of betrayal – great or small as the opportunity offers. Love of power it is impossible to be free of, at any rate in the diminished form of love of importance. When I was given my present job – which was announced to me out of the blue in a perfect style for such things, in a minor key, almost off-hand – I was for weeks in a state of elated incredulity. I was beginning to exercise a power much greater than I had ever exercised before; there was nothing I particularly wanted to do with it, but the importance of it was intoxicating. The intoxication soon abated, but should I now accommodate myself to a more junior position? There is of course a sense in which it is difficult to hold a senior position – it means a pressure of work quite unlike that to be found in even the busier jobs lower down. But there is a sense in which life near the top is easier. One's own odd ways of thinking become things that other people have to accommodate themselves to, instead of merely things one has always to be painfully bending to fit the devices of some superior. There is the exhilarating possibility that what one thinks may happen; but this is a fear as well as an exhilaration, for very few thoughts can safely be acted upon. Part of the business of being fifty, with some years of service behind one, is that one has some

15

perception of the possible. I hope I have not given an exaggerated view of the grandeurs and servitudes of my position. These things are relative – and that goes for situations much more eminent than mine.

One delusion which enters easily into the head of the man in a position of power is that the more or less acquiescence which surrounds him signifies approval. In earlier years, I had the impression that at least one holder of my present office was a tyrant of the most irresponsible kind. The main evidence for this was his apparent distrust of, perhaps even contempt for, myself. There is no way now of testing how subjective my impressions of him were. But it is certain that the effects, from which I drew my conclusions, have their counterparts in the office now that I am responsible for these things, and that there must be people to whom my own reign seems tyrannical and unjust. The only remedy for injustice is to win, and that is not something that everyone can do. At any rate if one has been an oppressor, as well as being oppressed, one has a clearer notion of these relationships.

First, there is the folly of earning money
In order to have what is called independence

I DO not belong to one of those clubs in Pall Mall which are the lunchtime habitat of a number of my colleagues. I eat in the canteen, where messengers and senior officials are served from the same hot-plate and share the same crumby tables. If I go out to lunch, it is to enter a different universe of discourse. But having escaped from my stream of visitors, telephone calls, meetings, on the occasions when I do get more than the minimal eating space I am not anxious to talk to anyone. Of course in the canteen one does talk, with a conversation always bordering on shop, but one can escape from that quickly and into the street. The fascination of streets is in anonymity. It is the human race, *tout court*, that one observes there. Of course one sees people one knows, coming out of the crowd, but that is rather an irruption from the world of identities, or pretended identities, which spoils the pleasure of anonymous perambulation. Of course this emergence, if it is sufficiently unexpected, can bring its own pleasure. I was walking the other day out of Soho into Shaftesbury Avenue when a soft-spoken gentleman with a velvet coat collar drew up beside me and addressed me by my name. I cannot tell you from what a different world he came, or how long it was since I had seen him. Within a stone's throw of Piccadilly I have met, at various times, several figures who would

16

never have separated themselves from the crowd had we not once, wearing the same uniform, sailed in the same ship or sweated around the same camp, which is enough to give the illusion, or it may be the perception, of something in common.

Sometimes I wander into the picture galleries of Bond Street and around. I know nothing about painting, but then many people who know nothing about writing know what they like, and why not? Apart from the ineluctable defect of not practising the art of painting, I have a great ignorance of the past, like the public for whom the literary pages of the Sunday newspapers are written (that is to say, I know a *little* about it, I am educated you see). It is occasionally borne in upon me, when I look at some good work by an older master, that much modern work that I have taken for good is trivial. However I do not regret my occasional purchases of pictures, for one learns something by the simple test of durability, if one lives with a picture. My natural tropism, however, is towards the secondhand bookshops of the Charing Cross Road. Here I move as an expert. I do not know what I am looking for but I know when I have found it. My knowledge of the editions of all the more valuable productions of the English poets, miscellanists, producers of odds and ends, theological, biographical, what have you, would make me a respectable bookseller in no time. After a glance over the shelves I know infallibly whether a bookseller is one to be taken seriously, and whether he is cheap or dear. But I look only for books that can be read, and in order to read them; the bibliophile who is a sort of stamp-collector is nothing to me. I have one friend whose mode of operating in bookshops I recognize as exactly of the same kind as my own, but I do not wish to introduce his name too often.

There is also the London Library. It would be impossible to exaggerate the value of this institution. Certainly for someone with no time to sit in the British Museum, to be able to walk among the shelves any day and come out with ten books under your arm is, at any rate, a preventive against the worst illiteracy.

But I must get back to the office. A certain modesty, as well as prudence, prevents me from telling you much about it – as it prevents one recounting at all circumstantially one's domestic arrangements. It would be fair to say, however, that to my colleagues collectively I owe a large part of my education, which has consisted in the suppression of my private interests. When I first entered this establishment, years ago, I did not hesitate to talk to people about the things that interested me – about Dante or about Tourneur, if I happened to be reading them. I then learned that it was no business of theirs what I

17

read, and that the thoughts to be cultivated were those which were generally accepted as such and so of some practical use. The other kind of thought worth cultivating (but privately) was that which explained the mechanism of public behaviour. For many years life in the office seemed to me to be a sort of tight-rope turn; it consisted wholly of trying to move in accordance with laws imposed by the circus-master. It is not that the circus-master was wrong and I was right; but after all he knew what would make one fall off the rope and if the laws of nature didn't, he could give you a push. So I learned simultaneously to keep my counsel and to do as I was bid. Of late years the situation is somewhat different, but I wonder how much? Certainly I feel more at ease; there are fewer people I have to please and more people who have to please me. I can alter a number of things to my liking – but it is not really my liking, but to the laws of operation of this kind of enterprise, which I have perceived, or am held to have perceived because I am now one of the persons who can legitimately alter them.

But anyone who has had to do with the running of an organization of any size will know that the freedom of choice is small, that direction consists in an infinite multitude of little adjustments, carefully and tiresomely prepared, and not in the carefree abandonment to the will which is sometimes supposed to go with the word "boss". If people don't see my jokes, so much the worse for them. But my poems, written at odd moments in trains, in my room or on the staircase at home, or while walking through the town, represent a world quite different from the one I have learned to inhabit in the office. So in principle I remain organized as a dichotomy, only each term in the contrast is more rigorously drawn than before. There is some going and coming between these several worlds, however. All the disturbances of superficial life settle in the end like a sediment on the bottom of the lake – the level at which, if at all, poems are constructed. And then not all discourse about business is superficial. In the judgement of men and events there are junctures at which one touches deep below the surface of opinion. It is these junctures which make the fascination of business for a man of intelligence. There is such a thing as a genius for affairs, though it is very rarely found. It is something like the operation of a plumb-line, testing the depths, while the ordinary man of ability sails on. The man of ability may sail on and come like a fool to port, with a career in which nothing has gone wrong. So many chances prevent the detection of fraud – I mean fraud of quality – in the conduct of affairs. But the difference between this smooth sailor, so quick to turn his plastic boat around, and the man with the plumb-line, is absolute. It is of the same kind as the difference between the writer everybody reads, for ten years, and the writer some people read, over a hundred years or more. I suppose this is not surprising. There is one reality, if there is one at all.

About your table three or four who beg
Bully or trade

OCCASIONALLY after the office – on a Friday evening, most commonly, when the pressure ahead gives for a day or two, with any luck – I go to a pub where I may meet poets. More specifically, I go to meet David Wright, and if there are any others it is because they are circulating about him. David is certainly one of the most accomplished men of letters of the age – though the expression is one he disapproves of. He exhibits, in the field of letters, the same surefootedness, and the same absolute freedom from theory and other nonsense, that I have encountered in the odd administrative wizard in Whitehall. I mean that while an ordinary literary man, and an ordinary civil servant, might be expected to make pretty poor company for one another, one can imagine, at the level of competence of which I am talking, the two oddities being brought together and being merely interested in one another's proceedings. I do not mean that you would mistake David for a civil servant. It would not surprise you to be told, if you saw him leaning against a bar, that he is a poet. If you know nothing about poetry you would recognize the practical features of his attire – a sheepskin jacket with the pockets bulging with manuscripts or books – as easily as you might, if you knew nothing about Whitehall, recognize the civil servant by his bowler hat and rolled umbrella. If on the other hand you knew about poetry – and this, I am afraid, is a less probable hypothesis – you would recognize from the first gesture, certainly from the first words, that you were in the presence of *l'authenticité, le seul luxe*, as de Montherlant – himself less certainly authentic – called it. For a moment one might be shaken into believing in the existence of the human personality. If there is such a thing, this would be a specimen. Whether or not there is such a thing, there is, under the name of David Wright, a literary instrument of precision. The electronic device which has not yet been invented, for detecting the faulty rhythm or the unsuitable word – this is it, with a sympathetic dial placed between the sheepskin jacket and the turbulent white hair. Consequently if I have a poem which needs testing, I bring it along to the pub with me. Or I post it

19

to the mechanism beforehand, and with a slow movement he brings it out of the sheepskin pocket and, smoothing it on the bar, points an accusing finger, infallibly, to what will not do.

Among the minor advantages of the David Wright machine, derived from long use as editor, anthologist, friend of every poet worth knowing and student of and in the pubs of Soho and beyond, is its value as an indicator to the inexperienced traveller in the literary world. My education in this department had been neglected until a very late stage and – the machine taking the initiative – I was propelled round a series of pubs in the hope of effecting the necessary introductions. After getting back one draught Guinness the machine would become restive; its tentacles would shake as if it were the victim of some tropical storm. The dial would register a profound disquiet, and the machine would charge out into the road, completely out of control. It would walk into the middle of the traffic, quite unaware that no man with ears, and a normal sense of self-preservation, could follow. The trouble would be that X or Y, poets, who should have been drinking at that pub, were not. They were not at the French pub, but they might be at the Plough: they were not at the Plough, might they not be at the Salisbury? I never learned my lesson very well and I may not have got the names right.

At last we would reach a haven in which, perhaps, Patrick Kavanagh was brooding uncertainly in a haze of whisky and tobacco smoke, pretending that he was not thinking of his bog and that he was not the peasant poet of Ireland. I would be instructed in the proper way of approaching the master – which is with a large whisky in one's outstretched hand. When I first conducted this ceremony I do not think the poet had, in the hand not holding the whisky, the little glass of stomach powder which became his other defence against the evils of the world. It was always a little difficult to determine whether there was a look of recognition in that glazed eye. Was it therefore me he was addressing when, once, he told me that he was willing to tolerate certain poems of mine? I replied that I greatly admired certain things he had written, but I could see at once that was the wrong reply. That I should admire the works of the Irish sage, that was *selbstverständlich*; it was an impertinence for me to say so; he could not have taken my whisky had it been otherwise; but when he said he had tolerated certain poems of mine (whether or not it was me he was in fact addressing from the recesses of his smoke-laden cabin) he was conferring something, and the only correct attitude would have been that of one evidently sensible that something was being conferred. I do not question the propriety of these Irish judgements; I give them merely as a trait of character, for that is what Kavanagh would be said to have. Or if Kavanagh were not run to earth, we might reach a point in our peregrination in which David would point out MacBryde or would be almost on the point of seeing Colquhoun, though painters were not strictly in our line. Somehow the ambience was always creeping in upon us. Indeed David, himself a South African and married to a New Zealander, Phillipa Reid, used to allege that I was the only person of impeccable English ancestry he knew. I had to explain that the race was becoming extinct.

David's *piece de résistance*, which was often about to be produced but in the end was reported in some pub just out of reach, or in Rome performing the rites of fatherhood yet once more, was George Barker. There was one evening in the Red Lion, almost opposite my office, when this prodigy at last appeared, wearing a check suit and cap, all very new, as if in the course of an attempt to prove that he was not a poet but a bookmaker. The attempt could not be successful, however, for half a sentence made it plain that one was in the presence of a profound and subtle humourist. I was presented to George Barker as being a poet, a claim which he must often have heard advanced and which he would not be imprudent enough to receive without scepticism. But he enquired after my small poems, as it seemed to me, with charm and benignity. He has long been used to the adulation of the young, and he could not expect the same from me, not far off from being his contemporary. Although he can hardly have known it, he was, however, in the presence of something rarer. For, already on the declining side of forty-five, I had not then published a volume of verse and, in spite of the initial treatment I had already received at David's hands, I was still ingenuous enough to think of poets as people who wrote books, and it had hardly occurred to me that one could meet – save by the merest accident – the bearers of one of the names which had been larger than life for me since my student days. George Barker was, in fact, the first of those names ever to come to life for me in that way, casually, at a bar. I have not exaggerated my ingenuousness in the matter of literary society, though I do not claim a similar ingenuousness for what I had by that time written. I believe it was on this occasion that I first met Patrick Swift. Dom Moraes certainly passed that way on the same evening, then I suppose really in that dewy youth which has since become permanent, wearing dark glasses and a beatific smile and propelling before him, as I remember, two young ladies.

The order of this history is getting a little awry, but the chapter will serve to indicate that other range of facts within my awareness (though here it is I who am peripheral): the world of poets, men of letters who regard themselves as such, in contradistinction to myself who, if asked what I am, will reply by naming the calling which brings me the most money. The evening at the Red Lion – I expect because George Barker turned up – appears in my memory as in some sort a stone dropped in a pond, making a circle which as it extended embraced John Heath-Stubbs, Brian Higgins, Anthony Cronin – enough to make me appreciate the force of Patrick Kavanagh's definition of a poet as an original of which in time there are millions of copies. For each of these people was, in some sort, a new invention. Incidentally I find it difficult to see why, with Heath-Stubbs in the offing, David Wright should ever have regarded me as the only man of unarguably English ancestry within his circle of acquaintance.

If we have reasons, they lie deep

I MET today, in a village I hold too dear to mention but which looks out on the Vale of Blackmore, a man who in fact was the English residue. Seventy at least, he was astride an old horse – thirty years old, he told me – bareback, with a bit of rope for a bridle. He had bought the horse in Sherborne twenty-nine years before. He did not like to see an animal suffer that had worked for him. He had had one or two like that. There was a mare he had buried up in that field there. She had had lockjaw, and the vet in Blandford thought she was finished. She was stiff as a board. But she had come round, and in the end had died of old age. He had seen the last of her. To see the last of an animal that had served him seemed to be a duty he had put upon himself. No doubt he would bury that old horse in the meadow too, if he outlived him. Had we been in the church? I had often been there, and we talked about the Book of Homilies in a glass case of which you can get the key at the rectory. My interlocutor told me about a recent arrival in the village – "a Roman Catholic, I had wished he had been Church of England". I approved this regret for a man who could never be more than a foreigner, in English terms. My interlocutor said that if he had to choose (a communion other than the Church) it would be Wesleyan; he had worshipped with them with some of his family in Shaftesbury. "It is a pity if we don't all worship the same Maker, the place we're going." I went into the pub and drank two pints of beer while a young butcher from Sturminster Newton described how he had ejected certain rowdy characters – they were Yeovil men I think – from the bar at the Legion. "Out." And he demonstrated with his knee how it was done.

This country which persists – ever more faintly – under the technological England which is the centre of my daily calculations, can still be visited but it recedes before discovery. The fury of destruction is immense, and it is held to be outrageous not to believe – not least for one who earns his living as I do – that economic good resides in the destruction of our assets. There is little to be done about this except not to believe what one is supposed to. In this Dorset, to which I retreat as often as I can and where I have a cottage which makes that possible, there are enough green tracks left for one to be put in mind frequently of the time – more recent than one can easily believe – when roads were not metalled and natural ills found the body more defenceless. It is sobering to reflect on the modest scale of things in the seventeenth century. A book like the *Proceedings of the Dorset Standing Committee* – the parliamentary committee which, during the rebellion, supervised the sequestration of the livings and livelihoods of loyal persons – makes it alive. One shows the members of the committee coming and going, to Dorchester or Blandford, to settle the claims of the wives and families of ejected parsons to a fifth of the stipend – a tiny provision which the incoming Puritan preacher seems quite often to have been unwilling to pay. Or one can see in Walker's *Suffering of the Clergy* the Puritan troops coming into a parsonage and putting the baby son of the place to roast in a pan before the fire – only a playful bit of torture probably, because a woman came into the room and was allowed to snatch up the child and carry it off in her apron.

This small, discreet England of particular events lives still under the reign of technological processes, but it is as if the country had developed a carapace. Literature worth making is made far under this carapace; my own arrangements – by no clever design but the way things have worked out – provide for such writing as I do to shoot out, if it can't be helped, in such moments as are missed by the forces which organize my life as administrator and *père de famille*. This scheme is carried so far that I recognize that I have a duty to cut the grass, which I do not think necessary, and regard the writing of books as a frivolity which must come last on a long list of priorities. Put another way, the most serious concerns of my life – which is what my writing, in one way or another, is about – have little connection with the life I ordinarily lead. There are of course literary saints – dervishes perhaps would be a better word – who live on the assumption that there are not two worlds but one. But even Brian Higgins did not succeed in filling the world with his subjective vision, which would mean not only the general removal of the epidermis, but everyone standing round with silver spoons feeding the poet and saying to one another that he deserves every spoonful because he is a poet.

The attachment to a vanishing past is generally held to be a mark of inability to see the shape of the present. It is, however, an element in our sense of being human – though it may be that that is a luxury we are about to abandon. It is not peculiar to our own days. What will be peculiar will be the days without it. For the moment, what interests me is my identity with the men who made the giant of Cerne Abbas. Drayton in *Polyolbion* bemoaned the destruction of forests. It may be that civilization is the product of a certain tension between man and his natural surroundings. At certain stages of his destructive progress it is about right. The terrifying thing about our age is that, in this battle between ourselves and the rest of nature, we are about to win. You have to think very highly of the human race to believe that that is a good thing.

For now I know, only the past is true

WHEN I had been a week in the house of which I have described one room and the entrance hall, I went off to Geneva for a month and left my wife to sort things out. This was not a deliberate act of policy, though it had the air of being one. For several years I was in the habit of going to Geneva for conferences and committees of varying magnitudes. At the conference of greatest magnitude there might be a thousand delegates, advisers and the like obstructing one another in the committee rooms and *couloirs* of the Palais des Nations. This scene of so many political imbecilities would be fitted up with all the well-known paraphernalia of the international conference. One went to one's place, put on the headphones, and adjusted the switch to listen to whatever oratory was going on, either in the original language or in one of the recognized interpretations. The translators, impassive behind glass except on the rare occasions when, behind glass, they grew distracted or contemptuous, carried out their duties, it would seem, in a sort of trance. They showed signs of coming out of their trance only if there was a technical hitch or the orator got beside himself or lost his way, when one might in exasperation (or it may be only with deliberate intent to preserve his professional reputation) say: "I can't follow, he's lost himself, he's talking nonsense". With certain orators one could switch off for ten minutes or half an hour at a time, keeping the headphones on to preserve appearances, and go on with one's correspondence or read the *Journal de Genève*.

At every conference new nations appeared; they would be people who, in the language of the century, had just been liberated. The representatives of these countries, speaking in the language of the European power by which they had recently been oppressed or liberated, – generally both – have as a class a notably derivative style of political sentiment. The amateur of pre-war European politics will recognize at once the social-democratic style. The right thinking of the pre-war European left has, by and large, made its home in these heads and bosoms – though the performance is coloured by provincial blood and passions, rather as one imagines the oratory of the more outlandish demagogues in the days when the Roman Empire was drawing its energy from the outer reaches. In the *couloirs* and the cocktail party these usually lively and charming representatives of what are called "new" countries rarely disclose the things one would like to know. They are full of their hydro-electric schemes, broadcasting stations and other European detritus which they have learned to regard as the proper accompaniments of power, but reticent about the things by which they differ from Europe and through which alone they are likely to make any contribution to the civilization of the future, if there is to be one. The giant trauma of Africa, the suppression from consciousness of her real life, looks like becoming the great destructive force of the next fifty years.

The other group which, when one first begins to frequent international conferences, one expects to find interesting is of course that formed by the Russians and their associates. I greatly regretted not being able to follow any of these gentlemen in their native language; a man of letters, however profoundly suppressed by present business his interests might be, is bound to regret acutely the lack of those involuntary indications which can only be acquired by listening to the inflections of actual speech. I cannot imagine that much of the Communist oratory at international conferences is very interesting in any language, but in the flat interpretations of the gifted linguists in the glass boxes it is, generally speaking, dull in the extreme. The deadening effect which bureaucratic caution and the need for endless consultation are apt to have on the pronouncements of British officials is to be seen, in these Communist speeches, as a vast incrustation of speech. Of course in some ways the speeches of Russians are very unlike those of the *Royaume-Uni*. In place of the gentlemanly chill they favour the abusive word. But it is a regulation abuse they use; it is rarely incalculable, and so fails of poetic effect. The briefing of

25

Communist delegates is usually on a scale which makes our own look amateurish. Briefs are generally so boring that on the whole I was grateful for our comparative amateurism. The real arcana of the international conference are, of course, procedural and the Russians are great students of all the ways of making life difficult for their opponents. Whatever the nominal subject under discussion everybody is really engaged, after all, in a rollicking game of keeping his end up, and on this abstract ground at least the nations have found a common interest. The notion that international conferences increase understanding between peoples is not one that is likely to appeal to anyone with an inkling of what peoples, or people for that matter, are likely to have to say. Strictly speaking such conferences have nothing to do with understanding at all. They are a *performance*; or rather, a bit of technological arrangement necessary for co-*operation*. Essentially they do the same work as the consultations which go on in any big organization; they keep the thing going, but as to where it is going, that is another matter.

The smaller meetings which I also used to attend at Geneva about this time often took place in a building in some ways even more notable than the Palais for its social-democratic ethos. The peculiarity of this establishment is the profusion of hulking forms in paint or, more indestructibly, in metal, symbolizing a labour which is becoming extinct and an amity which is not yet noticeable. The only comparable series of grotesques known to me, as deifications of prejudice, is the row of German emperors which before the war decorated the Siegesallee in Berlin. Decidedly, nineteenth- and twentieth-century Europe has not been happy in its ideals, as they are called, if the grace of their expression is any indication of their quality, as I believe it is.

I pass in silence the Bergues and the Beau-Rivage, hotels which, in various capacities, I inhabited as a member of United Kingdom delegations. My wish – too rarely achieved – was to leave these establishments as well as the conference rooms behind and wander across the river while the bookshops were still open. Geneva has a number of good ones. They are not all across the river; there are indeed two in the neighbourhood of the Hotel Beau-Rivage which are excellent and to which I owe, among other things, my splendid quatercentenary edition of Ronsard and one or two odd volumes of René Béhaine – would that I could find the lot. But to cross the Rhône in full daylight, with the windows of the Bergues scowling on my back, represented an exodus from the world of international obfuscation and pseudo-communication to human life in a less perverted condition. The Rhône is impressive at the weir leading out of the lake; and on the lake side itself you can watch such trout as have not yet been caught and served *en beurre* by Monsieur Piguet. On the other side of the Rhône there is also the old town – Geneva proper – which remains as the prim centre of this city of international luxury. Well, perhaps prim will be thought not to be the word, for the place is infested by the usual nightclubs and restaurants for the international gang, and there is the Cave du Hot-Club. There is also the university, and cafés in which young men and women of several nationalities act out a pre-fabricated European Student Life. The residual inhabitants of Geneva are said to keep to themselves, with a sort of Edinburgh reserve, only giving the international gang as much attention as is necessary in order to make money out of them. I cannot say that I think that that is an unintelligent policy. The *Journal de Genève* occasionally gives glimpses of this autochthonous world; one may read there of the horror properly excited by young people wearing masks and disguises to celebrate the *Escalade*. I have never known too precisely what happened on the night of the *Escalade*, but there was a scaling of the walls of the city with results which were very good for the Calvinist cause, the independence of the Genevois (though how good it is to become independent depends on what you are becoming independent of, and who you are who become independent) and ultimately for the commerce of the international city. The Genevois are not forgetful of these blessings. One night by accident, in the neighbourhood of the desecrated cathedral – for extreme Protestants hate their church buildings – I came across what was surely the most native of Genevois bourgeoisie, on horseback and got up to kill in the costume of the sixteenth century. There was torchlight and a bonfire – that pagan thing – which nearly did not light because of an understandable desire to economize in the petrol used for starting it. Then a metrical psalm was sung, a proclamation was read, and the élite of the true Geneva went home to change into more sober clothes, or perhaps to go early to bed so that in the morning they could resume the labour of making money out of foreigners who, truth to tell, would never have been there at all but for the worldwide diffusion of liberal-protestant ideas.

This is the pot-bellied bankrupt
Naked upon the stage

I CANNOT tell this story without many offences against strict chronology but there was in fact an occasion when, as I crossed the Pont du Rhône, I was elated by the knowledge that a book of verse of mine

27

was to be published. These feelings would have been more appropriate to a young man. I was forty-six; forty-seven when *The London Zoo* appeared: old enough to keep quiet about it but without enough sense not to be more pleased than I ought. I wrote one or two bad poems at the *Bergues* on the strength of this publication. I can therefore understand the error of those who reason that *because* they have published poems, *therefore* they are poets. This seems to be one of the prevalent errors of our times. Although I fell into it far enough to write these mediocrities (not to publish them, but that perhaps was only through lack of opportunity to exhibit my swelled head immediately), my general history in this matter is more creditable. The poems I wrote in my later thirties I put away in a drawer. Perhaps if I had had literary friends who were interested in these things, and knew how they were published, I should have published them, or been tempted to write more on being informed that I was a poet. As it was, however, I remember saying to myself that if they were any good they would keep. They came at considerable intervals and were short, so they did not make great demands on house-space nor indeed have to be thought about very much by anyone. It was only after several years that I began to hanker after putting them on the record, in some form.

I made approaches to a publisher-bookseller, himself a poet; my letter said, to the best of my recollection, that it was not that I had ideas above my station about being a poet (this was not irony but awe) but that there were, so to speak, a few *pensées* which I should like to set down. The arrangement was made; my poet-publisher thought, rather to my surprise, that these few *pensées* were not bad. I corrected the galley proofs in high expectation. Then absolutely nothing happened. I will not trouble you with the hypotheses I formed to account for this *lacuna*. Meanwhile I went on setting down my few *pensées* as they came, until there were a few pages more for the record, but still no record for them to appear on. Since I was interested in the record rather than in publication, and had reason anyway to think that my prospects of attaining commercial publication were derisory, I resolved this time merely to get the poems printed myself by a local printer. This is generally supposed to be a very shameful thing to do, and if publishing makes poets it is. I was fortunate in having the Westerham Press within a few miles of my doorstep and I entrusted this bit of printing to them. They performed with punctuality and technical skill; I had at once the feeling of being in the presence of competence, not to say expertise. The pamphlet was duly delivered. I was conscious of my duty of sending a copy to the British Museum and one to the Bodleian; it was not at all clear what I should do with the considerable number of copies left on my hands. I distributed a few to those I thought qualified to benefit by the present, well aware of the predisposition to judge hardly the man who would print his own poems.

By good fortune (or discrimination) the recipients I selected included the editors of a literary review then rather new and it was, indeed, never very old. *X* had an office of its own, off the Charing Cross Road, and my missive must have reclined for a little while among the sumptuous notepaper and the piles of manuscripts awaiting the moment of rejection. Then one day, so I have been told, several contributors were standing around in the office, deploring with the editors the lack of new poets. Tony Cronin picked up my pamphlet from the surrounding waste paper (that is how I see this historic moment) and began to read. The consequence of that was that David Wright wrote to me, since when I have been a regular recipient of some of the best letters of the century. In due course some of my poems appeared in *X*. Moreover, through the offices of the same editor, and with no more effort on my part than is required for grateful acquiescence, the firm of Abelard-Schuman agreed to publish *The London Zoo*.

It was this publication I was meditating as I crossed the Pont du Rhône. After Abelard-Schuman had accepted the book, and before it appeared, an odd thing happened. One lunchtime I walked into a shop in the Charing Cross Road and found on sale, in a yellow cover, a copy of the little volume of poems the page-proofs of which I had corrected two or three years before. I asked the manager where it came from and learned that the publisher had himself brought half-a-dozen for sale or, I suppose, return. The other five had been sold. Not a little pleased at the appearance of my small volume, but formally indignant because of the way the thing had been done and highly embarrassed as to my position *vis-à-vis* Abelard-Schuman (since the volume contained poems which were to appear in *The London Zoo*), I bought the remaining copy for five shillings and wrote in firm language to my first and now suddenly resuscitated publisher. I was told that review copies of the yellow pamphlet were about to be sent out. This made things worse. I therefore wrote magisterially saying that if the volume were published I should write to the *Times Literary Supplement* disowning it. This produced the necessary assurance. This rare pamphlet can now be bought from an address in East Berlin.

CERTAINLY the chronology has gone awry for I had intended to say something about the period – which fell towards the end of the years in which I was going to Geneva – when Patrick Swift painted my portrait. I did not then inhabit the office I described to you earlier, but a darker, much more peaceful one on another side of Saint James's Square. There was always work to be done there, much of it in preparation for or as a consequence of my own or other people's sorties to Geneva. On the other hand, with much of the work it did not matter – except immediately before one of our *sorties* – whether it was done today or tomorrow, or even next week. This puts considerable strain on a character as weak as mine. It is only the absolute necessity of work that makes it tolerable at all; the less urgent file seems actually to weigh heavier in the hand than the one that has to be dealt with straight away. I must have done quite a lot of work at the time but there is a distinct air of somnolence about my recollection of that particular office, in which I spent only a year, though my voyages to Geneva were spread over several years. It was from this peaceful spot that I made my way to Paddy Swift's basement flat. Paddy was going to do a pencil drawing. He did in fact do one, but it left him ill-satisfied at the time and one day I arrived to find the paraphernalia of oils. Shortly afterwards the scene of action moved to the empty third-floor room at the other end of Westbourne Terrace which Paddy was then using as a point of vantage from which to paint the trees below. The trees stayed where they were; the poets had to come up to him.

Paddy had done his glowering and veridical, but slightly decorative, portrait of George Barker some time before; it looked down at one from under glass in the living room of his basement. A rather bulbous David Wright was gradually being reduced to order on another canvas. Higgins was under treatment, either then or shortly afterwards – no doubt, as the classic man with all the time in the world, the perfect sitter. Indeed, if Brian Higgins could have borne the thought of a second occupation, one step in dignity below that of being a poet, it would, I imagine, have been *sitting* in some form. I was not obliging in the time I gave but Paddy seemed to accommodate himself to anything. Indeed I got the impression that, so long as he was painting, it did not matter what. In fact it always turned out to be a tree or a poet, but it was as if to lie in the line of vision of that eye inevitably involved translation on to canvas. Paddy fussed about none of the things I imagined a painter who kept his reference to the external world would fuss about. He did not mind if the sitting was short; he did not mind if the times and so the light were different. He ignored the state of the light, so far as I could make out, with his trees, for he started early and worked all day at them, except when a poet crossed his path. These variations were part of the nuisance of reality. The finished picture would perhaps be one that captured enough of the nuisance. On these matters I speculate ignorantly. The finished picture, on Paddy's own account, had to be one that looked ordinary but proved in the end not to be so. I have not put it as he did.

While he painted, Paddy talked about the stream of friends which flowed through his flat or whom he met in the pubs. Hugh MacDiarmid had been there one morning; I regretted not having met him. (I had first noticed a poem of his, quoted somewhere, in about 1934, so this would have been the incorporation of a spirit). John Heath-Stubbs at that time lived under a pavement round the corner, and made tea in a cavern too obscure for any but a half-blind man. It was and is unintelligible to me that so much learning can go with so little sight. One day I arrived to find his carapace beginning to take shape on another canvas, though it was still a little while before we met. For Paddy the human character exists, I suppose; at any rate when he had finished with them his sitters had betrayed themselves. Although when painting Paddy appeared to be all eye, with the hand just doing the necessary, unobtrusively, the conversation which ran in parallel with this performance showed a rare lucidity. Paddy hated great dollops of reading matter, as far as I could make out, but operated powerfully on a piece big enough to be brought within his line of vision at one time. I also judged that, but for a deep-seated instinct of generosity, Paddy would have had some talent for affairs. Decidedly this was not a man who had taken to painting through an incapacity for other things.

The world evoked by Patrick Swift's conversation was the natural antithesis of the one I inhabit. In it, people put the business of being poets or painters first and other things organized themselves round that. Paddy appeared to be able to manage this while holding himself equally responsible for his family. I greatly admired the economic nonchalance of this world, and this admiration (combined with the accident of buying a copy of Mathurin Régnier in Geneva) accounted for *The London Zoo*, I mean for the title poem. Of course a closer examination of the world of writers shows up the defects of the system. A place in the ordinary social world has at any rate a certain purgative effect. One worries less about trivialities of reputation, because reputation is not what you count on for your keep. The imbecile rivalries of unimportant people who happen to have written a book (usually a bad one) are much like the rivalries of any other profession, and certainly not managed with more decorum or charity. Among those who give themselves out as having abandoned all for art (in his case, poetry) the most excessive case known to me or perhaps to the world at large is Brian Higgins. This footballer and former teacher of mathematics gave himself out as a northern proletarian, and came to London from Batley via Hull and Ankara in this character. In fact the large soft centre was coddled, it is believed, in an off-licence, and you do not have to know your Marx very well to see that there is nothing proletarian about that. This specimen of the human race combined the characteristics of a baby banging with a wooden spoon and shouting for more with a mental surface of great limpidity and sensitivity when it was not clouded by the operation of some too powerful natural need. Brian I am told made an excellent babysitter and would help with the pools; beyond that I have not heard of him doing anything. He wrote poems, of which I can enjoy even the most subjective, but his education stopped short of accepting the full consequence of the remark of Helvétius which Stendhal noted in *Henri Brulard: La societé paie les services qu'elle voit.* Brian was a character who could properly be called disarming, even disarmed. He had no right to disregard the rules of social responsibility so completely; it was very inconvenient to his friends. As a busy man, I happily had very little time for friendship, and could not allow my arrangements to be upset by appeals to Christian charity. So I not only walked by on the other side, but did so hurriedly, with time for no more than a good-natured kick on the way.

I came and went
As a person without mystery, gifted with reason

BEFORE my present house I lived in one about three or four miles away. It stood by the main road, and looked out on fields at front and back. On one side of it was a small terrace of cottages; on the other houses, none of them of great elegance, built about the turn of the century. The agglomeration was part of a village, however – by some regarded as a socially superior part, though its pretensions hung by a thread. The bulk of the population lived about three quarters of a mile down the road, and there, it is true, the ambience was a little more proletarian. In the gap between the upper and lower village were a farm, a biggish house standing well back from the road, and a church; I mention only the main features. The rest was fields.

I was no disturber of the peace in this village. On the contrary, when I left it I was well on the way to becoming one of those reliable figures to whom people turn when there is a job to be done. I was Vicar's Warden, and could be counted on in that capacity to be in my place at Matins to read the lessons. If there were a fête or a sale to raise money for the church, I would conceive it my duty to put in an appearance. When the old people had their tea, I would be there. A man who is thoroughly broken in to doing his duty in exchange for money can easily be persuaded that he must do it on other occasions. When a new trustee was wanted for the (non-ecclesiastical) village hall, and for the property which houses the Working Men's Club, I fell for it; these not very onerous offices I still retain.

The social organization of the village was complex. I expect for most of the inhabitants it did not exist at all. They came and went, did their work, ate, slept and amused themselves and were unaware of *organization*. But that is not how the matter appeared to responsible people like myself. The village was full of parties – Guelfs and Ghibellines, to mention only two of them. Titanic struggles could be staged on the smallest pretext. You could watch people moving fatally to a brawl over nothing. While everyone would pretend that a *solution* was what was wanted when there was a *problem*, in fact what most people wanted was trouble. You would be wasting your time trying to prevent it. The fatal addiction of the human race to trouble is something which, even at fifty, has not ceased to amaze me. What people like is a sort of Dodgems, the real game being not to dodge at all but to cause a crash involving as many people as possible. Without such crashes most people do not feel alive. Rather gross stimuli are required to reassure them; the ordinary operation of sticking a pin in oneself to make sure one is still awake is not enough for them. Still less do they want to spend their time contemplatively; that is a quite exceptional taste. It does not escape me that doing one's duty is a refined form of this addiction to trouble. Of course one's intentions might be eirenic, but the fatal lure of the crash is likely to be a motive. I admired the old naval captain, now dead, who before the local election came and stood for a while in our sitting room. We had then not been long in the village; the captain did not say what he wanted. After a while he went away. It was only then that it dawned on me (or more probably my wife) that he had come to solicit our vote. He was a man who might properly look for trouble. He also understood

33

duty as something you did because it was there to do, and something that had to be done in the proper forms, not determined by oneself. So he stood there like Coriolanus in the market place; the thing had to be done, but he did not consider it was for a man like him to ask. He was my predecessor as Vicar's Warden.

Really I suppose my years in this village coincided with a time when one or two older people who had long done things there were looking around for shoulder on which their mantles could fall. There were mantles, and the number of possible shoulders was limited – no wonder if one or two mantles, or edges of them, fell on me. I had not been long in the village when this same naval captain, no doubt with an eye open for anyone who would not flatly deny the existence of duty, persuaded me to agree to audit the accounts of the trust of which I later became a trustee. I hate accounts, and nothing more grotesquely inappropriate could have been found, but it was only one evening once a year. My major involvement, however, came from a dangerous internal source. It was because I felt the need to go to church that I did not refuse the invitation to become church warden, and I was so ingenuous as not to understand that this was an office which other people could actually want.

The church was a small one, built of brick and put in the wrong place, some sixty years ago, from an anachronistic sense of the relationship with the only residence which could pass for the big house. It was halfway between the two parts of the village. It was therefore, so to speak, *there* for nobody; anyone who wanted it had to go some distance to it. Not many people did want it. But the congregation was diverse and intimate. The old man who took round newspapers was there as well as the naval captain. Because of the size, no one was physically far from anyone else; and those who went there to worship worshipped *with* one another. There was no party non-sense about High and Low; this was the Church and if you went to it you went there. The differences which arose were those which must arise, anywhere, from the limited inter-adaptability of human machines operating in proximity. I count myself fortunate to have started life, as a member of the Church, in that establishment, for that is where I did start it.

We had an excellent system for cutting the churchyard grass in that parish. The verges were kept tidy, but the rest grew long and matted. The vicar, an Alexandrine Cypriot who had been given treatment at Harrow, brought a crate of beer into the glebe and there was a bottle for every hour's work. The evenings of the Churchyard Week thus became an agreeable if strenuous social occasion; I had to get home as early as I could to join in. The vicar had been in the cotton trade and a civil servant; he had also, it seemed to me, a communicable talent for prayer.

Although there may be treacherous men
Who in the churchyard swing their mattocks

AT THIS time I had frequently to go to Westmorland to visit my parents. They lived in a house my father had built in the Kentmere valley, about a mile and a half from Over Staveley. So I would get out of the train at Over Staveley and walk through this little town, which always seemed to sleep pretty profoundly each side of the busy Kendal-Windermere road. With the grey stone and slate of the houses, and the pale wet grass of the valley itself, one was at once in a country that was not the south. I remember the walk in rain or mist, though no doubt it was not always like that, the sheep on the hills and the refreshing sound of the fast river. For several years before my visits ended these sensations were underpinned by a heavy anxiety. My parents had reached that stage when, after even a relatively short interval, some new deterioration was sure to be visible. The journey was immense but my visits were usually short. I would try to make myself useful, not so much out of kindness as a distraction from the cares of mortality. I would cut the grass, which was sure to need that attention, and it would often happen that my father had been making adjustments to the mower and had lost a nut. I would tell my mother about the children and talk over whatever there was to be talked over.

For my mother, Kentmere was a sort of exile. She had never wanted to go there. On the other hand, she had never had so pleasant a house and liked that. Moreover, as a farmer's daughter she was perfectly at home in the country. She watched the late hay-making of those parts with critical interest and liked the cattle. I think the more rocky and instinctive local characters were more accessible to her than they were to my father. But it was he who was the native here, and it was to satisfy his outrageous passion for the place that the house had been built where it was. He was, more precisely, a native of Kendal, and I had been taken in and out of the yards of that bracing, granite town attempting to see how it looked to the boy who had been brought up there seventy or eighty years before. My father looked for the past in vain, or it never contented him, but I think those surroundings meant more to him in his closing years than any others would have done. He had loved walking over those hills, and used to boast rather

35

inaccurately about the feats he had performed, but his circle of movement had become restricted and I remember the horrifying effects of his weakened, uncertain gait and his sudden, unexpected fatigues.

When I went to bury him it was with a sense of relief. It happened that my brother was in America, so my wife and I went alone. My father's body was lying in his room in one of those terrible but no doubt serviceable institutions where old people go to die. I had had reason to know it well in the last year or two; my mother as well as my father had had a spell in it before. It was a perfectly good nursing home, I suppose, for its purpose, and one cannot blame the muscular Westmorland women who staffed it if they lived their own lives among much decrepitude. But I did not like the place, and it was only a moderate relief to go and spend the night at my father's now empty house. He was buried in the fell-side cemetery where, with my brother and a sister since dead, I had stood two years before at my mother's open grave. My mother had retained her passionate will to live until the last; in the two years which followed her death my father entered a world of fantasy. I remember, when I took leave of him after my mother's funeral, that his hand had a new coldness. We were exercised about his future and there were various plans. But in the end he stayed. The woman who had helped my mother, and who lived only a few yards away, came in each day, made him his main meals, and tidied up. It was a bit rough, but it was better than staying in the death-house in Kendal and it enabled my father to look out on his own hillside. It was only at the end that he went back to the nursing home, and died there.

The Kendal in which my father was born in 1876 cannot have been so different, in its main features, from the one he died in. There were new houses on the periphery; there had been, no doubt, much tarting up of shop-fronts and the like, as the progress of commerce demands. But much of the old stone building was the same; and there were the same hills and declivities. The nursing home was not far from where my father's school had been, and one of the ghosts that visited him there was his old schoolmaster, a figure of menace. My father had not been much educated, as these things are counted. He had left school at thirteen. His own father and grandfather had, I imagine, been at the local grammar school; at any rate a surviving letter of my grandfather's shows him to have been able to write with what would no doubt have been considered some polish. Besides, my grandfather must have been a person who counted in the town. He owned and ran the local comb mill, which had descended to him in direct line since the end of the eighteenth century.

My father once met, in a walk on the fells not many years before he died, an old man who remembered going with a cart to collect horn shavings at the old mill. But my grandfather died when my father was only eleven years old, and left little, having, I have been told, been involved in lawsuits over a fallen chimney-stack. There were a good many children, and my father was the eldest. So my grandmother opened a grocer's shop and Richard had soon to go out to work. He was apprenticed to a clock-maker, and my father always regarded with special pride the town hall clock, which he had helped to put in and which he used to wind each day, adopting various devices to make out that it kept perfect time. My grandmother's family seems also to have been in the town for several generations; they were coach-builders, and it was said that they had built the first coach that went from Kendal to London. A perfect bourgeois background, but in a sense of the term different from, and more precise than, the sense in which it would be understood in my commuter town.

South of the march parts my father

TTHERE was a year when I was free of the office. In the summer of that year I met the family at Avignon and took them to eat rolls and drink coffee in recognition of the fact that they were in France, and in the early morning. They had got off the night train from Paris. I had come from Milan, with a volume of administrative law and the poems of Ferdinand Cogni and Sandro Penna, less bulky but more to my taste. I had arrived in Avignon the evening before, and had slept in a third-floor room in a cheap hotel. The room could not have been better chosen. It looked out on alleyways and rooftops, and in particular on a family who were eating their supper in a room giving on to a bit of flat rooftop where the washing hung. The man slouched over a bottle of wine and his newspaper; the woman came and went busily, as beseems. The night was hot and smelt of the south.

It will be very odd if you are not more given to holidaying in the south of France than I am, and the scene was neither more nor less than what you go to see, in order to feel *abroad*. But it was in fact the first time I had been in Provence. I had not lacked the orthodox longings. Indeed, Provence was a name which inspired awe in the same way as did those admired literary names the bearers of which I had never met. It was the heart of Latinity and I was or had been a passionate Francophile, literary and political. So the specimens of the unimproved poverty of the south presented by the wine-stained newspaper and the washing on the line were not lost on me. It cannot be necessary to have read Villon in order to love France, for half Europe wants to get to the Mediterranean coast whenever it can. The streets of Avignon were full of tourists then; no doubt one cannot move there now. It is the rich south – the international hotels of Cannes and Monte Carlo – and of course the sun – which appeal to the vulgar, but you have to have taken only a tiny step on the road to sophistication to know that this is not the thing. You then like food and wine and, the stomach full, admire nothing so much as peasants and fishermen.

Each year the more prosperous go further and further afield in quest of this spectacle. It is nice to get to countries where the lower orders are poor enough to be respectful or pretend to be for the benefit of someone who will pay them. This appealed strongly, in the years immediately after the war, to people who found themselves less petted at home than they had been before. But no doubt the desire to see some remnants of human life, before it vanishes from the planet, is genuine enough. People do not love the technological world. They are rapacious for it because it mitigates the pains and itches of life, or would do if the irritability of the human system did not find new causes for unease as soon as one is removed.

We were in fact going to Languedoc. When we reached Leucate, we had all the pleasures of contemplating the residual life of the south combined with the amenities of a (rather elementary) *plage*. We had what we called a villa and was in fact the first floor of a small house built for letting as seaside *appartements*. We had the pouring sun, and women from authentic life coming to sell us, each morning, peaches, almonds and a newly-caught fish. It was on the *plage* that we spent our time; it was the old town, perhaps a couple of miles away, which excited my passion. There was nothing to it. A square, a *bistro* or two, a charming baker's; but in the back streets you could see the lineaments of a Roman town, and a woman going to cast water into a deep stone gulley which had no doubt passed as a miracle of sanitation in its time. It was this spectacle which evoked the poem called *Maurras Young and Old*, for in me the Latin south was inadequately dissociated from the extraordinary Royalist who had been condemned for what he regards as *une résistance comme les autres. Moins romanesque, peut-être*, during the German occupation, as he had been condemned earlier by the Vatican for his apologetics for a dechristianized, but extremely Roman, Catholicism.

I knew that it was not polite to mention his name, and I did not mention it, in my dealings with Frenchmen – they were mostly officials – about this time. But I had been told that there were towns in the south where the *libération* of 1944-5 had cost more lives than the revolution of 1789, the Communists having taken out and shot, in the confusion, those with whom they had scores to settle. I was then, as now, far from thinking it any of my business to take sides in these internecine French quarrels, but I did not admire the one-sided view of French affairs which made it so difficult, for most people in England, to see what De Gaulle was up to, politically, and made them, at that time, so ridiculously complacent about the future of the Fourth Republic. The main political developments, ever since I became conscious of them, seem to me to have been carried on by collective suppressions of unpopular views. I dare say this is part of the inevitable mechanism, in a world of newsprint and broadcasting, but a residual human attachment to consciousness made me for many years inclined to rage against the phenomenon. One can console oneself with the thought that it must always be uncertain whether things would turn out better if people saw events more clearly.

It had been part of my intention, obsessed as usual by the possibility of making time for writing, to have done with the manuscript of *The Spirit of British Administration* in time to write something else before I had to return to my office. I suppose this aspiration after liberty was strictly criminal, since I had leave from my work in order to make the enquiries which are the subject of that book. In any case my malice was defeated. The draft gave me more trouble than I had expected. It was even, at this stage, the subject of something like grief, which must have been rather boring for my family, who were having a holiday. The point was that I looked to this book to end a course of disappointments so long that it had become habitual. It was, I hoped, actually to achieve publication. If it was not I should be left with nothing to show for my year's work, and should return to the office and a future which would be exactly like the past, only more so, because the hope of ever establishing myself as someone with a right occasionally to put out a book would have gone. So I was anxious about this book. I was forty-three.

I wrote a few poems at Leucate, and at that stage I did not think in terms of publishing poems. I basked in the sun and in the penumbra of my official enquiries. When my younger daughter scalded herself with boiling soup it was to one of the private secretaries of the French Prime Minister of the day that I applied for help in getting a doctor. Another official and his wife drove several hundred kilometres to spend a Sunday afternoon with us on the beach. Decidedly I was not a man in a literary ambience. When *The Spirit of British Administration* at last appeared I decided that if I had a future in book-making it must be in books about matters related, more or less directly, to the office affairs on which, after all, I spent nearly all my time and energy and which could be said to be the only things I really knew anything about. A vast phoney science of management was rearing its ugly head and I would write inscriptions on that. Happily the sort of enquiries which would have been necessary proved to be incompatible with my ordinary employment. I suppose the decision to put my poems on a printed record, come what may, was a consequence of that. At any rate the decision to print my own poems was, what such things are usually thought to be, the last despairing gesture of a failed literary man.

– As if a man could be identified
At least for his folly after he had died

IN THE autumn before my stay at Leucate, I had arrived in Paris with no more serious object than to enquire, in whatever way seemed good to me, into the working of the French system of administration and the ways in which it differed from our own.

My taxi set me down at the door of a little hotel in the Place St-Sulpice, and I walked out on to the Boulevard St-Germain with an immense feeling of leisure. It is very odd, when one is accustomed to work, to have the disposal of one's time. No doubt I bought newspapers and ordered my coffee like a prince. But the habit of industry is invincible, and I soon began arranging a series of troubles for myself. My first call was at the Ecole Nationale d'Administration, this post-war invention which academics in England were beginning to recommend as a model for the training of our own civil service, though it owed its origin to the desire of some Frenchmen, who had been in London during the war, to transplant into France some of the advantages of the English system.

There is something comic about all institutions which exist for the manufacture of an intellectual *élite*. In the nature of the case, they can never be quite what they are cracked up to be. There are never a hundred immortals at the Académie; the man who sets up to produce an *élite* is in effect announcing that the standards by which he operates are modest. If on the other hand one thinks of a school which is to produce a *haute élite intellectuelle* as a factory producing a standard component for some current piece of social engineering, it can look very respectable indeed, and by these standards the Ecole Nationale d'Administration was very respectable.

The director and his assistant were, it goes without saying, men of the highest professional qualifications. They understood what mechanical properties were needed in the component they were producing, and they displayed great skill and intelligence in the production. It was explained to me that to have powerful technical administrators assisted by general administrators, as at the Ministère des Mines et des Ponts et Chaussées, was *"sortir de l'ordre"*. The pupils of the Ecole Polytechnique being often people of high intellectual value, this unsatisfactory order had easily established itself. It was hoped that, now that there was the Ecole Nationale d'Administration with a prestige as great as that of the Polytechnique, relations would change and the specialists would be kept inside their specialities. This seemed to me an intelligible objective, and the Ecole Nationale the intelligent headquarters of a campaign. Another day I found myself in the Ministère de l'Intérieur, where an admittedly not very senior member of the *corps préfectoral* elucidated the nature of the prefectoral system. It was the pre-revolutionary system of *intendants*. It mattered little that the king was no longer there; in spite of its revolutions, France remained the country of traditions. It was as if the *haute élite intellectuelle*, having lost the realities of order, was consoling itself with an intellectual fiction. That perhaps does not express the matter very well. But there is no doubt that, under the Fourth Republic, officials comforted themselves in a remarkable way with the belief that they, the *élite*, ran the state and in some sense were it, and that the nominal guardians of affairs, the president and the ministers, did not matter. This did not seem to me to be a sign of political health. The inner sanctuary of this belief was the Conseil d'Etat. I made my way, as directed, to the Palais-Royal – *pas le théâtre, mais le bâtiment lui-même qui est situé sur la Place du Palais-Royal* – and walked through those gilded chambers with a distinguished official. If the officials had saved France, in its many upheavals, the Conseil d'Etat had saved the officials. It had assured the continuity of the state. It was not really the official it defended, but the *fonction*. It acted as a conscience, and under the Fourth Republic, or under the Third, you could not expect ministers or parliament to do that.

I did not want to restrict my enquiries to Paris, and the efficient staff officers at the Ecole Nationale readily arranged for me to visit one or two *préfectures*. The first was Toulouse so that, if my night in a hotel at Avignon was the first occasion on which I set foot in Provence, I had already made the acquaintance, a few months before, of the land

41

on the right bank of the Rhône. The Ecole Nationale must have made me out to be rather more magnificent than I was, because the *préfecture* booked a disagreeably expensive room for me at the hotel. I lay awake in a magnificent bed and listened to a chorus of girls' voices singing vigorously what sounded like the accompaniment of a country dance, though I do not suppose it was. Next day I set off for the *préfecture*. The programme lasted a week. I will not give an account of the *exposés*, fascinating in their kind but of specialist interest, to which I was subjected. I circulated in the main departments in and about the *préfecture*; I discussed things with the prefect himself, who was no mere prefect but Monsieur l'Inspecteur Général, for Toulouse was the centre of a region although, since regions had been established by the Vichy régime, some tact had to be exercised about the nature of his function of controlling the lesser prefects of the area. Monsieur l'Inspecteur Général was evidently a man of great ability and the tasks he had to do in co-ordinating the development of the resources of this area of gathering economic forces seemed more relevant to the functions of government as I understood them than the refined delib-erations of the Palais-Royal. The traditional life of the south was to be blown up in an explosion of natural gas. The peasants scratching in their vineyards were a drag on the economic life of France. The south did not even produce much in the way of wine that could be exported. At the weekend an official car was put at my disposal – no doubt that would be the expression – to go to Carcassonne. So I saw this splendid relic as the guest of the Republic. I also attended, among the privileged spectators, a *défilé* of troops, I no longer remember for what purpose, where there was much in the way of salutations and pinning on of medals, and much chattering at important moments. I hope my somewhat vague recollection of this occasion does not do dishonour to the Republic. The point is that I was drifting among the eddies of provincial official life.

My second visit to a *préfecture*, organized shortly after my return to Paris, was less like drifting in eddies than reclining in a beautiful pool. I was invited to go to Nevers. La Nièvre is, I suppose, one of the more agricultural and untroubled of the *départements*. To a casual visitor life in the *préfecture* seemed idyllic. The building stood back, behind railings, in its own courtyard. With the tricoleur flying it was the very image of French provincial authority. My visit coincided with a meeting of the *Conseil Général*, and although the prefect excused himself for not being able to give me, on that account, all the attention he would have wished, it gave me an opportunity of being the spec-tator of scenes which were heavy with local colour. The notables – big

42

farmers and others – assembled for the meeting were entertained to lunch by the prefect and Madame, and I was also a guest. Madame's drawing-room was like a little court. As an immense cattle-owner kissed her hand I felt I was for a moment in the presence of civilities which no doubt surrounded the lady of the *intendant* under the *ancien régime*. The dining-room was a scene of great splendour, the walls dazzling with mirrors. I slept in the *préfecture* and never before or since have I been bedded in such splendour of velvet hangings. It was hard to remind myself that the master of this establishment was a civil servant of, after all, no very over-powering grade. Certainly I was in a country which had inherited a different notion of officialdom from the one to which I had been accustomed.

Which shows that in liberating the human spirit
The grands ancêtres *provided amusement for centuries*

MY ENQUIRIES into public administration took me into several countries – I will not tell the whole story. One day I arrived in Bonn just as lunch was being served in the early spring sunshine. The terrace I remember had a theatrical quality; I was about to walk on stage among the prosperous German eaters. Not on stage in the sense that anyone was going to look at me, but in the sense that I was about to enter a theatrical world. It was not that these solid burgesses were not solid in their pursuit of *Bratwurst* and *Schinken*, garni of course for lightness with a little salad. The atmosphere had its proper loading of *Kartoffel*. But I was conscious of a dramatic encounter with Germany. It was over twenty years since we had seen one another. How my friend had changed! There are people who will not allow one to be acquainted with a nation in this way. They assert dogmatically that there are only people, *individuals*, as if these great collectivities did not exist. I wish I could think the human race so highly evolved. Or perhaps I do not. At any rate, as things are, the collectivities are there, and the national ones not least, to my eye. The Teuton has as definite an existence as all but a very few of the individuals who compose him. I have always had a sense of a particularly powerful collectivity, when I have encountered him. Since I had last seen him, there had been a war, and he had replaced what everybody now knew to be wrong ideas of how to conduct oneself by right, that is to say democratic, ideas. As I observed him eating his lunch I thought this new diet suited him. He looked fat and well.

It had been my intention to lounge in Bonn for a day or two before

I launched myself on my enquiries. I wanted to grow a little accustomed to this new world and, moreover, try to regain a little facility in speaking the language, of which my mastery had at best been imperfect. I counted without the zeal of the British Embassy. When I got in touch with them I found that they had arranged for me to pay my first visit to a German ministry that very afternoon. I imagine that my interlocutors in that ministry understood English, but that we were at that stage of post-war relationships in which they made no show of this knowledge, to make it clear that they were not an occupied country and that if Englishmen wished to address them it must be in the language of the country. I picked up a few technical terms as we went along and so managed to put some questions at appropriate points in the naturally weighty discourses these helpful officials emitted. I emerged from this first interview with mild exhaustion but the complacency which the trained performers of duty feel when, after any brief pause, they again begin their tricks:

Once set on this course, I persisted in what I had to do. I attended a sitting of the *Bundestag*, and a waiter in the restaurant told me, showing his teeth, that the Germans now ate better than the English. There was a considerable shininess everywhere of cars and new buildings. I took tea with a German official and his wife in their house on a new estate, modest and antiseptic. They were cultured, and brought out volumes of reproductions for me to admire. I admired them for I do not much enjoy this form of cultural ware. They were reconstituting the cultural international. They were very charming, and I do not wish to seem ungrateful. I am still in the realm of collective impressions. If I were talking of persons I should record that the face and figure of the lady of the house touched my susceptible heart and that I thought of her as I made my way back to Bonn.

My visits to ministries and the odd embassy party were interlarded with browsings in the bookshops. There is comedy even in books of administrative law, and the little manuals I acquired were rich in it. To translate some of the splendid sentences I found there is to denature them. *"Nur vorübergehend gibt es Beamte ohne Amt und Ämter ohne Beamte"* – it is only temporarily that there are officials without functions and functions without officials. Well, yes. Here in solemn array I found a whole philosophy of what was involved in being that splendid animal, the *Beamte*. His duties – not the work he might have to do but so many categorical imperatives defining what, in the abstract, it was his nature to be – were set out in paragraphs numbered one to five, and the full complement was more, as the later paragraphs explained. The introductory paragraph said that the basis and basic duty was fidelity. From that were derived the duty of obedience and the duty of actually doing the work: *Grundlage und Grundpflicht ist die Treue. Daraus ergeben sich Gehorsamspflichten und Dienstleistungspflichten.* I did not greatly regret that British officials were not expected to mug up such stuff.

The impression of the first days in Bonn was one of great oddity. Either there had not been a war at all, or the Germans had been on our side. No doubt there had been great changes in the ministries, but many of the people I met must have been there before 1945. No one exhibited a shadow of sympathy for the recent *régime*. Contrary to the impression I had received twenty years before, Hitlerism must have been a minority movement. Either that, or I was again in the presence of one of those monumental *voltes-face* which are characteristic of modern societies. It is no use talking to me about individuals when such phenomena are to be seen. I went on to Munich, to explore a little the administration of a *Land*, for the dispositions taken in Bonn were hedged with all sorts of constitutional guarantees aimed at installing a certain powerlessness at the centre. No doubt like other constitutional safeguards they can be got round, by the skilful practitioner. None the less, the peculiarities of these arrangements did put a stamp on the operations of Bonn. If France was *la femme sans tête,* as Maurras alleged, the Federal Republic was *die Frau ohne Unterleib,* she was really only a top part. It is surprising what can be done with these ladies of imperfect physiology.

I went on to Vienna, and was received with great urbanity in the chancellery of that truncated empire, which had all experience, enough and to spare, of the ways of conducting a bureaucracy. But even more than by these relics of greatness I was impressed by the huge, shoddy monument erected by the Russians to celebrate their presence on the banks of the Danube. On my way back, I went to the school of administration in Speier, the *Hochschule für Verwaltungswissenschaften Speier.* Here everybody was actively forgetting that the school had been set up by the French occupation authorities in imitation of the *Ecole Nationale d'Administration.* We discussed the usual matters. But the professor told off to take me out to lunch did not mention administration from start to finish of our meal. He had read Joyce and Eliot and wanted to know what new names there were, now that the war was over. I could not remember that there were any. He could not produce the name of a young man himself, but talked with enthusiasm of Gottfried Benn. I added one or two volumes of Benn to my luggage and on my way out of Germany I read: "In my view the west is going to its ruin not because of totalitarian

systems or the crimes of the S.S., and not because of material impover-
ishment at the hands of Gottwald or Molotov, but because of the
cur-like crawling of its intelligence before political ideas".

The turning and deceits of time
Do not allow to catch full face
Even the face of agony

THERE IS no subject on which a thesis can be written which does not
risk in time becoming the speciality of a professor, a reader or a
lecturer, and since it is supposed to be a good thing for people with
those designations to be *free*, there seems to be no end to the multipli-
cation of such specialists.

The innocent taxpayer puts his hand in his pocket and says, Ah,
education: leaving it to Dr. X and Professor Y to decide what that
is. In fact, education has become a matter of the initiation and cultivation of subjects, and a subject is anything which one academic can
persuade another to allow to grow. The modern university is a great
garden in which there are no weeds, because anything that grows is
by definition good. This is probably as good a definition as can be
found of what it is good to grow, and since many specialities are
directly related to the making of money and the diffusion of the pro-
ducts of industry, an air of plausibility hangs over the whole proceedings and there is much that is useful by the standards to which we
are accustomed. One of the specialities which has, of recent years,
pullulated with some success, is the study of government, and at the
moment of writing there are said to be about a hundred and fifty
people on the staffs of universities in this country who give themselves
out for experts in this field. Even at the time of which I am writing
there were quite a few, and it was to this happy circumstance that I
owed my liberty to wander around Europe. I was given a fellowship
by the University of Manchester, which had one of the most respectable of Departments of Government, in the hope that I would contribute to thought on the subject. Incidentally I was to be given the
opportunity to consort with experts for whom this was a *subject*, while
I was merely, so to speak, a fitter who earned his living by doing
some of the jobs which have to be done about the boiler-room if the
machine is to be kept running at all and the ship of state navigating
on its course, no one knows exactly where.

The city of Manchester is one of those disgraces by which the
human race advertises the squalor and turpitude of its mind. In this

46

town whose chief honour is to have been the birthplace of De Quincey are miles and miles of the trash of nineteenth century industrialism, which is being replaced, at a modest but increasing speed, by the trash of the twentieth century. Out of the rows of dirty and generally hideous houses rise the monuments of prosperity erected by the corporation and by insurance companies. Frock-coated statues of men who were figures of fun for Matthew Arnold still strut, with the prostitutes, in Manchester's Piccadilly – or so it was a few years ago when I had the honour of taking up my fellowship.

The Department of Government was housed in a shoddy building in Dover Street, which is just opposite that point in Manchester's Oxford Street which is embellished by the piles of the university itself. I dare say this last expression does not correctly designate the original heaps, for the university is a spiritual thing diffusing itself like a gas over an ever wider and indefinite area. But it will be clear enough that I mean those acres where once grass grew no doubt, but over which any manifestation of nature has long been concealed by Owen's College, the original nineteenth century foundation, the library, the refectories, and buildings which house various other mechanisms which prove the place to be a university. The central buildings of Owen's College are in a vaguely ecclesiastical style, but there is no sign of a church of any kind belonging to the university, which was founded at a time when men were already putting such nonsense out of their heads. I suppose the builders still associated ecclesiastical architecture with dignity, in a vague way, and it was certainly their intention that the College should have that.

When I arrived I was directed to an unlicensed hotel in Fallowfield, a couple of miles up the road, as likely to be the place most conducive to my studious peace when I was not actually in the thick of intellectual activity in the university itself. At Dover Street I was offered a share in the room of an eminent authority, not merely on government, but on civil services. This learned doctor knew how they should work. With an immense contempt for everything that went on in Whitehall, with which he could hardly be said to be familiar, he had only to cross the Channel to find officials operating according to rules which caused him to emit little cries of admiration, and to print enormous books explaining how justice could be secured for the people of England by almost any device which ran counter to the habits and traditions of the country. As a corrosive substance, eating away at the prejudices on which our institutions are based, he was I suppose mildly useful, for the technological world requires the destruction of the subtler traditions of mankind, not the understanding of them. As a

47

guide to the construction of any new edifice, or to possible ways of tinkering with the old ones, the learned doctor was less reliable, for he had his own set of prejudices, stiffer in the joints and less fit for the exercise of any practical work. Innocent young ladies came in considerable numbers to be instructed by him, and what notions of the operations of government they carried away with them I cannot say, for when they came tapping at my door I made myself scarce, and took refuge in the library where Subjects of all kinds were being studied, to all appearances.

My own orientation in this field of academic study was uncertain enough, and when I went into the library I was astonished to find row on row of books which purported to describe just the activities I had lived with for the best part of twenty years. There were many splendid American volumes, bound in solid buckram against the risk that someone might actually read them and written in a prose which gave the impression of having been translated from the German. These volumes contain the purest thought which has yet been invented on the subject of administration. No doubt the technological disintegration of learning has gone even further in the United States, and money is thrown away even more recklessly in the elaboration of new subjects. It must be like the dream of a nineteenth century German professor come true in a happier and more carefree world.

I collected a pile of these books and began to draw what enlightenment I could from them. In the end I felt obliged to retire from the higher peaks of this subject and consider those laws and institutions which were the speciality of my learned room-mate. I avoided America altogether because it had been made plain to me that the university was not going to be so reckless with its money as to pay my fare across the Atlantic. Privately, my desire was to get away from Manchester whenever I could and for as long as possible. Not that I lacked a proper seriousness about my obligations to the place. Once again the ineluctable and persistent habit of doing what was supposed to be my duty saw to that. I had been told that part of the benefit the university hoped – rather faintly, I imagine – to get from my presence was that I would be about to converse with the staff of the Department of Government and no doubt of the circumjacent schools. I imagined that, if I could not enlighten them they would at least, as men inured to research, find me a not unuseful object of study. So I made myself available. I went every morning to the Senior Common Room, which was full for an hour or more every morning of droves of lecturers and the like drinking coffee and exchanging ideas. They were certainly drinking coffee. In the evening it was not so easy. When five o'clock came, all these learned men went home like a wave of commuters, no doubt to continue their researches by their own firesides. The first weekend I remained in my private hotel in Fallowfield, imagining that during the ten weeks of term time the minds would be interacting even on Saturdays and Sundays. I daresay they were, but the process was not apparent to the eye of a visitor. The doves were released from Dover Street at five o'clock on Friday evening, and they were not going to be seen again until they came fluttering back, no doubt with their little messages, some time after nine on Monday morning. So I went home as often as I could, although it was a long way. Twice in the course of my intermittent stay I was invited by learned authorities to their homes; once I went to a university cocktail party and was introduced to a professor who remarked, on being introduced to me, that it was nice to know how the university was spending "their" – the staff's – money. But I should not complain for there were watercolours by Blake in the gallery up the road and after all it was from here that I was released to idle in Paris, Bonn, even in Madrid and Stockholm.

---

and the big mouths of learning
Open and close over my thoughts without biting.

ALTHOUGH THE essay from which my book on administration had grown had appeared in the *Cambridge Review* – under a pseudonym, because Michael Oakeshott thought it had a flavour of impropriety, for a man employed as I was – three years before I took up my fellowship at Manchester University, my reading during the intervening years had not been of a kind which could have met with approval in the Department of Government. It included a number of books illustrating the antecedents and family connections of *The Book of Common Prayer*. What one of my authors called "the revival of a taste for history" in the first half of the nineteenth century has left in the bookshops, here and there, relics which are still of interest to the uneducated churchman.

William Pickering, who must have been one of the most useful men of his day, produced in 1842 *Liturgiae Britannicae*, or the several editions of the Prayer Book from its compilation to its last revision, and in 1844 *The Ancient Liturgy of the Church of England*, according to the use of Sarum, Bangor, York and Hereford, together with the modern Roman Liturgy. In 1846 and 7 he likewise published *Monumenta Ritualia Ecclesiae Anglicanae* – the occasional offices of the Church of England according to the ancient use of Salisbury, the Prymer in English and other prayers and forms. The latter volumes contained a discourse on the old service books of the Church of England by the editor, the Rev. William Maskell. If one had browsed over these volumes one had a new sense of the depth and resonances of the English Prayer Book and the continuity of the English Church from mediaeval times, and a sharper feeling for the impertinence of the nineteenth-century Roman – or should one say Irish-Italian – intrusion. The fashions of the times I suppose demand the exclusion of liturgiology from the history taught in schools and even, often, in universities but once one has the thread of this subject, however insecurely, it becomes a guide which then appears indispensable.

Two other small collections of liturgical documents came my way about this time. These were the *Reliquiae Liturgicae* and *Fragmenta Liturgica* produced by the Rev. Peter Hall in 1847 and 1848. These volumes contain the text of the emendations and substitutions for the English Liturgy which have been proposed from time to time, and partially adopted, whether at home or abroad. Here one can find, for example the *Directory* put out by Parliament in 1644 together with an ordinance "for the taking away of the Book of Common-Prayer" and add sensibly to one's understanding of Puritanism past and present; or the Non-Jurors' Liturgy, and see how certain currents from the seventeenth century ran on through the eighteenth, until Coleridge came to reintegrate the English mind. With the *Fragmenta Liturgica* I achieved one of the triumphs of secondhand book buying – finding some of the seven volumes in London and the rest, later, in Tunbridge Wells.

At this time also I was subject to another addiction – Ford Madox Ford. I had read *It was the Nightingale* before the war, *The Critical Attitude* in 1940, and one or two other books by the same author at various times, and these I had turned to frequently for the comfort of easy, balmy reading, when that was what I wanted, rather as one might take Relaxa-tabs or some other mild preparation to soothe the nerves. But about this time volumes of Ford Madox Ford, Ford Madox Hueffer, began to pour in on me. There were soon nearly forty of them on my shelves. It was a true addiction. This insinuating style made its way to every corner of my mind. If there is such a thing as a capacity to write, without necessarily having anything to say, Ford had it. "He breathed Letters, ate letters, dreamt Letters", as Wyndham Lewis said of Ezra Pound. "A very rare kind of man". Wyndham Lewis also somewhere described Ford as "an invention of Ezra's," no doubt out of contempt for the inadequacy of his content and perhaps some failure in his reference to the outside world. There is plenty to be said against Ford Madox Ford, but so far as I was concerned at this time it was like the objections one might raise as one sank into the arms of an octopus. These are poisons that one has to take. There is even the possibility that Ford Madox Ford is not entirely poison. If I were recovering from flu I might still reach for *The Rash Act*. There is an appalling technical facility about such books, and God keep me from it. I suppose the perfect novelist would have all the immense skill which Ford disposed of, and somehow succeed in not using it. There is however some content in Ford. The writers he mentions casually in passing almost always turn out to be good ones. He directs the mind to good things, seen a little askew and out of context. What he really presents is a kind of caricature, in pretended variety but dominated by the style of the author. The four Tietjens books, *Some Do Not, No More Parades, A Man Could Stand Up*, and *Last Post* are even a great work of some kind, in this kind. The hero of course is Ford himself, as he hoped he was but as, by all accounts, he was not. The shadow of personal obsession hangs over the whole production. Aspiration and delusion mingle in the portraiture. The son of a cultivated German who was music critic to *The Times*, and a Roman Catholic, he was out of the stream of English life for more reasons than his temperamental peculiarities; so Tietjens had to be a tremendous English Tory, a landed gentleman of the most magnificent and discreet kind. There was a real man called Marwood who has sometimes been indicated as the model for Tietjens but he must have been the merest occasion of Ford's delusive portrait. Everything in the Tietjens books is marked by the same excess. Every detail shows a defective correspondence with reality. There is no reason why it should not be so, but it makes for a singular type of art. Think of the Imperial Department of Statistics which was served by those two young men "of the English public official class", Tietjens and Macmaster. It and its operations are idiotic. It is so with everything in the book. Yet somehow the book manages to be about the impact on England of the 1914 war and for some exposed nerves Ford's books at large will remain, deleterious, seductive, beneficent, for a good many years, as the duration of books goes.

If I write with some fury about this strange figure it is perhaps because there is in manuscript a book which, to my mind, bears the taint, particularly in its soft middle part, of his influence. For the first and I hope the only time in my life I was constructing a novel. *Christopher Homm* had been the round of the publishers and come home to rest. I had given up trying to write, not for the first time. Then one day I resolved, as it were in defiance of publishers, that I would write one more novel. *Christopher Homm* had proved to my satisfaction that I could write, but an itch remained to find someone else to assent to this proposition. I determined to write a novel which even a publisher would recognize as being one. I suppose this was a moment of defection. I organized the superficies in a way that was supposed to look publishable. Apparently after all my novel did not look like that. No doubt that served me right. I was trying to use skills I had acquired instead of abandoning them in favour of new ones to be picked up on the way.

Last time I looked at this novel I thought it was better than it ought to be. It presents a form of military life of which I had had a profound experience. So it is not about nothing.

His head has gone inside a volume
And he is no more than a margin

SOME TIME – and it would be at about this point in the backward march of events – I shall have to tell you how I came to be a member of the Church. In one sense this is a thing I cannot do; in another, it is a thing I cannot do in one chapter, if the whole book does not do it; but in a third sense, you might as well know that one Sunday afternoon *anno aetatis meae* XXXIX, in the small brick church I have described, I was baptized, and shortly afterwards, in the small, but this time ancient, church of a neighbouring parish, I was confirmed by Christopher, Bishop of Rochester. The approach to these mysteries was something like giving oneself up to the police. I mean that I had committed the crime – if it is one – of yielding to the persuasions of the Creed, some time before, gradually, I am not sure when. And when the great festivals came round, year after year, I felt a growing deprivation. It was to cure that that I submitted to the public regulation of my position.

The priest I asked for baptism was not one with whom much oral communication was possible. The predecessor of the vicar with whom I cut the churchyard grass, at the price of a bottle of beer an hour, was a man fit to have orders, like the centurion, and most of his life he had been an army officer. He did what he had to do with punctilio, and I have never been able to stomach a priest who does not. At a certain point in the instruction he gave me before confirmation he said: "I am not going to discuss that", as if he feared that his catechumen, sitting under the shadow of numerous and perhaps rather clever books, might wish to argue. But I approved this silence before the inexpressible. All manner of expression, from all manner of ages, had brought me to that point. We had taken our children, who had been baptized, to church, sitting near the back, and the vicar did not mind if we took them out before the sermon. He did not regard that as the important part.

There is a modern mind which finds it impossible to justify joining the Church. What makes Augustine so attractive is that he was acquainted with something very like the modern mind, and turned his back on it. There is a part of our reasonableness which is against it, or so it seems. The basic incomprehension of enlightened people comes from a belief – for which the superficial evidence is admittedly plentiful – that the man who abandons himself to the Church is wilfully shutting out half the world of facts, like an ostrich which has managed to bury one eye in the sand. That is entirely to misunderstand the subjective process. At any rate when I joined the Church it was because it seemed to me that the world was as the creed said it was. Nothing was excluded; one was merely removing a prejudice which concealed the miraculous nature of the creation. People talk about the Christian doctrine of marriage as if it were a moral rule invented to crush tender feelings and healthy appetites. Actually it is a fact about the nature of man and woman. You can do something different; all but saints in some sort do. The fact will remain; all you can do is to deflect your mind from it, and our wobbly minds naturally find it pleasant to be deflected. It is so with the creed. It says what it is; it does not say anything else. No one can surprise you with a fact that is inconsistent with it, because there are no such facts. There is no question of having to deny that the world is round; if the world is round, then that is what the creed says. The ordinary modern objections to the Church are simply irrelevant.

It is because the Christian is concerned with the same objective world, precisely, as anyone else that the difference between Christian and non-Christian is, in one sense, subjective. Subjective in the proper sense of pertaining to the subject and not on that account any less real. If we exist at all, in the sense in which we think of our*selves*, it is in that existence that the Christian faith has meaning. If on the other hand one manages to attach meaning to *cogito* without a *sum*, then certainly the Church is a nonsense. I cannot get this clearer. Sometimes it seems possible to reckon with our activity without our existence, and that is doubt.

Given a sort of Christian resolution, what should one do with it? It is the sacraments which tie one to the world; without them one would wander unassured in a sort of limbo which is, no doubt, the impersonal world of the mechanism with no subjective part. This may be hell. It is what the religionists of the technological world are trying to imitate, as artists were once thought to imitate the creation of God. The sacramental life is the alternative. In practice this means joining people not of your choosing, but who in some sort have chosen what you have chosen, and turning up at inconvenient times to perform a corporate act with them. The theology of it is that you have not chosen at all but been chosen, so it is none of your business whether the silly sheep that are with you have caught sight of the shepherd. Have you caught sight of him yourself? My woolly head is buried in the sides of the other sheep.

Of these matters one must always say too much or too little, or both as I have done. Something like this chapter had to be written, if this book was to be written at all – and that condition only shows the frivolity of one's excuses. The best I can do, short of scrapping the whole thing is to stop now and make the chapter a short one.

I ought, however, to add that about this time I was writing *Christopher Homm*.

He was last seen passing by Aldebaran

LOOKING around for something for which I could write an occasional article I must have come across – no doubt in the Charing Cross Road – an early copy of *Catacomb*. Not being sanguine of editorial welcomes, I did not invent anything specially for this periodical, but sent them, thinking it was barely worth the stamp, seven paragraphs I must somewhen have written to amuse myself. They were described as "relics of futurity discovered in the course of recent excavations in Whitehall" and were the text of an official document drawing attention to "certain features of the living arrangements of a number of workers" which had "given rise to difficulties". These arrangements were marriage and the production of children, which the future officials to whom the document was attributed saw as an impediment to the proper organization of industry. The normal arrangement, at the period in question, was for children to be produced on state farms by artificial insemination, a record to be kept of the mother's identity number and of the stud number of the father; and the children were "graded and regraded at the ages of three and ten respectively" and received "at each stage the training appropriate to their grade". The authors of the document conceded that arrangements were "being made in most districts for the prompt collection by local herdsmen of children not born on state farms", but since the system was not perfect they prescribed that "every effort must be made by local officials to identify cases of childbirth and to destroy the issue wherever transfer to a state farm could not immediately be effected". All kinds of difficulty were foreseen in cases where this did not happen. Some "off-farm" parents, who had kept the product of their connections for considerable periods, called them names. Some children had received various forms of training which did not correspond with that given on the state farms. In some cases "responses to verbal combinations other than official orders" were found. Some of the children moved irregularly, in a way which would be an embarrassment when they were turned over to industry. This meant they had to be destroyed, which was a waste of trainers' time and of the feeding stuff that had been fed to them.

It was a rollicking little fantasy. To my surprise Rob Lyle, who with an apparently dormant Roy Campbell edited the magazine, not only printed it but was interested enough to suggest that we met. We did so and Rob Lyle, having like a serious editor explored my interests, asked me to write an essay on Charles Maurras. With the help of the London Library, and of the eight or ten volumes of Maurras (including the trial) on my own shelves, this was done. I was glad to set down what I knew of this siren of my youth, because it still seemed to me that a reading of him could provide several clues to the understanding of Europe which were missing from the usual British interpretations. I was glad of course to be asked to write at all. And greatly surprised.

The contributors to *Catacomb* were a strange gang, and I hope it will not be offensive to say that I did not altogether like being associated with them. It is true that the number in which my relic of futurity appeared contained a *Letter from T.S. Eliot* which for a little review was the touch which must surely remove any possible taint of King's Evil, but there were contributors who shook more convulsively than I liked when socialism was mentioned, some of them even dreamed of the Holy Roman Empire; Rob Lyle himself wished devoutly for a Carlist restoration. I never met any of the major contributors except Rob Lyle himself, and I did not and do not readily see myself in the company of Manuel Reverte or of Erik von Kuehnelt-Leddihn. I suppose the magazine was a hotbed of international reactionary Popery, and that is not where my sympathies lie. I fitted to the extent that I was illiberal in my outlook on politics and the arts, but at the end of my essay on Maurras I saluted Hooker, whom I regarded as having saved us from some of the political troubles of the Roman countries. I do not know whether the managers of *Catacomb* noticed or would have minded this act of dissociation. Anyhow I was asked to write another article and since I had been reading Filmer's *Patriarcha* and the *Discourses concerning Government* in which Algernon Sydney, like almost everyone else, had treated Filmer with contempt, it took the form of some notes about those two which crystallized around Marvell's *Horatian Ode on Cromwell's Return from Ireland*. So *Catacomb* served the purpose of making me do two solid pieces of work. It must have come to an end soon afterwards. This often happens to papers I write for.

Please leave indignation alone.
It is enough if you are a stone

THE *New English Weekly* had come to an end a year before the date of my first contribution to *Catacomb*. The issue of 8 September 1949 was the last. The causes of its *démise* were the usual ones.

> When we started, the production of a weekly independent journal was possible, at a sacrifice no greater than we felt it was fair to ask: in these days the demands it makes upon its patrons and producers are greater than they can be expected to fulfil.

The *New English Weekly* was the successor of *The New Age*, and when I first started to write for it it had borne that name as well as its own on the title page. So its traditions went back to the Enlightenment of 1912 or thereabouts. It was outside the stream of commercial journalism. *The New Age* under the editorship of Orage had no doubt been inventive in a degree which the *New English Weekly* never achieved. It had had Pound and Hulme among its early contributors. But Orage was a fine intelligence in his own right and by all accounts an editor of exceptional integrity and independence.

In the volume of Wyndham Lewis's *Letters* there is one on the subject of the decay of Arnold Bennett which contrasts "the intelligent principles that governed the management of" the *New Age*, "that review *d'élite* under the editorship of Mr Orage", with the very different requirements of the *Evening Standard* to which Bennett took in his plutocratic decline. Lewis describes how "in the earlier stages of his latter labours Mr Bennett attempted, somewhat lamely and haltingly, to convert a page of a great booming daily into a not-too-businesslike page of the *New Age*". Bennett, however, "soon discovered, so it seems, the incompatibility of the standards of big-scale book-boosting and those appropriate to the duties he had discharged in the peaceful pages of the *New Age*". The *New English Weekly*, at its foundation in 1932, had had Orage as its editor, and though there could be no recurrence of the seminal activities of the period I have vaguely designated by the date 1912, Orage certainly carried into the new periodical the independence of the old – that freedom from commercial influence which has become so rare in the literature of our time as to be regarded as a dangerous eccentricity. The editor who succeeded on Orage's death in 1934 or 5, and was still in the chair at the time of the journal's decease, kept this spirit alive through the fifteen years of his tenure. He was Philip Mairet; I have never known a mind less deflected by money or ambition.

I have the last number of the *New English Weekly* before me now.

I think it was "done in" (Mairet said) by the forces of financial inflation which are overwhelming so many cultural efforts and liberating vitalities of a lower order. The continuous production of such a weekly forum is a task which grows no lighter; but whenever I have thought – as sometimes who would not? – that another editor might be better for the readers, I have been all the more ambitious to see such a firm establishment of the journal as might enable me to find a successor. The disappointment of this hope has coincided with one I find more painful – that of the younger writers who, since the war, have again been finding a means of expression in this journal only to have it now suddenly snatched away. Should it prove possible in any way to re-establish a connection between them and our circle of readers, this would be a leading motive for doing so.

The man who wrote that was, I think, nearly seventy. He was not very tall, slight, a little deaf, with a faint nervous *tic* in the mouth and a momentary impediment in his speech which, when it came, was lucid and vigorous. His words were thoughts. His eyes would light up as visibly as the bulbs on a pin-table, as the ideas rattled round; or he would break into a grin or a laugh as he touched with his scalpel some oddity of human behaviour. His face was of extraordinary mobility; and what made this crinkling of the tissue paper so impressive was that there was not even the remotest suggestion of affectation about it, or of the adoption of a social tone. He gave the impression of living very close to the truth. I wish I knew more about him; but how he got through those fifty-five years before he took the *New English Weekly* over from Orage I do not know. He is said once to have been a clown in a circus, and though I can imagine him in that rôle I do not suppose it accounted for many of the years. I am writing all this in the past, as at the point I am in my history, but I still occasionally see Mairet in the London Library. Approaching his mid-eighties, he is absolutely unchanged. When approached he deftly switches on his hearing aid. The wisp of white hair still straggles over his fragile skull. He lives in Sussex and occasionally comes up to collect books and to nose around. He is still working, I do not know exactly at what – the odd bit of translation, the odd review. He has plenty of work, and that is, so far as I have known him, all that he ever wanted. He once said to me, when he was writing his weekly editorials, that it was very odd, putting out that stuff week after week, and nothing ever came back. There were almost no reactions.

My own last contribution to the *New English Weekly* had been a review of the *Pisan Cantos*. Pound was still in his mad-house in America, having been incarcerated as a result of his activities in Italy during the war, and his name had been by no means entirely re-established in polite circles in this country. As his letters show, he had in the past occasionally written for and to the paper; he probably still saw it. Anyhow, Mairet was anxious that an early notice of the *Cantos* should appear, and before the volume came out I was given a copy of the proofs to study. Eliot was on the editorial committee of the paper and no doubt Fabers parted with the proofs easily. I was not a reviewer of poetry, but this book I was glad to do. Some weeks afterwards I received an air-letter with a United States stamp and no sender's address. Inside was scribbled in pencil: "Thank you for a pleasant surprise. E.P." I was profoundly touched.

My contributions to the *New English Weekly*, during its last few years, were numerous and I am surprised, looking back over the copies I have, to see how industrious I was. I reviewed books – sometimes those I asked for myself, often those Mairet asked me to do. My interests were those of the paper, that is to say, they were what might be called sociological if that word did not now carry the suggestion of pseudo-science and vain attempts to talk quantitatively of things whose only interest is qualitative. We were interested in books and events as evidences of what was happening to the human consciousness. That is not a very good way of putting it but perhaps it indicates the orientation. I reviewed a volume of Max Weber, a book about universities by Sir Walter Moberly, essays by Alex Comfort, an autobiography by Fred Copeman, a Communist turned Papist. Most of these books I should certainly not have read at all had I not been a reviewer; if it did nothing else this reading acquainted me with territories on the borders of my own where I might have ploughed if I had had the time and if publishers had not been so difficult about circulating what I wrote. Sometimes the books were of intrinsic interest. I was asked to review Eliot's *Notes towards the definition of Culture*, a book which Philip Mairet had read and commented on at various stages in its production and which Eliot dedicated to him. If I found something within the paper's general field of interest which would make an article, I could do that without the *corvée* of reading a contemporary book; Paul-Louis Courier provided as good an illustration of the tendencies of our society as an author of our own time.

The main benefit I got from the *New English Weekly* at this period was, however, a sense of the existence of other minds which operated in a manner not dissimilar to my own. A maturing writer does not need fame; it may be a nuisance; but the benefit of some association with other minds of like propensities is enormous. Except for Mairet himself, whom I saw or corresponded with fairly often, the association was a little remote. Some of the main pillars of the paper – Maurice Reckett, T.M. Heron, W.T. Symons – were like Mairet himself very much my seniors. Some of the more distinguished younger contributors – such as John Heath-Stubbs or George Every – were authors in their own right, so to speak, while I was merely a *New English Weekly* writer, and such was my diffidence that it did not occur to me to try to get to know them. The occasional *rassemblements* of *New English Weekly* writers and readers did not produce much, and it was a world I entered on tip-toe. There was, I am no longer quite sure at what stage, but it was after the war, the odd dinner or two at P.E.P. in Queen Anne's Gate. It must have been there that I met Montgomery Belgion. Ronald Duncan turned up, but he was a poet, apparently a familiar of Eliot, in general one too great for me to approach. Eliot himself put in an appearance on these occasions, and I can be said to have met him once or twice, though it must remain uncertain whether he ever met me. This was not for lack of condescension, however, and I remember one night, as I stepped into the fog of Queen Anne's Gate, he came up behind me and spoke to me, I expect about the weather. As we walked along the pavement we were overtaken by Montgomery Belgion, who addressed Eliot as if he had been human. All three of us paused on the corner, then Eliot made off in the fog to St James's Park station and I walked across the park with Montgomery Belgion, who called at the Athenaeum to pick up a pair of boots. I think these great events must have taken place earlier than the epoch I am now talking of – perhaps 1946 or 7 rather than 1949. It feels at least as remote as that.

59

THE LAST summer of the *New English Weekly* was the first summer of my second daughter, who was born in the middle of it. A year before that we had moved into our village in order to rear children there. We also reared chickens, and one year ducks.

Since we had lived in flats, this house was our first. We went through the suffering which seems to be inseparable from a first acquaintance with property. Having mobilized every available pound to get into the house, we found it agitating to be repaired the moment we got in. The faint smell in the sitting room was dry rot; beside the mousehole the skirting board gave softly to the touch of a penknife. We sent for a local builder who, rather appropriately, was grave but reassuring like a doctor. Soon the boards were up all over the place. Some of the joists had gone, and the rotting, cobwebby wood sneered up at us from a floor that was little but bare earth. I remember one Saturday afternoon, when we were wondering how to pay for the renewal of the timber, climbing with my wife and then only child to a chalk pit to sun ourselves among the remarkable flowers. When we had sat for a little while I took a lump of chalk, wrote on the soles of my shoes, DRY ROT, and stretched out my feet for my wife to see. That was what was on our minds.

However, all these troubles pass and the house was in many ways a very eligible one. A lane rich in cow parsley ran along the bottom of the garden, beyond the hen house. In the field beyond were rabbits, for no one had yet thought of destroying them by myxomatosis. The cat we had a year or two later spent a long summer afternoon bringing baby rabbits back alive to play with in the garden. In such natural struggles it ought to be very difficult to know which side to take, but brought up in the sporting morality of the (later) English we knew at once that the weaker party had to be defended, and so rescued the rabbits and returned them to the field. Every Sunday morning I cleaned out the hen house. I rather like such mucky tasks in the proximity of animals, even animals so low in the scale of human affections as the pecking, unintelligent hen. We reared one or two cockerels of great splendour, and ate them when they were at their most beautiful. Hedgehogs went panting round the garden on summer nights, and I have wakened there to hear the nightingale in full song. All this was beside the A21, where before we left the house the traffic was bumper to bumper at the weekends and a man was killed travelling at high speed a few feet from our front door.

In those days I had some of the virtues a father should have. When the swing became rickety I built another with my own hands, making what seemed to me to be expert joints so that there was no risk that the thing should collapse on my precious offspring. I also wrote a novel. Or rather finished it, for I had written the opening chapter before we moved into the house, and then came the inevitable pause until we were settled. I carried the manuscript with me and, if my train into town were early enough, I would write a bit more in a coffee-shop on the way to the office. It was clipping coins; the few minutes I got each time amounted to a useful sum, in the end. But in the main the book was written at home. This was *An Asiatic Romance*, which was of course to establish my place as a writer. In a mild way I was avenging myself on the office, which took all my time, by making my most villainous character an eminent civil servant. His original name, in my manuscript, was Sir Wisdom Tooth, but when at last the book came to be printed the printer objected to that, on the to me extraordinary grounds that it might be considered a libel on a politician whose rather dissimilar name had certainly never entered my head. My most conscious purpose, however, as with later productions of the novel kind, was technical. I thought the best possible way of getting away from the soppiness of the commercial novel was to write the straightest possible objective narrative. I suppose in the background of my cogitations were Wyndham Lewis, Smollett and Defoe, but they were certainly much in the background, if there at all. The more immediate indication I had acted on was that a distinguished publisher, in rejecting a non-fictional book I had produced a couple of years before, had used the word "narrative" in a context which did not altogether convey disapproval. Towards such slight straws may the unsuccessful author clutch. There was, of course, an element of technical device in the juxtaposition of the *actualités* of the news bulletin and administration and a story taken from Golding's *Metamorphoses*. Too much so, perhaps, but it was also part of such substance as the book had.

Once it was completed, this manuscript like its predecessor set off on a round of visits to publishers. It did not please any of them, or at any rate it did not give them whatever impulse it is publishers have to have before they see fit to add a book to their list. From time to time I would come home to find a parcel of familiar size and shape awaiting me. There was usually no indication of the publisher's displeasure other than a rejection slip. I imagine that it must be very unpleasant to be at the receiving end of a lot of manuscripts, but my sympathies were less extensive at that time. The book came to rest in a drawer, or the equivalent. It was two or three years later that – I can no longer remember on what chance – I entered into negotiation with the Gaberbocchus Press. After a few weeks I followed, but there was nothing to be seen, for the address was only the company's registered office. The real work was done from an address in Maida Vale, to which I penetrated in due course. Up several flights of stairs I discovered that Gaberbocchus was supposed to be a Latin translation of Jabberwocky and that behind this device were Stefan and Francizska Themerson. By origin Polish Jews, they had come to this country as refugees after the Germans reached Paris and Stefan had served with the army during the war. They were charming, gentle, even a trifle whimsical. Of the two, Francizska seemed to me the more fortunate, if I may say so. It is probably not quite exact to say that painting looks the same anywhere but anyhow the painter in exile does not suffer the deprivations of the writer who is not allowed the use of his native language. Stefan was an intellectual, and thought in terms of ideas transferable from one speech to another and indeed all exercises in semantics seemed to fascinate him. Francizska devised the dust-cover of my book and then decided to do a sketch of the author to go inside the flap. I thought she made me look a little like Bertrand Russell, who a few weeks before had also climbed those stairs and sat in that studio for a sketch which was to go with the *Good Citizen's Alphabet*, likewise published by Gaberbocchus.

When with my host at last I redescend
After delicious talk

IT IS difficult to see the point of this recital of my life; but as it has often been like that in the living, as well as in the telling, perhaps that is not necessarily a bad sign. Before I bought the house of which I have made myself out to be so model a householder we lived in a flat in Earl's Court. This was a quarter of considerable squalor, as it seemed to me, after the war, though it was also the home of much solid respectability, ourselves for example. More than a faint air of the prolonged debauch of the war hung about the place, or perhaps I was imagining things. Anyhow, there was physical squalor, which is more readily identifiable. The tall house we lived in – a tall house in a tall street, in the manner of Earl's Court, was empty when we went there. It had few windows except in the top flat, which was to be ours. Intermittent workmen did jobs about the rest of the place, intermittently, or at least the landlord came and looked at the stains on the walls, and other symptoms of decay. Still, a flat was a flat. We had walked round what seemed an immense number of house agents and been treated with derision when we asked for a flat we could rent. It wasn't the rent we couldn't pay but the large sum – usually measured in hundreds of pounds – which one had to find before one could get in at all. Occasionally in the course of these visits to house agents one would encounter other enquirers better equipped who, after what had no doubt been a splendid war in some racket or other, unpacked suitcases containing more paper money than I thought could exist outside of a bank. I expect the envy which the modest salary-earner must always feel for the man who lays hands on large dollops of money by force, fraud or mere smart-alecry contributed to my impression of the decadence of the times. There was also a more impersonal perception. I remember walking down Piccadilly one autumn day and having – I do not remember why I should have done, on that particular occasion – a sort of vision of the whole world – well, London – caught in a gale of inflation. Nothing stood still. Perhaps it was the bits of newspaper blowing about which started it.

We established ourselves in this flat towards the end of 1946, so we were able to enjoy the fresh air which whistled through the window frames below and met us when we opened the bedroom door. For this, as the historian will recognize, was the winter when there was no fuel, or not enough to boil a kettle at any hour of the day, and also a winter which was cold enough by our standards anyway. Of course everything froze and remained frozen for weeks. We had to fetch water from the basement flat next door. Into the midst of these amenities came a Swiss girl *au pair*, with shining luggage and an air of hardly approving of us. We were certainly deficient in prosperity, and no doubt in other ways. When she came she thought the snow on the roof of the Exhibition building was a mountain, so her guile-lessness should have made our hearts bleed. She also tried to put her bedding out to air on the window sill each morning, to receive the smuts of London instead of the breeze from the *edelweiss*. She told us about the suffering of Switzerland during the war. How should she not? Our subdued resentment was part of the confusion of the times.

In the office the temperature often did not reach fifty at mid-day, so there was that boring mixture of people complaining and enjoying their complaint, bearing up bravely and finding excuses for doing less than they might, which had been characteristic of the civilians' war. The hours of work were long (though, come to think of it, not as long as I now work) and the pace, my impression was, less than it might have been. In one way and another what pass for the purposes of life were a little obscured. However, since I could get to the office in twenty minutes I had some advantages which I have not known since I went to the periphery to rear children.

The literary machine ground on, in its intermittent way. Not only did I write the first chapter of *An Asiatic Romance* in this flat; before that there were other operations, though I find it difficult to synchronize them precisely with my somewhat frequent movements in the two or three years after the war. At some time I wrote *One Eye on India*, in which no one was interested, though I had even made the paragraphs short in my anxiety not to bore. That I should have thought of writing concrete prose of this kind at all was due partly to the fact that Philip Mairet, who was editing – with Denis Saurat – a volume of short stories from France, asked me to translate four stories of Supervielle. He gave me *L'Enfant de la haute mer* in his office in Regent's Park saying, "Of course I don't know that you can do this sort of thing". He asked me to try a few pages and let him see the result. I felt this request as an immense boon, and indeed the work was useful to me because in the course of it I got a slightly different hold on English prose. It felt like that, anyway, and I had the impression that I carried this experience with me when I began *One Eye on India*.

Translation is the best of literary exercises, perhaps the only serious one. It is strictly impossible, and the scope for the apprentice's ingenuity is therefore unlimited. At the same time the translator can have before him a competent model, not to copy but to study and to make something of his own out of. One of the games I played in the slow reorientation after coming out of the army was making verses out of bits of mediaeval French verse. I did very little of this, but even so it gave me a notion of a plainness one could aim at. I read a number of French books at that time; it was part of my rehabilitation and the result of once more having access to the *London Library*. It was partly also that I was interested in what had happened to France, though I could not go there. I must have read most of Montherlant, though I think without at that time being able to get hold of *Solstice de Juin* which stated his position in 1940. I think I should very much dislike this shiny egotist if I tried to read him now. A much greater charmer was Péguy, then in resuscitated fashion. With all this oiling of the wheels it was not until nearly the end of 1946 that I resumed my place as a contributor to the *New English Weekly*.

The shorter post-war was not spent entirely in Earl's Court. I had a month or two there *solus*, my wife and child remaining where they were outside Reading until we could find some possible place to live in. At this epoch I occupied one of those dowdy furnished rooms in a house in which most of the other rooms were occupied by people about whom nothing was clear except that they belonged to worlds barely contiguous to my own. Then we acquired a large, nominally furnished but somewhat empty flat near the Crystal Palace. This establishment was remarkable enough to deserve a brief description.

The house stood in a garden of a couple of acres at least. It had been built to be impressive, I suppose somewhen in the last decades of the nineteenth century. No doubt it had known splendour in its time. Now it was half-derelict, the garden entirely so. The downstairs was inhabited by the owner and his considerable family. He combined the activities of a post-war speculator in property with the sanctity of a peculiar ultra-protestant sect. The children had the air of a separated people, and they were kept in holy ignorance. In these pastures our landlord kept a cow, which had been known to wander off and had had to be retrieved from the Crystal Palace line, low level. One day as we stood in the doorway with my landlord and his hulking sixteen-year-old son it occurred to me to ask what happened when they had to change the cow. It had not been revealed to the young man that cows dry up, or why. My landlord gave me a warning look and went indoors. I was not to sully that young man's mind by talking of cows.

Before we left there was a little affray between worldliness, as represented by myself, and the more spiritual forces which owned the property. I had made some enquiry of the local authority about rent restriction. One day I came home to find the reply, and that it had been opened by my landlord. I taxed him with this but he was invulnerable. He did not deny opening the letter, but instead of exhibiting any shame at the discovery he counter-taxed me with ingratitude for having asked when a rent tribunal was to be set up in the district. It had been charitable of him to let me in, it seems. His expression exhibited all the mechanics of sanctimoniousness. The eyes rolled up. He then told me out of his nearly infinite mercy that no doubt I knew more of the world than he did. I certainly did not know as much about property. Whatever my worldly knowledge, my landlord went on to explain, he had one ineluctable advantage. He was saved and so could not do anything wrong. It was certainly a convenient way of keeping the rent up.

Perhaps something was said

65

I GOT my demob suit at York, where I did not have long inside the cathedral. We were almost at once back over the tail-board of the three-tonner which had brought me as from Wentworth Wodehouse. That evening, as I walked back from the village, I was hailed by three utterly unfamiliar toughs. Between the trilby hats and the stripy shirts I made out with difficulty the features of my fellow-N.C.O.s. The change was complete. Once they had abandoned their uniforms they became socially differentiated in a way which had not been noticeable before. The political impetus of the years immediately after the war was to abolish that differentiation. It was a powerful motive. An even more powerful motive was to make sure that there were no bleeding officers any more – a very understandable wish. Civvy street was to be a place where those bastards fell into their proper place. Hardly surprising that when, a year or two later, the owner of Wentworth was received by Attlee at 10, Downing Street it was to be told that the acres in front of his house would be torn up at once by open-cast mining. After that an earl would know that it was not worth his train fare to London to defend his estate. It was generally agreed that you shouldn't ought to have had an estate. Meanwhile, the collection of less visible wealth became no more difficult, nor the envy with which every man was entitled to regard his neighbour.

Around the stables of Wentworth I mounted guard. The recruits I commanded on these occasions seemed incredibly young. I was thirty-one, and back from two-and-a-half years' service overseas. When I considered these recruits I felt like a man of profound experience. It was generally agreed among those with whom I had returned from overseas that such lads should get some service in. It was half a joke, half a serious joy that someone else was to enter upon a course of deprivation which for us was supposed to be finishing. Certainly these recruits seemed odd at the first encounter. When they got fell in, it was not with the alacrity I expected; nor was it with the accomplished reluctance of the seasoned man. They were soft boys who had grown up in the war. When I first paraded a party of them for guard duty and marched them back to the guard-room I was astonished to find that they expected to scatter to their barrack-room or the canteen the moment they were not visibly on duty. I had expected them to lie on their backs in full kit in the guard-room, waiting to be turned out at a moment's notice. They, however, had learned the scrounging habits of the old soldier before they had learned anything else. With that observation I entered, I suppose, on middle age.

My own exit from the army was a kind of impeccable scrounge.

I had served for only three-and-a-half years which, though it seemed long enough at the time, was nothing to the five or six years which was common enough or to the seven which was usual with those who had been unfortunate enough to be called up with the militia in 1938. I had sailed into Greenock in a P. & O. boat turned trooper, and such was my relief to be back that when we went ashore I did not notice that I was not in my native land. I observed that the girls who waved to us as we marched in were not brown. They seemed luscious. After some necessary pieces of organization at the transit camp we took a train to the south, and I went to the outskirts of Reading where my wife and a daughter I had not seen were awaiting me. I shall say nothing about that evening, or the following morning when a child of mine climbed on my bed for the first time.

I was supposed to have come on a month's leave. My wife and daughter had been squeezed into a single room; the rest of the house was occupied by a civilian and his family whose life had pursued a more even tenor. I think they must have expected the worst of a returned soldier; at any rate when I passed the woman of the house on the stairs she thought that it was an insult such as she had expected. We went to spend some of my month in the Cotswolds. No sooner had we arrived than I was summoned by telegram to attend for an interview at the War Office. I had to get off the train at Reading and change back into uniform. The interview was about a matter of interest. While I had still been in India my employers had asked for my release, under one of those schemes intended to enable the peace-time world to re-start itself as quickly as might be. I had been told, first that I would be released, and then that I would not; they preferred to release people who had not been so inconsiderate as to go so far as India. So on arriving in England I wrote to my employers to say that I was no longer far away, and that they had one month in which to lay hands on me. I assumed, correctly, that the interview at the War Office was about this business. A pale lance-corporal received me in an ante-chamber. Presently I was introduced into a room where a major was sitting at a table. He was a man who had recruited me to the Intelligence Corps, three and a half years before, only then he was a captain. He had throughout this time preserved a certain military punctilio. His first words were: "Where's your badge?" I replied that there were none issued, where I came from. He asked me where that was, and I told him, India. He then said he understood there was some business about my getting out of the army, and asked me what my release number was. These numbers were calculated on age and length of service; they embodied a sort of arithmetized justice. I told the major my number, and he said there could be no question of my release, the number was too low. I began to get worried; I saw myself back on that draft and sailing out of Greenock again. So I explained with appropriate interlarded Sirs! what I knew about the correspondence which he held in his hands but apparently had not read. He looked at me with considerable displeasure and sent me to wait outside. For a considerable number of minutes I consorted with the pale lance-corporal. Then I was sent for again. A thin bowed colonel now paced behind the major at the desk. It seemed that, while I was out of the room, these two had at last got round to reading their papers. The major was too military to admit his mistake. He told me firmly that if I heard no more from them I was to report back to the transit camp at Greenock. But I could see that it was all right. As soon as I got back to my wife I received a telegram, no doubt despatched by the pale lance-corporal, telling me to report instead to the depôt at Wentworth Wodehouse.

Before I left Reading I told my wife to expect the military police. They would obviously be busy picking up the deserters off that draft. And while I was dutifully mounting guard at Wentworth, sure enough they arrived. They brought their van and left it discreetly a few yards down the road. Then one red-cap came and thundered at the front door while another doubled round to the back to cut off my escape route across the fields. They must have been men of experience too. My wife told the man at the front door that her husband had told her to expect them. This he thought a joke in poor taste. However, he took note of the address of the depôt at Wentworth. When I came home on a weekend leave an ordinary blue policeman came round to see me. He too took down a great many particulars and went off to report somewhere. Neither system of reporting can have been free from defect because the authorities in the transit camp at Greenock started to send me insulting letters. They made it clear one way and another that my desertion would receive its proper reward. As time went on the voice of authority grew fainter or its mind more wily. The last communication I received was merely a list of the times of trains from King's Cross to Glasgow, where no doubt I was intended to give myself up. When I finally became a civilian my first act was to write to the commandant of the transit camp in Glasgow telling him it was time he improved his organization.

I remember that, when I reached London after my release the taxi man asked for more than his fare and I refused to pay him. We exchanged courtesies with vigour, and reflecting on the matter afterwards I recognized that while in the army I had received a certain

68

education. When I got back to the office I studied the organization chart and found it full of names I did not know. I also found that other names I did know had, some of them, been climbing the family tree with remarkable speed.

We who have been in chains
Accepting bitterness for every day
Now walk as free as any men can be

II   One Eye on India

They are already made
Why should they go
Into boring society
Among the soldiery?
But I, whose imperfection
Is evident and admitted
Needing further assurance
Must year-long be pitted
Against fool and trooper
Practising my integrity
In awkward places,
Walking till I walk easily
Among uncomprehended faces
Extracting the root
Of the matter from the diverse engines
That in an oath, a gesture or a song
Inadequately approximate to the human norm.

On a Voyage

THE PALE blue of a fine January day hung over the little town and the encircling hills. The air was not without moisture, and the ground was sodden. Drenched matted grass held the observer's eye and invited the noses of the cattle; what was dead or dowdy among it had a sheen not less than that of the living grass. A soldier standing upon it leapt into a slit trench to bring the grass to his eye-level, and the pearls became monsters.

When his eyes tired of the microcosm he raised them, and bare trees with bent-elbow branches swung into the mirror.

The soldier climbed slowly out of the trench and looked at the obstacles littered over the grass – fences for vaulting, walls for climbing, logs designed as tightropes, ditches to be leapt across. A vivid pool that was itself a mercurial sky.

All this lay evidently on an upland, for jutting above the near horizon were one or two house-tops and, a little more remote, the tip of a church spire. The soldier advanced to what had been his horizon and looked over. A grey town lay below, shaped to the muscles of the hills like a growth in an armpit. The series of roofs, elsewhere packed densely like fish-scales, was riven across to allow the passage of a stream, and a road became visible for a little space where the bridge walls clamped it and it leapt from its hiding on one bank to hiding on the other. Across the bridge people were passing, with a slowness consonant with the heaviness of the valley air. Occasionally a van hurried between them or (could it be?) a fish leapt in the stream.

"Remember that we are English, that we are Christian." The air above the little town was heavy with Christianity. The soldier shook his long limbs, and the weight of his boots rippled the muscles to his shoulder-blades. He was at least English.

He turned back to camp and entered one of the Nissen huts. In place of the vault of the sky was an arch of corrugated iron. It was as if he were inside the ribs of the whale.

Wooden beds, a few inches from the ground and militarily spaced, stood on each side of the hut, their noses to the wall and their tails to the gangway, like cows in a milking-shed. On each bed were four blankets, neatly folded, three in a pile wrapt up in the fourth, and webbing equipment was laid out in order upon them. Lengthwise in the middle of each bed, in rigid sleep, lay a rifle. A scabbarded bayonet was placed crosswise below.

The draft was to leave at sundown. The soldier, who was Pearce, tried to attach meaning to this, but could summon only an immense nostalgia. This was what he had chosen.

For several weeks he had ruminated on this departure. His occupations had allowed him opportunity. The exertion of intermittent performances on the assault course or of swinging them arms on the barrack square were not of a nature to stir one's fundamental thoughts, and the idleness of long mikes had made him think as thoroughly as a cow eats. His only preoccupation while he held for hours a wet knife and a solitary potato had been that he didn't accidentally finish the job by peeling the potato.

Kitbags were put on a truck and the men were assembled in full marching order. The column moved down the bended path and was beckoned out by the regimental policeman on duty there. It swung right, and soon the boots under its centipede tail as well as those under its head clattered on the road, and the head inclined gently over the edge of the hill as the column started its descent into the little town. A few passers stopped; a few heads popped from windows. The draft was unmistakable. It went into the station as into a morgue. The usual orders were obeyed with the rhythm of laden men who had a thousand times obeyed these orders' brothers. The men fell out: the train came, and they piled into their places.

They had to change trains at 0100 hrs. and stood for an hour on the junction platform. One or two unstrapped their mugs and queued for tea at a little canteen. The rest merely smoked and waited. Another train took the draft to the port, and at dawn they were under a loading shed at the quayside. The air was smoky and wet, and the sky grey. Above towered the ship's side, the rails lined with men who had already embarked. Here and there the blue serge of a matelot threaded its way among the khaki. But the sailors were distinguished less by their uniform than by their gait; theirs were the comings and goings of men who were about some business that they understood.

The gangway was down, and at the shore end of it was a little group of men with papers. An officer sat at a table writing. A sergeant-major stood behind him. Two military policemen guarded the approach to the ship.

Presently the draft filed on board. Each man carried a kitbag on his shoulder and dragged another with the hand that was free of the rifle. At a snail's pace, and with frequent halts, the file moved up the crowded companionways, along the open deck until they were well aft, and then started a descent. Below the lid of the deck were the chambers and passages of an ant-hill. Men and their baggage were

74

moving around in dim spaces dotted with electric light bulbs. They were crowded so close that they seemed to intermingle and to travel over and under each other. The draft passed down another companion-way. The second circle, where the damned moved in the same restless confusion. Then down again. The deck revealed by the last descent was similarly crowded but for a bare patch at the far end. Towards this the file moved bearing their ants-eggs. They covered the bare patch exactly. They had arrived.

The deck space they filled was covered, but for spaces eighteen inches wide at regular intervals, with narrow tables flanked by benches. Eight men fitted without elbow room on each side of each of the tables. The ceiling was 6ft. 6ins. from the deck level.

Living in these burrows, the body acquired a habit of economy in its movements. When hammocks were slung criss-cross over the mess-decks, the smallness of the gaps between one's own and neighbouring bodies predetermined the muscular action by which one could gain access to a hammock, or get down from it in the morning. When the ship nosed and crashed among the waters of the wintry Atlantic, a false movement would send one's vomit spraying over the men below.

And the mind acquired a ductile quality akin to the dexterity of the body. As the body learned to thread its way among the trunks of the devilish and uncertain forest of surrounding bodies, the mind became retractile from the simple conversation of the lips, but could be extended at will to counter a falling kitbag or to answer a jest.

Queues formed outside the latrines that were awash with sea-water and vomit.

On the open deck, the eye caught a rolling world where great ships rose and fell mast-high in the Atlantic gulfs. Occasionally there was the crackle of light Ack–Ack or the zoom of a plane. For weeks nothing but Atlantic grey, the rise and fall of the sea, and the savourless wind.

Then the convoy moved into the calm and light of Dantean latitudes. The sea sparkled, and once as it greyed at nightfall Teneriffe loomed out of it and the convoy passed breathlessly through the Canaries.

South of that began a miracle of tropical waters, a smoothness of mercury which for all its blue resembled nothing that had hitherto entered into Pearce's notion of the sea. The only imperfections on this surface were the ripples made by the plodding ships, or the sudden emergence of flying fish that skimmed the water like mechanical swallows.

The destroyers played like ducks and dropped depth charges that sent up spouts of water like great whales.

At dawn and sunset the sun poured across the sea all the colours that swim sometimes for a moment in a bubble blown from a bubble-pipe.

The body washed only with sea-water grew rough to the touch and the blood grew thirsty and scorbutic.

One morning the convoy rode into Freetown harbour. The eyes, tired of the water, had at last something to look at, but the foliage on the low hills seemed, behind its hazy veil of heat, to have no quality of slaking.

The ships took fuel and water on board and one night sailed out, with little warning, into the Ocean.

The southern passage passed in an easy routine. Below deck, sweat trickled continuously off bared chests and backs. It soaked the shorts as if one had peed oneself. It smoothed the hair on bared calves.

Stacking and re-stacking kitbags in the crowded hold Pearce studied the pile with his eye lest he might make a movement of which some element was superfluous.

At night he lay on his back on the open deck and plucked the stars. At dawn he leaned easily over the rail, sipping a mug of tea.

Certain imbecilities salvaged from barrack life persisted. Officers were ordered to appear on duty in Sam Brownes, which were no longer an item in their scale of equipment. On a ship where water for washing or even for drinking was scarce and precious, the men were ordered to scrub their belts and gaiters. At a church parade the chaplain, illustrating the meaning of "faith", said: "We have faith, for example, in the captain of this ship," and added as an afterthought, and out of politeness: "And in the O.C. Troops."

Pearce had not counted on making the personal acquaintance of the O.C. Troops, but a curious occurrence brought him that piece of good fortune. When his draft had been on board only a few days and the ship was lying in the Firth of Clyde while the rest of the convoy collected, some stir had been caused on the chock-a-block troop-deck by the indignant circulation of a report that a senior officer, inspecting the deck, had replied to a man who complained: "You've got more bloody room than you deserve!"

After which, as the story was told, the officer retired to a private cabin and the Sybaritic conditions of the officers' mess.

After giving such account as he thought the censor would stomach of the conditions he found himself in, Pearce inadvertently recorded this remark in a letter, which was handed in for despatch before the convoy sailed.

Two weeks later, the monotony of the day's routine was broken by a summons to the orderly room.

"Are you 271 etc Pte. Pearce X.Y.?"

"Sir," replied Pearce.

"Are you the author of this letter?" pursued the adjutant, waving one or two sheets which were covered with what was indubitably Pearce's handwriting.

"It appears to be mine, sir."

"The O.C. Troops would like to see you. You will come here at 0900 hrs. tomorrow."

"Sir!"

Pearce saluted and withdrew. On the following day he appeared smart and punctual. The adjutant accompanied him personally to the cabin of the O.C. Troops.

The O.C. Troops, who was sitting at a table covered with papers, passed a hand rapidly over his grey hair and looked at Pearce with eyes of the type that are called understanding.

"In order to understand something of what the men on this ship are thinking and feeling," he began in a tone that was evidently *reasonable*, "I have sent to me a cross-section of the letters put in for censorship." Then after a pause: "There is something in one of your letters that hurt me very much indeed."

Pearce defended himself against a rising smile, and strained his already rigid posture to show that he was a soldier.

"Stand easy," said the O.C. Troops in a kindly voice.

Pearce obeyed the order as if he had been on the barrack square. No fraternisation!

The O.C. Troops read out from Pearce's letter the passage about "more bloody room",

"Did you write that?" he asked.

(It seemed to be difficult to credit anyone with such effrontery.)

"Sir!"

"Do you know who made the remark you have put down here?"

"No sir!"

"Did you yourself actually hear it made?"

Pearce had to admit that he hadn't.

"There you see," said the O.C. Troops, perhaps relieved, in his *handling men* tone of voice. "You should know better, you know, than to repeat an idle rumour like that. It might give people at home quite a false impression. They might think that no one cared for the welfare of the men on this ship."

"I did not actually hear the remark made," Pearce said modestly, "but I had good evidence that it was made."

The O.C. dismissed him and the letter with him.

Back on the troop-deck, Pearce questioned one or two men till he found the draft to whom the remark in question had been addressed. From this draft he chose two likely lads and told them what had happened. Then he returned to the Orderly Room. The adjutant scowled.

"Is it about this letter again?"

"Sir!"

"Well, what?"

"This morning I withdrew the letter because I was not in a position to substantiate a remark that I had made in it. I am now in a position to do so and I should like the letter to go forward. Sir!"

The adjutant dismissed Pearce, and told him that he would be summoned on the following morning.

The second visit found the O.C. in a different mood. He addressed Pearce angrily without waiting for further explanations.

"And you spread idle rumours," he shouted, "without evidence you could produce in a court of law."

This was Pearce's cue. He produced a slip of paper.

"These are the names and numbers of two men who heard the remark made. I have their permission to give them to you."

The O.C. evidently didn't like this.

"What have *you* done," he asked, "for the four thousand men on this ship?"

Pearce could not imagine what, from his residence near the keel, he could have been expected to do. He said nothing.

"But do you know who made this remark?" asked the O.C.

By this time Pearce had a pretty good idea but he replied: "I did not think it my business to enquire. It was sufficient for my purpose that it had been made."

Next day the O.C. Troops summoned the two men. Pearce was not present but what happened was reported to him.

"Well, who made this remark?" asked the O.C. Troops.

"You did, Sir!" they replied.

The laughter that followed had the air of having been prepared.

The laughter was evoked again when Pearce was interviewed on the following day.

"Of course I didn't mean what you took me to mean. You can send your letter if you like."

Pearce thought the time had come to be magnanimous.

"If you think it is liable to be misconstrued, Sir..."

It is the nature of combats for liberty that, once they are won, one wonders why they were ever fought.

A sudden change in the ship's routine was the Noah's dove that heralded the approach of land.

Pearce closed his eyes and in dream buried his face in long wet grass. Fresh dew ran in the salted wrinkles of his face and trickled to the tongue through parched lips.

Suddenly there was a cry. Table Mountain had appeared to starboard.

The men lined the rails and gazed at the growing land, but before it burst on their vision in all the reality of detail it had started again to diminish. The ship Pearce was in kept the sea for three more days and put in at Durban.

Land seemed not to have been truly reached until, some miles out of the town, the men dumped their bags outside a tent and were free to run over the grass to the canteen, where they buried their noses in grapes, fruit pies, and bottles of pop.

As he came out of the canteen, Pearce observed trees the green of a more meaty foliage than is to be found in English latitudes, and sand showed between the dune grasses where the earth was growing bald under many footfalls. He was lightly clad, and the air that was at blood heat played on his body. The blue sky mantled him. But it was, in Nathaniel Hawthorne's phrase, "by noting things too small for record" that he became aware that he was in a new country.

Tents with the brailing up and kits exposed in the sun before them were aligned on the bare sand. Pearce extracted some soap and a dirty towel from his small pack, pulled his shirt over his head, and sauntered off to look for a shower.

Fresh water after salt, water sparkling from taps and hoses after the unshining puddles in the wash-hand basins in the ship's lavatories, was itself a miracle. Pearce kicked off his shoes and delighted his bare foot in the sand. He dropped his dirty shorts to the ground and stood naked in the sunlight. With a sigh he turned the hose on himself, soaped and sluiced himself again until the last salt had left the skin.

Back at his tent, Pearce laid his new body gently on the ground and pillowed his head on a kitbag. Then, after a moment's reflection, he rose and made his way across broken ground to the station.

On the platform he learned from the inscriptions above the little hutches that served as waiting rooms that the world was divided between two kinds of animal. One inscription said *Blankes* and the other *Nie-Blankes*. (He liked this better than the alternative *Europeans* and *Non-Europeans* and wondered whether the latter inscription could fairly be called by contrast *colourless*.)

By an error he got into a negro compartment of the train. The negroes clucked and gabbled around him, doubtless astonished by the descent of an English soldier to their quarters. He felt very *blank*. Looking out of the window as the train approached the town he saw little groups of negroes, scraggy and dejected, who had evidently suffered defeat at the hands of the city.

Pearce was tempted to buy apples, oranges, grapefruit, grapes and a dozen other fruit, but bought instead the *Natal Daily News* and read the history of a couple "who used to play bridge with us" who had handed their children over to the care of a native nurse. While the parents were going two no trumps the children caught syphilis and both died of it. From these particulars one was meant to draw the general conclusions. Evidently one need not hesitate to insult the blacks in print.

The town surprised Pearce, always susceptible to that emotion of unguarded minds. The broad streets soaked up sunshine and emitted it again; the pavements were thronged with women in bright dresses and men in uniform. The red flashes on the shoulders of the South African troops bore witness to a less mechanical conscription than ours, and their carriage gave a suggestion of superior height and swagger. But the men had not the compactness of some of the English troops.

Turning the corner into a side street he found himself in an Indian town. (A guidebook informed him that the population of Durban was one-third European, one-third Negro, and one-third Indian).

Indians are *nie-blankes*. In buses they sit on the seats reserved for the coloured. On one bus Pearce saw two women in elegant saris pulling one another's hair. Such manners are not *blank*. The women were put off with little ceremony.

An Indian lady returning from Oxford, after spending two years in the comparatively high civilization of that place, talked for years afterwards in Calcutta of the Durban bus service, which she considered demonstrated a bitter irony in the "British fair-play spirit".

Too much vegetation, thought Pearce, and a coastline not sufficiently variegated: sand dunes, trees, bushes, and flowers (great red flowers in the bushes). Butterflies. The Indian Ocean beyond.

The country one drove through was raw in comparison with a European landscape. The ladies spoke of England as home and of the natives with irritation.

Days passed in the usual avocations of a camp where there is nothing to do, but in an atmosphere of relaxation and luxury. Route marches ended with bathes and ices at Isipingo. Laundry was done in a froth of Lux and rinsed in a limitless gush of water, and in no time was ready to wear again.

At night Pearce had sometimes to stick a pistol in his belt and patrol the camp, which was enclosed by wire and illuminated at the main gate by a searchlight.

One night, dressed in a pyjama jacket, P.T. shorts, and a belt with a pistol in it, he got out under the fence and amused himself by walking back into the blare of the searchlight past immaculate policemen too scandalized to complain.

One night he fell into a pond used by negroes as a latrine and by flies as a stud-farm.

When he went to the town he looked for food. Determined to relish the contrast with the troop-deck, he walked into the most expensive hotel he could find. A commissionaire tried to dissuade him: "You can get a drink round the corner, Johnny."

"Are you telling me this place is out of bounds to other ranks?" asked Pearce.

"Not out of bounds," said the commissionaire equivocally, "but I bet you a pound they won't serve you."

An hour later he came out replete, and said as he passed the commissionaire: "It would have been a shame to take your money."

On other days he explored the numerous and excellent canteens whereby the pro-war inhabitants of the town exhibited their loyalty. The Jewish canteen exhibited a balance sheet showing its losses. It was there that Pearce read in the *Palestine Review*: "In spite of the Englishman's alleged feeling of superiority towards the foreigner, he is loath to practise self-advertisement."

The proximity of Madagascar was reflected in the Free French canteen, where on Sundays wine was served with the admirable lunch. An English soldier, and who speaks French! Madame was delighted.

One evening he dined with the van B.s., whose acquaintance he had made. In a flat overlooking the sea, they drank South African wine and dinner was served by a black woman. The family consisted of van B., his wife, and his wife's father, who had come out from England

81

forty years before. The old man had been for years in the British army, and a photograph showed him in the present war in the uniform of the local defence force. He discussed military equipment with Pearce, and said that he had come out on a diet of ship's biscuits. He was not highly literate, and replied to the remark that Indians "practised" fire-walking in Durban by saying that he had never heard of them *practising* but that they did in fact walk through fires.

Mrs van B. explained that the old man had worked on the railways, night-work, and that his health had been bad. He had come to them, nearly dying, six months before. She and her husband had had a plan: they had found the old man a job in their little factory, and had brought him to live with them. Now his cough had almost gone.

"Oh he is happy now," she added, in a phrase usually reserved for the dead.

The car was brought round and Pearce was taken to visit Philippe and Denise, whose flat was a petty France in Durban. Denise was a woman of great vivacity and beauty, or, as for beauty there is Heine's remark that no one could say whether the women of Paris are beautiful because their liveliness and wit stops one examining their features for immobile beauty. Denise talked to Pearce of her daughter of 17, which astonished him. But she explained that she was married at 16, and that when she went to her first dance at the age of 23 she was already the mother of three children. She divorced her first husband and had married Philippe four years before.

Van. B. showed a film he had made. It showed, among other things, Indians walking through fire at Rossburgh. Denise, at whose knees Pearce was sitting, expressed herself forcibly as disgusted by such spectacles and as not interested in India. By this she won Pearce's heart. Fakirs lying on nails were to her merely diabolical. She had no wonder for what was remarkable in the spectacle. She had lived in Mauritius and Madagascar, and had left Paris in 1924; her travels and her nostalgia no doubt counted for something in the matter. But still more depended on the fact that she had a closed and classical mind, not interested in morbid deviations from human reason.

One day Pearce had to wander inspectorially among hundreds of sick Italian prisoners being embarked on a hospital ship. He admired the good humour of all ranks and the scent and silk underwear of the officers.

One man was carried raving on a stretcher, ahead of the rest.

"You see that bastard," said a British soldier, "laughing at us!"

These diversions ended with a sudden order to pack up and be ready for embarkation. It had been the good fortune of the previous draft to be slightly torpedoed just outside Durban, and to limp back for a further stretch in the transit camp, and there was speculation as to whether this draft would also be lucky.

Those who intended to desert made last-minute preparations in their kit and consciences, and slipped the train on its way to the docks.

Pearce's draft arrived on board intact, and the ship sailed without incident into and out of the Straits of Madagascar. The boat turned north as if to put in at Mombasa, but doubled back and steered out into the Ocean. It became clear that the draft was for India.

Indeed India was already on the ship, which was manned by Lascars. These gentlemen carried on an illicit trade in tea. Buckets of lovely stuff were prepared in the crew's quarters and sold to the troops at threepence a mug.

It was explained to the troops that it was not to their advantage etc., that the tea probably came out of their own rations.

Pearce and his fellows listened to these explanations and ordered another cup.

Sentries were posted at the entrances to the crew's quarters and one man was sentenced to a term of imprisonment for permitting the traffic to continue. But the remaining sentries merely said: "Not too near, mate. We're put here to stop this."

So the dry throats of the troops continued to be slaked. The sentries remained loyal, but not to the authorities.

Day after day the sea looked smooth and heavy as mercury. Sharks swam belly up beside the ship, showing their teeth. Night after night great stars hung over the mast-head, and moon-coloured phosphorescences played about the stern.

To keep the troops amused the authorities instituted pointless guards and organized tombolas.

Men sprawled on the burning decks and listened with avidity while the numbers were called out.

"Bed and breakfast, two and six!

"Doctor's delight, number nine!

"Legs eleven!

"Downing Street, number ten!

"Top of the 'ouse, ninety!"

Evidently it was a fragment of England that was being pushed slowly across the still sea.

When a fleet of dhows appeared to port it was evident that the trip was nearing its end. Next morning land was visible, and before many hours had passed the ship was lying under circling kite-hawks in Bombay harbour.

The man next to Pearce jumped up, and with a degree of irrelevance rare even in an Orangeman, shouted:

"Up King Billy!"

He repeated this several times, deafeningly, no doubt with the intention of frightening any Papishes that might be skulking in the Presidency.

I do not say this child
This child with grey mud
Plastering her rounded body
I do not say this child
For she walks poised and happy
But I say this
Who looks in at the carriage window
Her eyes are big
Too big
Her hair is touzled and her mouth is doubtful
And I say this
Who lies with open eyes upon the pavement
Can you hurt her?
Tread on those frightened eyes
Why should it frighten her to die?
This is a fault
This is a fault in which I have a part.

In Bengal

As a strictly practical traveller, Pearce was able to defer his zeal to examine the east until he had eaten and washed the sweat and the salt from his body. He found on the quayside a canteen suitable for his purpose.

As he went out he encountered an officer returning from his first inspection of the town. The officer reported: "I haven't seen a buck Indian yet that I wouldn't like to shoot at sight."

The road from the docks has the same squalor in all great ports. Pearce did not buy combs, watches, French letters, or dirty postcards, and he avoided with difficulty falling over the small boys who started to clean his boots as he walked.

A beggar squatted by the roadside and addressed Pearce as he passed. Pearce's sense of the indignity of curiosity did not permit him more than a glance at the man.

There was a very large number of Indians in India. That much was evident at once. Pearce who had not "farci d'impressions préalables son carnet de voyage" found himself surprised that Europeans were so rare in the streets.

Turning a corner, he came upon a procession; men and women singing and dancing, he was not sure whether in joy or sorrow. Then he saw, carried shoulder-high and decked with flowers, the figure of a girl, her red lips slightly parted, showing her teeth. The spectacle would perhaps have been less astonishing to one from a Latin country where people are accustomed to make much of the dead and of the images of saints.

Pearce took refuge in a restaurant run by Chinese, cool pale people with a talent for food and politeness.

On board his ship once more, he learned that the draft was to move. All arrangements had been made, and seats booked on the Calcutta express. A truck took the men to the station. They made their way among the hundreds who squatted inside, carpeting the place with their sweaty bodies, their clothes, their pots and their chatter. The train did not come. Enquiries were made. The men waited, sweated and smoked. Then the train came; but seats had not been reserved for the draft. A truck took them away to the transit camp at Kolaba.

When next day they did restart their journey, it was by a civilian train. The second class compartment, with its four bunks, seemed spacious and luxurious after the troop-deck. Pearce and his companions unpacked their kits and prepared for a residence of several days.

There were frequent stops, and the passengers could walk into the station restaurant and take a meal. At first some of the men were a little apprehensive that the train might leave while they were eating – a thing that never happens.

Each time the train halted, in however remote a place, beggars appeared, sometimes the aged, but usually little children whose job was evidently to turn an honest anna by frequenting the railroad. The train had only to slow to a walking pace for little cries to creep up from the track: "Sahib! sahib! do anne baksheesh sahib!"

The beggars were often very cheery children, different from town beggars. One little girl stood and rolled her eyes like a rather clever mechanical doll. One sang an obscene English song.

After the beggars, the most numerous class of the population that accosted the men at the stations were the sellers of tea. Tea could be had at all hours; Pearce found that he had only to put his head out of the window and shout "Chae wala!" for one to appear. And if he didn't put his head out, someone would put his head in and utter the same shout.

The brown lands they passed through settled in Pearce's mind like an atmosphere. He looked at the country, despite its monotony, with attention.

At Bilaspur was a man dancing; music; and women carrying on their heads bowls of new shoots, a pale green of the spring.

The lack of machines and plumbing was what struck the troops most forcibly.

The life of the villagers was evidently that of such unenlightened people as Our Lord Jesus Christ. No doubt, Pearce reflected, Jesus would have got around to preach the gospel better if he had had a car.

The brown lands changed to green, and the hot air grew damper. In place of the parched earth was a filthy proliferation of leaves and grasses. The sky line, always close at hand on account of the flatness of the country, was broken by tufted palms or the splayed leaves of banana plants. At frequent intervals the foreground was filled with rectangular tanks, into whose green water men with their loose white garments still about them descended to bathe. When the train stopped in the neighbourhood of a tank, a fastidious–looking man in spectacles and a spotless shirt and dhoti stepped down from the compartment next to Pearce's and immersed himself in the stinking water.

Here and there were small tanks from which steps arose to the lawns of green or ochrous bungalows that were crumbling under the teeth of the devouring climate.

87

At the end of the journey, coolies fought for the baggage. They snapped like dogs, whose eye-whites they had. Greed made them inattentive like preoccupied and hysterical women.

It is a merit of the military system that, in whatever strange circumstances the soldier may find himself, it demands of him the punctual performance of rites no less than if he were in a regimental barrack room at home, or if, as may often be the case, the observance of a large part of the rites goes by default, the sense of an Order remains of such force that whatever is actually done is enjoyed as a variant from it, much as the rhythm of verse may be enjoyed as the almost imperceptible variations from a formal scheme.

Pearce's first duty was to learn how to make up his bed. The next was to dine.

It was only later, when he lay smoking on his bed, that he summoned the recollections of the day and the camp built itself again in his mind.

The truck that had brought the draft from the station some miles away had slowed down on a metalled road that ran through a grassy stretch dotted with great red-brick buildings like warehouses out of Chirico. Before one of these buildings the truck had dropped its tailboard and the sweaty, loaded men had been pushed out like dung from under the tail of a horse. With the rest Pearce had mounted the few stone steps leading to the verandah, and had found a bed in the lofty room under a punkah that swept slowly to and fro from a creaking framework. In these barracks the Queen's red-coats had sworn and sweated; this was the site, Pearce was afterwards to learn, of an opening scene of the Mutiny of 1857; and of a more relevant mutiny during the First Burma War, when British soldiers refused to cross the river because, they said, the costs of transporting their baggage were too high.

The beds were aligned barrack-fashion, and along the room ran lines from which were suspended the mosquito nets. As Pearce entered the room, a dark-skinned man in loose white trousers and a coloured shirt (with the tail outside the trousers) rose from where he crouched on the floor beside a pile of boots and blacking brushes. The man had watched the draft dump their kit, and had then let it be known that he was the bearer. Quietly he carried away Pearce's boots.

For a rupee a week, Pearce learned, this man would clean his boots, make his bed, and arrange his mosquito net. Pearce's mind was not revolted by this purchase of services.

A small, very dark, bare-footed man had then appeared. He spoke no English but explained himself simply: "Dhobi, sahib."

Pearce shovelled on to the floor all the clothes he wasn't wearing and the dhobi carried them away. He looked enquiringly at the bearer, who at least seemed to have an address (in the barrack-room) and the bearer indicated his approval of the proceedings.

(A few days later Pearce discovered the dhobi ghats. Only a few hundred yards from the barrack-room the air was broken by the slap of wet clothes on stone. Half-a-dozen dark men were wielding shirts and towels and slacks like so many flails. All around the clothes were spread out to dry. In a little hut nearby it was pressed and folded into neat piles. It was here that Pearce learned to come to interview, not the men labouring with the flails, but a bright-eyed boy of eight who never forgot a face, and never failed to associate it with the correct mark, so that on a customer appearing the right pile of clothes was put before him. It was the talent of a waitress who never forgot which of two hundred customers take milk or sugar. This kind of memory is often granted to the illiterate.)

The second visitor to the barrack-room was the char wallah, a bearded man whose coming was regularly announced by the clink of his charcoal-heated urn and his box. The urn glinted as he put it down, like a cat winking before it goes to sleep. The box, of dull metal, hung by a strap from his neck when he walked: when he set it down and opened it one could see dozens of unappetising little cakes, some with splashes of coloured icing on them. The char wallah was accompanied by a small boy who collected the mugs and brought back the tea.

Pearce ordered a mug of tea, and two of the little cakes. The tea was a thick, dirty drink, whose least offensive taste was of smoke. Before he left India Pearce's blood was composed of this liquid.

On the roads outside the barrack-room circled the gharry-wallahs on tricycle rickshas. The men were short and dark, they pedalled barefoot, and their shirts were sodden with sweat. If one wanted their services one had merely to shout "Gharry!" or raise a hand. They stopped; one took one's seat: for a few annas they took one where one would along the level roads.

The temptation to call a gharry was strong in an atmosphere where no effort at all brought sweat trickling over one's body. It became a matter of routine, when Pearce came into the barrack room, to strip off his sodden shirt and hang it on the bedding line to dry. A shower bath kept the sweat off one's body only for a moment. And the water was always warm and did not refresh.

Pearce's bowels grew liquid and often his belly could hardly contain them. At night he was often forced out into the latrines to give vent to his diarrhoea. One or two others were sure to be on the same mission at the same time as he, hurrying with anxious look or returning happy, perhaps stopping to smoke a cigarette under the tropical stars. The latrine became a friendly place. Pearce wondered at the sweeper whose millennial descent had secured him the honour of carrying away the buckets.

The air was heavy with squalor and oppression; millions, it seemed, lived in an abjection from which nothing could raise them. Pearce scrutinized the faces of the passers for clues to their thoughts and identities. The coolies and sweepers with unlit eyes; the mincing babus; the Sikh tailor from under whose beard there broke, as he showed his teeth, an unmistakable girlish smile. It was impossible to comprehend this world; and clearly those who had lived long in it had lost the habit of comprehension. Sympathy, had it been possible, would have been exhausted by the multifarious calls that sapped it. Life seemed to be possible for an Englishman only by a shrinkage of the brain to the size of a walnut, so that he was left concerned only to defend the most evident self-interest against the encroaching strangeness. There was no new mode of feeling or thought to be learned, only a mode of action which was, it was patent, perversely limited, but which none the less bore traces of a social skill which had developed in two hundred years of occupation, and had reasonable claims as a wisdom to be learnt. But Pearce had not yet learnt it.

One day, in a local train taking him out of Calcutta, he had just taken his seat in an inter-class* compartment. At the last moment a coolie accompanied by two women and three small naked children pushed their way in. Pearce was on the point of offering one of the women his seat, forgetting that they were not ladies, "those monsters of European civilization and Christian-Germanic stupidity". But an outcry arose, and Pearce gathered that the coolie and his little flock had no right to be there at all. (Doubtless the third class was the place for them, or perhaps they should have ridden hanging on the outside of the train, as so many commonly did.) Pearce's next impulse was to offer his seat to the woman in spite of his perception that such a gesture would be socially unsuitable, just to observe the effects or perhaps in

---

* The inter-class is "inter" third and second, the latter being the lowest class in which anyone in the sahib class could possibly find himself. In general, it is axiomatic that the sahib travels first; sub-sahibs, such as B.O.R.s, may go second.

indulgence of a Puritan self-righteousness. He hesitated, however, guessing that there might be indignation if he gave up his seat to a coolie-woman and thinking at last that no one would have known what he was about if he gave up his seat. (A few months later he would have sworn at anyone who tried to make a gesture half as quixotic.) The women settled comfortably on the floor. At the first halt, one of the seated passengers got out. The coolie moved into the vacant seat and his conduct was clearly "right". Any other action would have been an absurdity. (When Pearce passed through London on his return to England after several years, he found that a similar code of conduct obtained there.)

When the coolie, his womenfolk and their children got out, a boy with cymbals got in and played and sung monotonously till the train reached the next station, when he asked for annas that nobody gave him. He got out with a smile that was almost cheery.

The issue of clothes to the men was somewhat meagre. One of the two pairs of boots Pearce had carried from England was withdrawn so that he was left with only one. He had never been given more than a single pair of long slacks, though the wearing of them was compulsory after sundown as an anti-malarial precaution and the K.D. didn't last more than a day or two without washing. For topee he had only the grotesque and heavy cardboard affair that had been issued to him in England.

It was therefore necessary to make purchases. For the officers, officers' shops were provided where that poverty-stricken class (on Indian rates of pay) could buy all that they wanted cheaply, but Pearce and his friends were subjected to the racketeering of the open market.

There were some who felt that a grateful country might have arranged things differently.

"And the cook-house."

But the cook-house was all right.

In the swelter of 1300 hrs. a truck might unload at the barracks. The men would fetch their plates and mugs from the barrack-room and make their way to dinner. The dining room was a low wooden hut with no punkah, and was about the temperature of the stew that was baled out at one end of it. Each man would collect a plateful and pick a blank space for himself on the bench beside the table. Sweat fell from foreheads, chins and arms and noses, and little pools stood wherever a man rested his arm on the table.

At one end of the room stood two dark-skinned gentlemen, each with a bucket of water and a dirty rag that was believed to be a tea-towel or a loin-cloth. As each man finished what he could eat he rose, handed his mug, plate and eating irons to these attendants, who dipped them in the stinking bucket, rubbed them in the tea-towel or loin-cloth, and handed them back to him. Evidently the British soldier was no menial.

Sometimes it was better to leave the dinner and take a slice of bread and jam (if there were any) back to the barrack-room.

As one carried it out of the dining room, with a swoop of the wings a kite-hawk might fall from the sky to devour it, its wing or beak hitting one's cheek or shoulder.

Of course the Orderly Officer visited the dining room: "Eggs are appreciated when issued. Could they be issued more often?" – No.

"The bacon is very fat and sometimes uneatable." – Same as in the Officers' Mess.

"The floor of the cook-house is dirty through smoke, etc. Could something be done about this?" – No.

"Washers-up have only two pails of water and two dish-cloths. This is considered unhygienic. Could more be issued?" – Take away the privilege and let the men wash their own dishes.

The most insidious evil of his condition seemed to Pearce to be the censorship, which put a barrier worse than that of time and distance between the soldier and the people at home. Pearce had experienced censorship in his first days in the army, in Ulster. But there the authorities had seemed concerned only with military secrets (and Pearce didn't know any); here they seemed concerned with morale – and any exposé of one's opinions could hardly be less than sedition.

Pearce amused himself one day by writing out, in courteous terms and without evidence that could lead to identification of the ship or the officer concerned, the story of his encounter with the O.C. Troops on his boat.

The story had a moral for censoring officers and the one who interviewed Pearce was cautious.

"I'm afraid I can't sign this. You could send it to the base censor of course, but I warn you there might be disciplinary action."

Pearce indicated that he was not picking a quarrel with anyone.

Coming off duty on a lucky evening, Pearce might go to the little swimming bath in the barracks and find that the water had been changed and was clean.

The bath-keeper was a soldier with twenty years service in, who had been seven years in India. He was stupid and dull and coarse, thought Pearce, but those are gifts of nature. He has acquired, from his long life in the army, what his fellow who stayed lounging in the streets at home would never have, a social education which makes him possible to live with. He was a man to have a pleasant word with, and not troublesome, probably, even when he was drunk.

Pearce would plunge in, and swim up and down once or twice. Then he would put on his shorts and put his towel about his neck and stroll back to the barrack-room.

One night he borrowed a pair of civilian shoes which made his evening's idleness a luxury.

He picked a book out of his kitbag and wandered slowly down the barrack steps. A circling gharry wallah stopped as he raised his hand, and he bowled along the road, the motion of the gharry making a small moist wind that was a pleasant relief to the body already sweaty again after the bathe.

The gharry wallah stopped as instructed before the gate of the Soldier's Club. Pearce proffered a rupee note. The gharry wallah indicated that he had no change.

A shortage of small change in the country in that time gave plausibility to the story*, but Pearce had already learned enough to pay no attention. He began to walk away.

"All right, sahib! Change!" called the gharry wallah, producing from under his shirt a heap of coins tied in a dirty rag. Pearce, pleased at these first-fruits of experience, walked back to the gharry and paid.

He strolled across the lawn and up the steps of the Soldier's Club and took his place on the verandah. There he drank lime-juice and ate eggs and tomatoes and chips, the diet of the legionaries on ticket-of-leave.

Night fell, and fruit-bats with gigantic wings emerged from the great trees and circled. A monkey or two popped out for a last chatter. The stars grew big.

Then was the moment of the most delicious cigarette. Pearce took out a packet. The sweat from his fingers moistened the rice-paper. Sweat trickling down his upper lip fell in a blob on the cigarette as he put it in his mouth. He scratched one damp match after another on the flimsy box, till one lit the night for a moment like a bubble of light slowly expanding and quickly burst. (Of these matches it was said that if you took one out of a new box and it struck, you should throw the box away, because *that was the one*.)

---

* Many Indians thought that the nickel coins represented real value (like gold) and hoarded them rather than take the notes of a tottering régime. Piles were found under dung-hills etc.

The cigarette was musty.

Presently two little Muslim boys whose eyes sparkled in the darkness came round begging cigarettes. Pearce shook his head. They insisted. He told them to be off and they made off like mice.

Pearce drew two or three times at his cigarette, and a voice at his elbow said: "Sahib!"

One of the small boys had come back.

It was understandable, the boy conceded, that one couldn't give cigarettes to two boys, but to *one*... that was a different matter.

Pearce saw the fallacy of this argument but, amused, threw the boy a cigarette.

No sooner was he alone than the other boy appeared.

Evidently, the argument ran, it had been impossible to give two boys... Pearce laughed and tossed the boy a cigarette to stop him talking.

Suddenly there arose out of the darkness of the lawn a man carrying a large bundle that might have been laundry. He went in at the lighted doorway and Pearce followed him.

The man set his bundle down and enquired of Pearce where the "contractor" was to be found. (Pearce did not yet know that there was always a contractor.) He referred the man to the mem sahib who appeared to be in charge of the place for the evening. Apparently the mem sahib gave the permission that was sought, for when the man came back to his bundle he opened it and lay the four corners of the covering cloth carefully on the ground. In the centre of the square was a pile of books. Pearce, with the hope readers have, looked at the titles. The books were: *Confessions of India*, *The Indian Harem*, etc.

The memsahib meanwhile had apparently had second thoughts, and came out to look at the books. After conference with a soldier who, apparently, had momentarily produced on her the impression of reliability, she decided that the books were pornographic and sent the vendor packing. Unperturbed, he folded up the cloth and re-tied the knots, explaining as he did so that he had also good books and would return.

"The British soldiery," explained the trustworthy soldier, "are sufficiently depraved. You should bring them the *Christian Science Monitor*."

The orthodox honour Brahma, Vishnu, and other deities. Sectarian votaries of Siva wear the *lingam* "fastened to the hair or around the arm, enclosed in a little silver tube; but more often they hang it around the neck, and the silver box containing it rests on the chest." Votaries of Vishnu paint the *namam* on their foreheads.

Pearce, playing blind-man's buff in an ignorance more hopeless than darkness, found the *lingam* on the arms of the gharry-wallahs and the *namam* on the foreheads of women passed in the street.

Were not these mysteries that assailed the Roman soldiers in Asia Minor, and finally flooded and destoyed the capital itself?

"It is incredible, it is impossible to believe, that in inventing this vile superstition the religious teachers of India intended that people should render devout worship to objects the very names of which, among civilized nations, are an insult to decency...

"What I have just said about the *lingam* applies also to the *namam*, another emblematic and not less abominable symbol."

The gloomy Abbé's book* evoked a world which answered to the stinking and sweltering atmosphere of the place Pearce found himself in. The Abbé had observed with a Christian and Roman anger that was both a nostalgia for and a defence of the France he had left for so long.

"It is only after long and serious reflection on the many eccentricities and inconsistencies of the human mind that one can look without astonishment..."

Pearce could not. Or if not astonishment, a suppressed wonder inhabited the back of his eyes where this strange world was reflected.

The brown children did not play, but sat hopelessly before the doorways, without vigour. The little ones were naked; those a little older had acquired a loincloth or a diminutive sari. The girls were slow and sober, no doubt busied early about their household vocations. They could be seen moving gravely along the streets with pots or parcels upon their heads.

One house with barred windows was a school, and the noisy chatter of human disorder came from it.

The utter flatness of the land nowhere afforded any long prospect, but a short walk took one from the squalid streets of the bazaar to open ground in which was sunk one of the large rectangular tanks which are a characteristic of the country. In this dead water men and women washed themselves and prayed. Beside it was a Muslim burial-ground, and sometimes along the rutted track might be seen coming a little group of coolies carrying a corpse whose shape was easily visible under the flimsy cloth that covered it. There could not be a humbler end to life than this.

---

* Hindu Manners, Customs and Ceremonies, by the Abbé Dubois. This famous work, as is well known, was the outcome of the Abbé's studies and work in Southern India at the end of the eighteenth and the beginning of the nineteenth centuries.

In the gathering heat before the monsoon rumours of famine reached even the soldiery.

"No one wants this scrap of bread, but if I take it I shall be punished."

On the streets of Calcutta the beggars lay as usual with hopeless eyes. Occasionally a body was found, but for people to starve was at any time hardly remarkable. And it would scarcely have been polite to enquire, of each one of a heap of bodies lying in the streets, whether he was alive.

Once Pearce saw a coolie running along the road with a handcart on which the almost naked body of another coolie was stretched.

"Dead?"

"You do not suppose he would be given a ride if he were alive!"

Looking out at a certain angle from the barrack-room window upon green tree-tops and blue sky one might have imagined (but for the lead in the sky and the stillness of the branches) that this was England. Oh to be in an August at home, lying on one's back in the delicious and scented breeze, looking up through waving branches at the "silk-sack" clouds! But here was the hostile sun; the heavy leathern buffaloes that stood like hippopotamuses in the pools, only the top of the head and the line of the back visible; the sweating Rama on his bullock-cart, crouching above his beasts and twisting their tails. Even by the river at evening watching the sampans, or sitting on the ver-andah of the Soldier's Club, eating fruit salad, one could not look out on anything that did not represent servitude.

For Pearce this seemed to be the prospect of many years. No one ever went home. There were regulars who had spent seven years in the Command and had no news of return. "Not a tenth part of whom," he had read in some account of the soldier's life in the days of John Company, "ever go home again."

Freedom was inconceivable. Pearce thought of it as existing thou-sands of miles away across the atlas world of Africa and the Mediter-ranean, and remote in time.

The pariahs and the Sudras (whose function is "general servitude") form ninety per cent of the population. Thus the Abbé.

But bright-eyed, bushy-tailed, rapid in their movements when they were not as still as stone, the tree-rats at least had found a way to live.

It is difficult for a European to like India, thought Pearce, who had not yet encountered one who did, though he had met those who liked the real or bogus authority that India indulged them with. The Abbé Dubois had expressed his dislike again and again. In his description the kites, with their cowardly disposition and their foul smell, were scarcely less repugnant than the evil customs of the people.

Nature in this country was as unwholesome as this rotted civilization itself.

Before coming to India Pearce had felt that, although the British should continue to govern the country to prevent worse, Indians and their creeds were perhaps best left alone. But in this atmosphere he felt the oppression of a tradition backed by centuries not of Christianity and respect for the human person but superstition, torture, even (not so far away) self-immolation and human sacrifice. The sacredness of kites, monkeys and cows became a nightmare; it was possible to watch these creatures moving among human beings and to see the human beings as of less account than they, and this transvaluation made them grotesque and frightful.

Pearce imagined too that he could feel the air (which was perhaps heavy only with heat and moisture) heavy with the self-satisfying doctrine of reincarnation (men are born unequal and they bloody well deserve to be), one caste spitting on another. At any rate he had seen in Calcutta reṣtaurants rich Hindus treating servants with a contemptuous impatience of which a European would hardly have been capable because he could not have entertained such feelings unmixed with shame.

Pearce's nostalgia at times took the form of a belief that a country like his own that had been Christian, and seemed still, for all its diseases, healthy compared with this one, should not tread lightly on the corns of India.

"I did not take office to preside over the dissolution of the British Empire."

But the British were leaving India because they lacked conviction. They no longer knew what they wanted in the country. If they had still a function to perform, the statesman who could inform them of it had not yet appeared.

The troops did not celebrate the sabbath, but on one day in eight they were allowed to substitute for military idleness such idleness as they could devise of their own.

On one such day Pearce wandered slowly down to the Hooghli banks.

"Don't wander along like that, corporal!"

He had omitted to salute some apoplectic officer.

When this nuisance had gone, Pearce resumed the pleasure of gazing at the great slow river, on which sampans steered or drifted.

A sampan came to rest near him with the surprised little jump of a boat that is suddenly grounded. It was the ferry boat for Serampore.

A little group of passengers collected – two or three coolies with great bundles, women in dowdy saris and with downcast eyes, and two young gentlemen with shell spectacles and billowing white shirts and dhotis who were voluble in Bengali interspersed with phrases or sentences in precise and inhuman English.

The ferryman motioned Pearce to a seat in the most eligible part of the boat. The bilge-water clipped and clopped under his feet as she was pushed off.

The watermen stood; two forrard, rowing with long oars – bamboo poles to which blades were lashed with strands of wire; another with a third oar aft steered.

The boat's movement was governed by an interplay of oarsmanship and current, and the regulated drift brought her to rest at the foot of the steps on the further bank.

Dotted around in the water where the boat came in, waist deep or armpit deep, men and women stood praying.

Pearce got out and dropped a bright four-anna piece into the boat-man's hand.

Then he ascended the steps, which were flanked at the top by gaudy and hideous images.

To this strand Mrs W. Carey had been wheeled in her bathchair to take the evening air of 18—, and then returned to Mr Carey whose industry had produced translations of the Bible into forty languages and dialects.

At present the town was famous for its prostitutes and its V.D. hospital.

Pearce walked through the streets to the station, and when he enquired for a train he was directed into the first-class lavatory.

He found the train after a little while and it took him through a country of tanks and banana plants to Chandernagore.

Outside the station gharry wallahs were waiting. He climbed into a machine and without a word of instruction the man took him to the College. Apparently he was suspected of academic connections. But Pearce was looking for the Café de Paris, of whose existence he had heard and whose name enticed him.

One place in the colony was as good as another to Pearce and he paid the man off.

The Hooghli waterfront was ornamented with a statue of Dupleix, a Prison Général and an Ecole de Jeunes Filles. Pearce was pleased with this evidence that he was out of British India. The shuttered windows tried to look as much as possible like France.

Then Pearce turned into the town and observed with regret that commercial notices were usually in English. At last he stumbled upon green double doors and a sign:

WHITE HORSE HOTEL
late
Café de Paris

Inside was a delicious little courtyard on one side of which was a verandah with tables and chairs.

The manager advanced, cleaning his teeth as he walked.

"Good day," he said in English, and Pearce ordered coffee.

As he drank it the manager approached again and Pearce enquired whether he spoke French.

The idea seemed a queer one to the babu.

"The governor comes here once a year," he said.

Then the electrician came, with a bicycle on the handlebars of which was a coil of wire big enough to rewire the whole of Chandernagore. Four or five men gathered round the fuse box, sometimes pulling out a fuse and sometimes taking a tug at the punkah above it.

A tray was brought for Pearce to put his money on, and the bearer was grateful for two annas.

Whereas I wander here among
Stone outcrops, rocks and roots
Below me tapers the peninsula
All India going to the sea.

Below, summer is a disease
Which seas surround whose glassy blue
Nothing can cool and nothing cure
But seize my heart

The jackal wandering in the woods
For I have speech and nothing said
The jackal sniffing in the plains
The vulture and the carrion crow

O jackal, howl about my bed.
O howl around my sleeping head.

In the Hills

IT WAS announced that Pearce, with three others, was to leave for the north.

The station he was destined for was said to be in the hills. For months he had not seen even an undulation.

The four men packed their kits and a truck took them to Calcutta. The army had, of course, arranged everything, only the seats had been booked on the wrong train going to the wrong place.

The four agreed at once that they wouldn't return to the bloody dump they'd come from, so they fought and bribed their way into a second-class compartment among Indians with vast bundles, cooking pots, beards and a smell of garlic.

There was no room for them to put their beds down.

Some miles north of Calcutta Pearce saw a hill rising like a blister out of the paddyfields. It was long before he saw another.

Green grew rarer in the countryside and the character of the houses changed. The bamboo disappeared. The buildings turned into the white blocks of the picture-book orient. As the train slowed down to cross the river at Benares Pearce saw the first camel. They were in a new country.

Just past the Sacred City an altercation arose between a British sergeant, who had a place to put his bed, and a V.C.O. who was asking for a little space on the floor. The sergeant desperately wanted to throw the V.C.O. off the train. The Indian, a fine-looking Punjabi, was civil; the British sergeant's strained voice and contorted face bore witness to passionate conviction of a rightness for which there was no other evidence.

A further altercation, between an Anglo-Indian and the V.C.O. ended in the former tugging hard at the communication cord. Nothing happened, and nobody seemed surprised.

At Delhi Pearce slept on the concrete floor of the passage outside the waiting room.

At Lahore he got out and rode around the town in a *tonga*, but it was too hot for enthusiasm and he concluded the venture by drinking lime-juice and closing his eyes.

After Lahore the ground began to break up a little, and the altitude increased perceptibly.

After Rawalpindi there were low grey hills, dotted with darker scrub, and a light which made Pearce think they were in the hills of Greece, which he had never seen.

Under this olive-green horizon was parched stony plough-land. Bearded men out of the Old Testament were at work on it with oxen and wooden ploughs.

It was early morning when they arrived at their terminal station. A truck was waiting for them – perhaps through some miscalculation, two wrongs making a right.

The men stretched their creaking limbs and opened their eyes wide in the lively sunlight. The air was hot, but not sodden like the air of the Hooghli bank. One could stamp in the dust a bit and swear and feel better for it.

They were unwashed and hungry after several days of life in railway trains and on platforms. Pearce felt so thirsty that he thought that if he cut himself no blood would come.

The driver of the truck, an Indian soldier dressed much as Pearce and his friends were, took up the non-committal attitude of one who was waiting for orders. After a bit the men took notice of him.

"Wait!" they said, using one of the few Urdu words in their vocabulary.

Then they made their way to the waiting room beside the station. At their entrance the place became alive.

A small boy started to pull a punkah-cord as if he were a bell-ringer. Bearers in whitish coats and soiled pugris appeared.

What would the sahibs have?

What could they have?

They were offered eggs and chips. They were offered tea, cereals, milk and sugar. They were offered toast and butter. And jam.

They each drank a glass of lime-juice and reflected. Then they ordered everything they had been offered.

The meal was delicious. Finally they smoked cigarettes while the food and drink soaked in.

Then came the bill. It was Rs. 2-8 a head, and they were prepared to pay and be glad. A young officer walked in, however, and in a stream of Urdu whose quality he no doubt rightly judged the men would not be able to distinguish from its quantity, interceded unasked and argued the bill item by item with evident relish, finally fixing the just price of the meal at Rs. 1-8.

Pearce felt no gratitude as the young man explained the necessity of "watching these wogs, who will always try and do you," but the thing was fixed and they paid the reduced bill and went out.

By this time the truck was crammed with Indian troops, mainly Sikhs with their baggage and belongings. The four men forced their way in.

The truck tore off and was soon climbing a winding road that appeared to be mounting some sort of valley. At many places the road was little more than a ledge, the earth banked steeply on one side and falling away precipitously on the other.

The racing speed was soon reduced to an uneasy and almost back-sliding crawl, and the whole vehicle shook and almost split up at each change of gear.

Finally the truck was running on almost level ground. The land had opened out between two hills.

There were signs of military occupation. Other trucks passed Pearce's vehicle on the road. From time to time there was a smart trot of hoofs.

The truck passed a sentry and went into a camp. The men were spilt out.

Pearce was aware of blue air dancing in a heat haze, and around him the grey-white tops of army huts.

After a pause which, on such occasions, a military establishment requires before its brain can decide what to do next, Pearce was shown into a low-built wooden hut which contained a few charpoys. He dumped his kitbag with a thud, sat down, swore a little (but in happy mood) and stripped off half his clothes and in the remainder went in search of a wash-place.

The first soldier he met was able to direct him, and added: "Some wog has shit in it."

But the next wash-place was all right and Pearce took off the rest of his clothes and let the water from an exiguous shower trickle over him.

When he got back to the hut a bearded man stood at the entrance. He was scarcely more articulate in Pearce's language than Pearce was in his, but he let it be understood that he was a bearer, "the bearer".

He was very attentive, and it was only with difficulty that he could be prevented from dusting Pearce's shoes every time the latter went in or out of the hut. Pearce, never very enthusiastic about cleaning his own shoes, admired the man's diligence but foresaw that it would be tiring.

The relations established were a little too pleasant.

That night the C.S.M. descended on the hut and informed the men that the bearer had not been vetted by the police. The bearer was interviewed next morning, after which he came to Pearce, sadly and said: "It is finished."

The four men gave him baksheesh and engaged a less fascinating character.

Pearce looked with delight on the Indians walking about the camp. They were men of a very different stamp from the abject race he had been accustomed to, from those who for centuries had sweated and rotted in a filthy climate and had hoped for nothing. These men were tall, many bearded – beards naturally black but some dyed red in compliment to the Prophet. They wore loose trousers and shirts and their pugris hung loose at one end.

Everyone had a shirt to his back.

On the road beside the camp a stream of traffic passed. There were tongas, sometimes with drivers standing, their pugris flying behind them; the ponies it is true were poor beasts but they were giants compared with the miserable creatures sometimes to be seen crawling around Calcutta. Many men on foot, sometimes in long pointed slippers like Aladdin's, more often in sandals known as chaplis.

There were tiny donkeys, many of them loaded with great bundles twice their size.

There were long strings of camels, led by pale-skinned Indian soldiers who held a rope one end of which was attached to the nose of the leading camel. Sometimes single camels dragged heavy carts, and Pearce saw one, who had lost its driver, racing along the road with the cart swinging dangerously from side to side.

There were strings of mules.

There were of course bullock carts. There were buffaloes. There was a great variety of Indian and Ghurka troops.

At evening, when the near hills darkened, the further hills were scarcely pencilled against the sky. But the world was merely a rustling tissue of images. Next day, at noon, the sky suddenly grew green, and overhead, black. The hills in the middle distance became purple, wedged between ridges of the nearer grey-green.

Torrents fell, and extinguished the scene like a safety curtain.

The stripe on Pearce's arm gave him admittance to a room that was specially reserved for corporals. Here a few fusty armchairs, relics no doubt of the peace-time soldiery, tried without much success to give an air of civilian luxury. And tea could be ordered from the frowsy bearer in a pot. It was very distinguished.

Pearce smelt round the room, which was empty. A few old Sunday papers and other periodicals sent from home were piled on the table, and beside them was an open exercise book with a few pages not yet ripped out of it.

On the open page Pearce saw where a shaky hand had written:

a b c d e f g h [etc].

1
2   Cooking apples
3   Cooking apples
4   Cooking apples
5
6
7
8   Tonga
9

Then in a firmer hand:

'Corporal Renn loves Tonga.'

A bearer came in. He was only a youth and his eyes and lips were those of a person quickly bashful and flustered. He closed the exercise book and prepared to go out with it.

Pearce ordered tea and entered into conversation with the boy about change. Before he had done two corporals Pearce was not yet acquainted with came in.

"Tonga!" they shouted.

"One minute, sahib" said the bearer.

Pearce continued to address him and the bearer listened.

Suddenly one of the corporals came across the room and seized Tonga by the shoulder.

"Don't you ever tell anyone to wait," said the corporal menacingly, out-staring the boy (which was not difficult). "That's an order."

He went back to his place.

Pearce, who was acquiring the habit of the country, which is to be quickly angry, felt affronted and kept the bearer another two minutes.

"He mustn't be allowed to tell anyone to wait," said the corporal when the bearer had gone.

"Try to talk sense," said Pearce.

Admission to the Corporals' Room was known as membership of the Corporals' Mess, although the corporals in fact took meals in the ordinary troops' dining room.

One day the Mess held a meeting. The sergeant-major took the chair.

The first question was, who had called the meeting. At first no one seemed to know, but after some murmuring it was discovered that one corporal had said something to an officer about lack of entertain-

105

ment and as a result a notice of the meeting had been put on orders.

The C.S.M. explained that there must be a social. He defined a social as dancing, a general beer-up and a tombola, but it seemed doubtful whether dancing could be arranged.

There was little enthusiasm for the project. At last someone asked: "Do we really want a social?"

The C.S.M. was a little affronted by this, but being a democrat put the matter to the vote.

11 voted for a social.

14 voted against.

3 did not vote.

The C.S.M. said that the abstention of the three meant that they didn't care whether there was a social or not, and concluded that he *therefore* had a casting vote. He cast it, adding as he declared the result: "And the social will be a Commanding Officer's parade."

One evening, when Pearce returned to his barrack-room, he found two ponies waiting outside, attended by a shiny-toothed black-bearded rogue who was blowing his nose in his pugri-cloth. Pearce consented to ride.

The horse-wallah did not expect his customers to know how to ride, and started explanations in an imperfect language. While he was talking, Pearce selected the stouter of the two ponies and climbed into the saddle. He was off at a brisk trot.

The clop of the hoofs on the stony path was delicious. Pearce stood in the saddle and shouted. The beast pushed out his neck and blew long through his nostrils. Pearce kicked encouragingly and they disappeared out of camp, down a slope and across a stream that increased the animal's excitement.

Occasional clouds billowed overhead and a brilliant light fell on the hills, which were, however, traversed from time to time by fleet shadows.

They came to a crossroads and Pearce turned left, following a road between acres of green zea. The green, the grey hills, and the enormous sky, sang round his head. Why worry where he was going? The horse was enchanted. The grey hills came nearer. He trotted smartly into a village and the hill was a wall before him. The track narrowed, and Pearce slackened the pony's pace to a walk. Old men rose from their places before the houses, their beards trembling with incipient advice.

A little ahead the road became a precipitous sheep-track, pointing upwards like the old men's monitory fingers.

Slowly, slowly Pearce turned his horse in the narrow street and leaned back contentedly in the saddle,

"Walk up, walk up," he murmured, and the little animal trod daintily as a funeral horse.

"O where shall we go, little beast?" he asked, and the pony seemed by his tugging to choose the west. The road went into the falling sun in whose glare nothing was visible but shapes and shadows. Houses and boys playing were adumbrated, suggested, but nothing seemed actual.

As they came again to the open country the animal broke into a trot. Pearce was on fire with ecstasy from crown to stirrup. He rode on almost in blindness.

Suddenly the pony shied. A few feet in front of them great bony legs were sprawling across the road, writhing like monstrous weeds lifted by a sea-swell. A slavering camel lay kicking on the ground. Pearce reined the pony tightly and carried its head to the extremest edge of the track. What he could see of the creature's eyes was wild with fear. It placed its hoofs with a fearful reluctance.

Then they had passed the danger. The pony's whole body relaxed into a laugh. Pearce gave him his head. The path turned, and put the sun on one side. The world became fully visible again. The brilliant pack of images was re-shuffled, and the high clouds fell to the horizon as if they had been weighted.

Darkness spread.

Pearce kept the tired pony awake with his legs. Soberly they crept back to camp. The horse wallah rose from the shadows to take the bridle. He was not two yards from where Pearce had left him.

The low wooden hut was stuffy at night, and inside the mosquito net one did not feel even such faint breaths as would sometimes steal from the hills.

Pearce lay watching the glow of his cigarette. Images of what he had seen chased one another in the darkness.

It was some time before he could distinguish, under the surface of a consciousness ablaze with happiness, an encroaching nausea creeping up from the belly.

But as the night passed the belly grew hard like a mountain. Pearce strolled into the full moonlight but he could not vomit. He looked at the hills. They were dark, but here and there in their quietness a flame showed. O people of villages! Pearce imagined the crouched figures beside the dung fires. The life of the legions could hardly touch them, it seemed; but he knew that they sent their sons to learn the drill he had learnt, and that without the pay so earned the families

107

could not live on the little crofts. And all around him, under a score of roofs, his mates were asleep beside photographs of girls whose smiles and affections were frozen in the amber of dreams.

Pearce went back and slept till the char-wallah with his chinking can sounded reveillé. The tea slaked a little and he sent the bearer for more.

When he stood up his suspicion that he had a temperature was confirmed. "I'm going sick," he said, thinking to himself that it was as good an occupation as another.

By eleven o'clock he was lying between sheets in the hospital. His mind burrowed into a sort of sleep and he paid to the visiting M.O. only the minimum attention of discipline and politeness.

The needs of nature were rather troublesome, and he groped in stupor to the latrine, but he was left alone and nobody worried him.

After a day or two he felt better and when his skin was a daffodil yellow the doctor diagnosed jaundice.

Days of ease and peace followed. An odd book or two came his way, and occasional copies of the *Civil and Military Gazette* and the *Statesman*. In the latter he read that the Calcutta Corporation had had four meetings that month, of which one had been adjourned for lack of a quorum and the other three out of respect for various eminent persons lately dead. Meanwhile in the streets and hospitals, people were dying of famine. He also read that a man in the I.C.S. had been dismissed as a result of the interception of a letter of his by the internal censorship. "Surely such things would not happen in democratic Britain."

Shiny copies of *The Onlooker* were left on his bed. He admired the photograph of the Brigadier M.F.H. "leading in hounds after a strenuous morning at one of the last meets of the season of the Lahore Hunt Club", and learned with regret that "petrol rationing and the need for economies had led to the reduction of hunt coverts from eleven to six". There was more cheering news of the Poona and Kirkee hounds, whose prospects, "for such troublous times as we are at present living in, looked particularly bright". He read with sympathy of the troubles caused to a Messing Committee by a visit from "that great and distinguished soldier, General Sir – –". The Committee "had to think out" a very special dinner for a very special guest. Hors d'oeuvre, cream of tomato soup, boiled salmon (fresh – none of your tinned variety) had already been decided on and we had come to the roast. Chicken, duck, goose, guinea-fowl, had all been suggested", etc. What problems! The women were suffering scarcely less.

"*Common-sense, not Convention.*

"Reduce the number of courses served at your dinner table.

"Put away some of your silver, thus saving cleaning powder and polishing cloths. Ditto brass.

"Give small intimate parties instead of large ones."

Further:

"*War-time Economies.*"

"Carry on with your war work as much as you are able, but don't overdo it if it means a lot of rushing about... If there are two or three of you within easy walking or cycling distance, meet say one or two mornings a week, for a bridge or mah jhong party – not forgetting to give your winnings, however small, to the Red Cross or some other War Relief Fund."

And did the local population try to make things any easier for the sahibate? Not at all. If gun-dogs were hard to get hold of, coolies were almost as bad. "In theory, there were always hundreds of coolies only too pleased to earn a few annas by acting as retrievers, but in practice the said coolies often lose more birds than they find. More often than not they 'lose' them for their own cooking-pots." The anguish of the sahibs and mem sahibs was such that it didn't even stop at poetry.

> Most things are expensive,
> And soaring every day;
> Coolies are offensive,
> Demanding double pay.

When the poet turned to the B.O.R., his voice broke with the pathos and the verse stumbled:

> 'Tis yours, we know, not to reason why.
> From you there never must be a reply,
> And your valour in verse we don't glorify,
> But yet, for freedom you gladly die.
> Did you guess? PRIVATE, you're the guy!

It was a pity, thought Pearce, that the fall of India would inconvenience England. The British out here were ripe for a kick in the seat of the pants. And of the knickers.

Pearce was idle as a lord. After tea in bed he would rise, shave in a leisurely fashion, and then walk a few paces to a neighbouring bungalow where, in a small pleasant dining room, breakfast was laid on white tablecloths. He sat in an armchair. Porridge was brought, swimming in milk and treacle; then eggs and tea and bread and butter. He strolled back and the day was spent as he wished, idling in a deckchair on the verandah or lying on his bed. All day to read and write: peace, and the hills to look at.

Silence was a thing to cherish.

Anonymity expressed its sweetness in the delicate line and colour of the hills and the enchantment of the tingling blood. That rawest youth, in which one is tempted to protest to all comers that one is such and such, but in fact conceals much, was away in a dim past. Pearce wished now to conceal nothing and to display nothing. What would be the use? For we are to people what they comprehend; it is a vanity to wish to be known. Even to the better sort one's resources need not be exhibited, for they are of interest only as the situation calls them into play. One is bored with irrelevance in others; why should one suppose one's own irrelevance of interest to those one meets? To be vain is to value opinion, and "opinion is not worth a rush". There are those who are aware of their own existence only in the imagined opinions of others; these are the people who are dominated by fear.

When he was first released from hospital, Pearce wandered back to camp and read Part 1 orders, with an agreeable feeling that they didn't concern him.

"Inadequate accounting is responsible for much *bad* messing in the case of men, and *expensive* messing in the case of officers."

Pearce relished the literary style of the pronouncement. He smiled and took a mug of tea from a passing char-wallah, and sat to drink it on the edge of the verandah of the hut he had formerly inhabited. He half closed his eyes. The heat haze buzzed like an enormous fly over the hills.

He rose and made his way back to hospital. Next morning he was to leave early for a convalescent camp further up in the hills.

As light was breaking the party assembled, three or four men and one or two officers, a little group bound together by no other purpose than the journey. An Indian driver lounged by the truck, blowing his hands as if it was cold. There was a pleasant air of departure.

"They make you do P.T. up there," one of the men was complaining.

They always do, thought Pearce. What the hell is he ticking about?

The truck went down to the plains as if it had been thrown, and bounced and rebounded like a pebble. There was a halt, and the men amused themselves by cheapening in the bazaar the hideous objects which were designed to decorate, as souvenirs, the front rooms of

British homes. Pearce went with his companions, but found it hard to show an interest in their purchases. These gallant soldiers were like a lot of old applewomen. Nothing, it seemed, was so disconcerting to the mass of mankind as to be left for a moment without practical object.

When the journey continued it was at the same hurtling speed as before, until the steady rise of the hills slowed it to a crawl.

The bare hills were left below and the vehicle entered a belt of coniferous woodland. Visibility was often only a few yards on either side to the wall of tree-trunks, but at times an opening or twist in the road would reveal dizzy valleys of an aqueous green. One might have been on the floor of the Atlantic.

When the truck stopped there was no sound from the chasms whose nature demanded a roar of waters.

The second stop followed a turn from the road up an unmetalled track. They had reached a bald eminence, and from the presence of a few huts it was clear that this was their destination.

They tumbled out and threw their bags on the ground in a heap. Little boys advanced, obviously anxious to act as coolies.

Pearce shooed them away much as one does sheep or cattle. Nearby, camels were being unloaded of bundles of firewood. Pearce watched and waited.

Presently a tall hatless man who, by his stripes and crown, was evidently the quartermaster, strolled up jauntily. The officers in the party, to whom delay seemed an indignity which honour obliged them to resent, had been wriggling uneasily as if their bladders were bursting. Now they were sent away contented to their mess.

"You can go up there and draw some blankets," said the quartermaster to the men who remained, indicating a hut that was obviously the store. "He'll tell you where to go."

The coolie boys came back like a tide and Pearce employed one. The boy ran off gaily with the kitbag on his head and the pack under his arm.

Inside the store a lance-corporal was keeping a crowd of shabby Indian troops at bay across a sort of counter.

"Don't be insistent," he was advising them, "when you change your colour it may be all right but don't come in here like that now."

"These black bastards..." he began an explanatory sentence as Pearce and his friends came in.

"Four blankets each," he said, doling them out with a thud on the counter. He indicated where the men should go and then returned with a scowl of distaste to his dark customers.

111

Pearce and his friends followed their coolie boys (who were now laden also with four blankets apiece) down a stony path to a stone-built barrack-room. The bungalow stood a little below the level of the track, on each side of which the ground fell rapidly away.

The inside of the barrack-room was neat and to Pearce's eyes even luxurious. In the middle of the room was a bare wooden table and two benches. Beds lined the walls and beside each bed was what Pearce had never seen in a barrack-room before, a bit of old carpet to serve as a bedside rug.

Pearce resolved to enjoy life.

The air outside was of a perfect clarity. There was no haze of heat, and the sunlight fell unimpeded on his face from the empyrean spaces. Under the trees walked a thin cold wind.

Pearce was confined to camp for the first days of his convalescence. But that was no confinement, for the boundaries of the camp enclosed acres of precipitous woodland undistinguishable from that beyond them, and Pearce would climb with a volume of Dante, whose light this sunlight was, and make his study under the pine-trees. Or he would sit back and gaze over tree-tops that were like the Harz that Dürer had made blue.

One day, strolling through the woods, he came on an opening where, over a little wall, were untended tombstones. He climbed the wall and read the inscriptions.

Privates and corporals of an English regiment, whose summer quarters this camp had been, were buried there. This was not where they had expected to die.

Pearce found it strange that, while he was still a child, these men from England should have found this place and died in it. What would they think when this spot in the Asiatic mountains had become unfindable and no comrades came from home to stand beside them?

Pearce thought he might organize a tombola on their tombstones.

In the camp nearby, tombolas were organized in the evenings, and Pearce sometimes took a card though he never won anything.

More often, he sat in the barrack-room and played chess by the light of a hurricane lamp. Half the men in the hut seemed to be learning to play. Most were not difficult subjects, but with one man Pearce played a game that lasted most of an evening. A little crowd gathered round the table, each man holding a mug of char and waving it as he encouraged or advised.

Two men whom Pearce had often seen playing together watched with particular attention. All they understood, they said, was playing like draughts, a man for a man; they would have had the board cleared

112

by now, but evidently (they added) Pearce and his opponent saw all manner of moves that they did not.

In the afternoons lectures or other improving entertainments were arranged. One day there was a brains trust, which considered among miscellaneous questions whether Shakespeare should be modernised.

"Modernise him!" shouted someone, "let every bastard understand him!"

One day there was a spelling bee. Pearce was detailed, and caused surprise by spelling "equilibrium" correctly. Two young officers murmured that that was pretty good for a B.O.R. Someone asked for a definition of "Syllogism" but as the officer commanding the spelling bee couldn't provide one Pearce thought it would be impolite to know.

Some days he went riding along tracks that seemed hung in the tree-tops over the pine-clad valleys.

Every day he did a little P.T.

One day he was summoned to the Orderly Room and informed that the office of sanitary corporal had been conferred upon him.

He went out and found the jamadar sweeper. A dirty pugri cloth of dark emerald trailed far over the old man's shoulder; his face was sprinkled with the shiny grey hairs of a beard that he had meant to shave. His teeth, though discoloured, looked white in their setting of dark skin, and he showed them often in a smile that was craven and cajoling, but was saved from abjectness by a light almost of irony in the eyes. The jamadar sweeper's trousers were of dirty white, his loose shirt a sweaty red brown. He carried a stick which at times he waved as he gesticulated orders to his men.

At Pearce's command the jamadar sweeper conducted him on a tour of the latrines and drains of the camp. With the latrines Pearce was already familiar in the rôle of customer; he now followed with interest the lines of the open drains that carried over the hillside water from the wash-places and cookhouses. The sweepers had to brush these drains free of obstructions with their short-handled besoms. (Because of the short handles of the brooms the Indian sweeper's characteristic posture is one of stooping, whenever he is not standing in abject attendance of an order.) They had also to clean the grease-traps of stone and straw that were built outside each of the cookhouses. Pearce soon discovered that these were the key points of his inspection. In the mid-morning, when the job was supposed to have been done, he would go round and lift off the lid of a grease-trap here and there, bawl to any sweeper in sight that it wasn't clean and stroll around smoking a cigarette while the thing was done properly. Occasionally if things went well he would give the jamadar sweeper a cigarette, and as they walked round the camp together the old man would tell him of the cattle he had in his village on the plains.

Pearce felt almost affectionately towards his band of ruffians. Every day they would bring their tin cans and put them outside the cook-house door to receive the scraps and messes left on the plates when the men had finished. These they carried away and devoured in out-of-the-way parts of the camp.

He liked the work, but it soon came to an end. The M.O. told him he was fit.

The next man to be examined came out smiling.

"I'm fit," he explained, "but I can't go back because there's been an outbreak of cholera in my station and they haven't the stuff to give me a shot before I go."

Pearce was going to the same station so he went in again to the M.O. He explained that he was apprehensive of the consequences to his health of going where there was cholera without taking proper precautions.

"Oh, have a shot when you get there if you like," said the M.O.

Pearce walked away with a sigh. He packed his bags.

When he arrived at his station he had as a matter of routine to report sick.

"Do I have to have a shot for cholera?" he enquired.

"You can if you like," said the M.O. "It's hardly worth while."

Pearce, already loaded with more shots than he could remember, said he wasn't fussy and withdrew.

He feigned occupation for several days, and then he was posted.

Jungle, scrub and paddy-field
And, looking up, I see
O shower of leaves in the sky
On the thinly-peopled tree

Ce pays où, a l'improviste...

Dust gets upon its feet behind the gharry
That starts, and leaves me standing in the roadway.

THE POSTING order instructed Pearce to report to his former station in Bengal, there to receive orders for joining his unit in a forward area.

He found a truck going to Rawalpindi and dumped his kit in the transit camp. Then he visited the R.T.O. and secured a booking on the Delhi train. He wandered along broad streets among the white of buildings and the green of trees. The air he sniffed was dusty, and heat sprang up from the pavement.

The platform was crowded with Punjabi troops leaving for the east.

When Pearce found his compartment he arranged his packages as if he were analysing them. He had learned to take up as much space as possible.

The train rolled away through the parched lands. When night came he laid his rifle beside him and slept with his arm over it like a lover.

At one stop in the darkness three or four Indians with huge baskets forced their way into the compartment. Pearce opened one eye and closed it again without comment.

In the morning he took a tray of tea through the open window.

Delhi announced itself by the Jumna on whose banks scores of dhobis were beating the linen of the capital. Behind them rose the Red Fort. The spectacle reminded Pearce of a print he had once seen of men working before the walls of Jerusalem.

In Delhi he swam and changed, and then continued his journey into Bengal. The moister air he encountered there was almost grateful. Though it was hot still this was the cool season.

He arrived at Howrah at night. A few trucks were drawn up at the station, but none that seemed to be for him. He made enquiries of the R.T.O., who suggested that he should get into one of the trucks and spend the rest of the night in a Calcutta transit camp.

The big truck crowded with men and kit moved off. Pearce noticed that the one or two men whom he could see by the lamplight were in the khaki of the R.A.F.

Presently the truck swung between double doors that closed behind it. The men got out and sorted out their kits.

The rest of the men seemed all to belong to a unit and went off under instructions from their N.C.O.s. Pearce went up to a camp policeman and asked whether he had to report anywhere.

"Where do you come from?" asked the policeman.

Pearce gave him some idea. On request he produced his papers.

"Army, eh?" said the policeman doubtfully.

It was an exclusively R.A.F. camp.

"Oh well, I can have a bed, can't I?" said Pearce, who was inclined to sleep.

The policeman informed himself as to Pearce's unit and said in the tone of a man still puzzling the thing out that he supposed it would be all right.

Pearce decided to look for a bed himself and soon found a palliasse on the floor of a large crowded hall. He put his head on his pack and fell asleep.

Next morning he awoke to a place that was like any other transit camp; nobody knew who anybody was. He took the breakfast that was doled out to all comers.

Then he found a truck that was going to Sealdah station. To find a truck was to find a lift, and he got in. The train was waiting and in a short time had dropped his kit in Chirico's barrack-room.

He informed himself of the fate of friends and was greeted with recognition by the char-wallah.

Beyond Calcutta there were no civilian trains, and it took three or four days to secure a place on the military train going east to the river. Before he left he was told: "You will take these two generators with you. We've been waiting for a chance to send them down."

The quartermaster indicated two small crates, heavy and compact. Pearce put his own kit on top of them and stood back to admire the effect. He wondered how he was to move with this mountain of luggage.

"We'll give you a truck to the station."

Soit!

Reservation of a place on the military train meant reservation of a place for your hams and not of space enough to lie down and sleep. The compartment was already full but after some shuffling of boots and rifles the regulation strip of 18 inches was revealed.

Coolies brought in the generators and blocked one end of the compartment. The crates were received with melancholy oaths.

At Golundo Ghats the rail terminates. The men climbed out of the train and Pearce shouted for coolies. Small boys whose backs might be broken by the weight were loaded with the packages and disappeared, followed by another boy carrying Pearce's kitbag.

Pearce tried to follow his packages through the crowd but lost sight of them. Following the surge of the crowd he found himself at the foot of the gangway of a paddle-steamer that lay close in to the bank. At the top of the gangway were the boys with the generators still on their heads. When Pearce came up he saw that they were sweaty and

117

exhausted. They tried to add to the pathos of their condition by showing the whites of their eyes. Suffering deserves money.

Pearce looked for an empty spot on the crowded deck, helped to lower the crates, and then sat on them. He paid the boys off and they complained, arguing that the baksheesh was too little. Pearce too thought that it was too little, but drove them away.

He looked out over the paddles on the miles of water.

Brown water, blue water, it flowed smoothly as if the movement were subcutaneous. The low banks were of a mud that shone grey and unwholesome. The river looked at them threateningly as if designed to change its course.

There is no constancy in their rivers, thought Pearce. The Severn flows between deep banks and is content with them.

On the shining water floated or obtruded piles of weed that were merely black against the falling sun, whose disc sent out across the water a lane of orange geometrically limited.

The lane was foreshortened into a square.

Night fell. An occasional searchlight lit up the sky and the river. The water plashed in the paddles. Pearce leaned on the rail and looked out into the darkness and occasionally, and as it were by an act of introspection, into the ship, that was crowded with crouched or recumbent Sikhs, their beards and faces lit up by lamplight as by a camp-fire.

The ship emptied itself in the night in Chandpur, and with the help of coolies Pearce got his crates and kit once more into a train. The third class compartment was stinking and crowded with troops. Taking turns, the men crouched in the Indian latrine that was simply a hole in the floor of the carriage.

Pearce slept lightly, and when he awoke the world outside the carriage window was the pale green of new paddy. The train was running slowly through wide fields, and in the background were small sudden hills specked with scrub.

The refreshment of beauty did not lessen the need for char. At the first opportunity Pearce swallowed a long draught.

Chittagong station was thronged with troops and coolies, and looked as if it was always so. Pearce secured coolies who unloaded his generators and kit on the platform.

As it was morning there seemed to be no hurry to do anything. Most of the men who had come on the train disappeared from the station. Pearce went to the R.T.O. and asked whether anything was known as to the whereabouts of his unit. It was suggested that he should enquire at the transit camp near the station. He once more summoned coolies and had the generators set down under the eye of the R.T.O. in the hope that it was a watchful one.

He crossed the bridge, carrying no baggage but his pistol, and in a little while found himself in a bamboo encampment. The sentry directed him to a kind of enquiry office, but the enquiry office had never heard of his unit.

"Probably the only people who know anything about it are X. Section here," said Pearce.

He went back to the R.T.O. and after some argument was allowed to use his telephone to ring up the section. They said they would send a truck down to collect him and his generators.

He wandered off the platform and looked at the station poor. Naked children, some of them deformed, some with great sores on them, crouched or gambolled round the entrance. Beggars with enormous eye-whites and the whining address of a mosquito extended for alms hands like bundles of wire.

There is such an emotion as pity, thought Pearce, but it does not endure. But there is such an emotion as pity.

Trucks came and went and Pearce saw one with the flashes he was looking for. He approached the Madrassee driver who was staring around apparently without much idea of what he was looking for.

Pearce had his goods loaded and moved in beside the driver.

In the town they went through there were everywhere lines of recently erected bamboo huts, another sign of military occupation.

The truck went through the town and climbed a hill. It stopped at the foot of the final bump of the hill, which was bald at this point and crowned with a stone bungalow and one or two bashers.

Pearce went in and reported, took out his plate and mug and then joined the men who were having dinner in one of the bashers.

After dinner he enquired where his unit was.

"It's just moved," he was told, "and we don't know, but it's a good way further on. We're sending a signal down and there'll be a truck to meet you at Cox's Bazaar."

Pearce also learned that the whereabouts of his unit would probably be known to — Corps Signals.

Next morning the picket woke him and he rose in the dark, took a mug of char from the cookhouse where the Indian cook was already stirring, and made his way down the first hillock to the M.T. park. There the picket was asleep. Pearce shook him and told him to help to load the truck. Presently the driver arrived from the world of sleep. After some minutes spent in prevarications of incompetence, the driver climbed into his place and the truck started. As dawn broke they reached the quay. Pearce was to continue his journey down the coast by sea.

At first they went to the wrong jetty. There was little time to spare and after Pearce had made some enquiries from a military policeman they raced off to another jetty, scattering coolies like chickens. This time they had found the right one and Pearce went aboard followed by three coolies.

They journeyed down the coast between low dark islands.

When they neared their destination, everything had to be transferred to a barge of shallow draft to go inshore. Pearce cursed the lack of dry land and coolies, but with help moved his belongings.

The barge went inshore at a drifting pace. When she stood before the river mouth dark men in sampans came to take off her load.

Three or four men got into each sampan but Pearce had one for himself and his generators. It was difficult to lower the crates without knocking the bottom out of the sampan or toppling the packages into the water.

The sampans were graceful craft, rising to a point at the bows like gondolas. The boatman stood at the stern, looking forward and leaning on the bamboo oars which were pivoted in simple rowlocks consisting of a ring of rope round an upright stick fastened to the boat's side. When the river was shallow and the sampan might have run into a mud bank, he girt as a loincloth the coloured skirt that trailed about his ankles and got into the water behind the boat and pushed, wading till the water again became too deep.

Pearce lay back and smoked, and looked at the flat green line of the further bank or the mud of the nearer one, and thought of home which he never forgot.

Some miles upstream the sampans were coming in at a little jetty. This was Cox's Bazaar where the gharry was to meet Pearce. He had his belongings piled on the land end of the jetty and looked around among the two or three waiting trucks. None was for him and soon they all drove off.

A dulling of the light warned him that night was about to fall. He chatted to the military policeman on duty.

"How do I find — Corps Signals?" he asked.

The policeman thought he should go to the transit camp a few hundred yards away.

Pearce made a sign that evoked coolies from nowhere and the party moved in file across broken ground to an encampment of bamboo huts. He found a hut with some space on the floor, stacked his goods, laid out a blanket on the ground and hooked up his mosquito net. Then he picked up his plate and mug and went off to look for food.

The Orderly Room had no idea where his unit might be but was able to tell him that a party was going tomorrow to — Corps Signals. He learned their time and place of starting and went off to sleep.

He was on his feet before dawn and found a group of signalmen with — Corps flashes. He thought he might as well go with them and with their help loaded his generators into one of the three-tonners lined up in the M.T. park.

The journey began. The rough, dusty road was of bare earth surfaced here and there with bricks or sleepers. It passed through a land of scrub, paddyfields and forest, in which it left raw scars.

Along the sides of the road filed the Arakanese; the women short and often plumpish, with sure, peaceable carriage, their hair worn in a coil at the nape. The men wore small beards, clean-cut near the point of the chin. The eyes were a little aslant.

As the truck passed, men, women and naked children sprang from the undergrowth to lay the clouding dust with water from rounded pitchers.

There were villages of bamboo, and some houses in them had a main storey of another wood. But everywhere bamboo, bamboo, bamboo. Here and there the bamboo huts of the occupation, where Indian or British troops sweated or idled. The whole country had an extraordinary air of improvisation.

Every ten miles there were gates guarded by military police, and while the gharries queued to go through them Pearce and his mates got out for a smoke or a piss.

The road full of dents and eminences threw the truck from side to side and the men hit their backs and heads against the sides and roof.

After some hours the truck fell out of the convoy while the men unloaded. The others disappeared into the undergrowth, having pointed to a path Pearce might take. The gharry went on.

Pearce stacked his belongings and started off down the track. Presently he saw under heavy foliage a tent where at a trestle table sat a man with a wireless set. Pearce went in and made enquiries.

This was indeed — Corps Signals. Pearce explained he had a couple of crates and asked if he could borrow a gharry. The man in the tent said he would fix it and in a short time Pearce was back on the road putting his things into a 15cwt. truck. — Corps Signals after some thought had recollected that they had heard of Pearce's unit and told him what track to follow to find it. Down this track, which looked hardly fit for a cow to pass, Pearce now directed the gharry. After

121

some see-sawing up and down little hillocks they came to a stop in a clearing. Pearce got out and walked down a path till he encountered a man dressed in boots and shorts, strolling through the undergrowth as one taking a turn in his garden. He recognized his O.C. and saluted.

There hadn't been any signal from Chittagong. The quartermaster seemed to recognize, however, that the generators might reasonably be intended for him.

The unit was distributed in tents buried in foliage on either side of a jungle track. Gharries were parked under the trees too, as part of the structure of the camp, and the place was invisible except on investigation.

There was just room for one more bed-space in one of the tents and Pearce fitted his groundsheet in and hung up his mosquito net. At night when he crawled under the net a lizard fell on his face.

Every morning his dry mouth was slaked by the sweet yellow tea that the cook stewed over a fire in a little clearing that was the cookhouse. A few yards from the fire was a bamboo table where the men sat at meals.

Nearby the Indian cook kept a monkey tied to the branch of a tree.

At night the approaches of the camp were guarded by pickets told off from among the Indian troops. A new password was given out each evening and the pickets were supposed to let no one pass without it.

One night as Pearce came into the encampment the sentry called "Halt!" and shouted at the top of his voice:

"The password is *piala*, sahib!"

"You ask me that," said Pearce as he passed.

The B.B.C. news: "On the borders of India and Burma is one of the strangest armies ever collected together."

"They've certainly got something there," was the comment.

One day at dinner somebody read out with derision from a newspaper sent from home a pathetic letter from a soldier in "a lonely part of England" and another from one "stranded in Somerset".

One day Pearce felled a small tree to make legs for a table.

One day he went out with the carrier trailer to collect water, hauling and heaving buckets of water till he was all sweat.

One day he went to the sea in a party like a Sunday school treat, and swam from the great sweep of sand that coasts the Bay of Bengal at this point.

Every day he went with his mates to bathe and dhobi in the dirty brook that trickled near the camp. In this stream, an hour before sun-

122

down, could always be seen half-a-dozen naked Europeans, sub-merged only to the knees, soaping themselves or beating articles of clothing in the surface of the water. In one place you could lie down and kick to get the soap off. Twenty yards upstream, the Indian troops would bathe, only partially stripped, retaining the white drawers that hid their shame.

And one day not long after Pearce's arrival the O.C. said to him:

"I've had a signal about you. You're to go back to the Frontier Province."

Only perhaps a couple of thousand miles.

He left the following day. A week later he encountered floods. Miles of land under water. Night fell, and along the side of the permanent way he saw fires alight and the inhabitants at their cooking. Telegraph wires were down, the road in places washed away, the embankment swept or fallen from under the sleepers so that here and there the line sagged in air. The train crawled forward, often along a line lifted many feet above the ground. Whole villages had evidently been destroyed, for family after family was to be seen camping out under tarpaulins on stations, along the line, or on any raised bank. The crops gone, a help for the famine.

Red fires under the cook-pots, and men and women squatting about them. At intervals were the yellow-white light of arc-lamps, and under the lamps a pillar of buzzing insects.

For many, all that they knew must be under water. It must have seemed like that to Noah.

When Pearce reached his destination an old Ghurka sentry was warming his hands by a fire at the gate of the camp. A real winter had come to the hills. Pearce found himself a bed and settled as best he could under his greatcoat, having till morning little else to keep out the chill.

The terraced and eroded country
Makes shadows in the evening sunlight
My horse trots smoothly and then falls

Courage is of no use against
The dust and falling mountains
The body feels its weakness and
Measures its tiny pace against
The Asiatic distances
In mind like Christ walks on the waters.

Kashmir

AFTER SOME months Pearce was granted such leave as is permitted to exiles. Several visits to a courteous Sikh patriarch who, with his sons and disciples, filled the main bare room of what served as the local bus depot, secured him a ticket to Kashmir.

Hours of travel along dizzy and uncertain roads scratched on the falling sides of the mountains, through villages where his ear was constantly delighted by the sound of cow-bells, took him to the frontier post of Domel. While he sat eating an omelette on a verandah that overhung the Jhelum river, he was called away by His Highness's servants to declare, on a great square form, certain particulars about himself. He described his profession as that of "soldier"; the other passengers from the bus described their nationality, not less queerly, (and yet prophetically) as "Hindu" or "Muslim".

A little later, His Highness's servants called him again to know whether he had in his baggage any "liquors, firearms or beef". ("They asked me whether I had any canned beef," said an American he encountered later; "*Now I wonder why that was?*")

The journey was resumed and the scene grew less wild until the bus was running smoothly between poplars in the approaches to Srinagar.

When at the terminus he descended from the bus he was surrounded by touts and sellers of every description, who offered him houseboats, tongas, lodgings, and everything else that a young sahib with rupees in his purse might be suspected of wanting. He stood still in the midst of them and closed his eyes. Puzzled and amused, they withdrew a little, but watched him still, for when cautiously he began to raise his eyelids they advanced again as one man. He snapped them down, and heard the sellers murmur and withdraw. The next time he re-opened his eyes it was with a purposeful look at the least strident of the tonga-wallahs, and a gesture that summoned him. He drove off to his lodgings across the river.

Next morning, in air that was fragile and almost cool, he walked down to the riverside and was ferried across by the house ferryman in a slim shikara, one of the gondola-like craft in which one travels the numerous waterways of Srinagar.

Willows and poplars stood at the water's edge; beyond them were the misty hills, one topped by a temple and another by a low, sand-coloured fort.

Arrived at the other bank, Pearce strolled without other aim than to look at the fish plopping among the water-lily leaves, at the ducks drawing a line through the green scum, or at the poplars that merely waited, and how elegantly!

In a city of touts and sellers it was exhausting not to succumb, and Pearce hired a shikara that at least took him away from the other sellers, except when, at the press of water-traffic about a lock gate, one leaned over from another vessel and offered him baskets where plums and peaches were set out in a nest of broad green leaves. Cleopatra's figs.

He passed miles of rat-eaten river bank, lined with rotting and decaying houses, with here and there a temple or a mosque. At frequent intervals were steps down to the river, where dhobis flattened clothes or little naked boys paused between plunges.

The boys were pale, as Kashmiris are, particularly before they have, as it were, ripened, and Pearce recollected the story in Nehru's autobiography of how, during some trouble, a party of British soldiers tried to take away from its nurse a Kashmiri child who was so pale that the soldiers thought it was a European child that had been kidnapped. Pearce could imagine the scene: "Hand over that baby, you black ------!"

There was no taint of oil on the river. Even the barges heavy with timber or stone were punted or paddled.

At Chatterbal Pearce disembarked. There was nothing unusual; the beautiful line of poplar and willow; the gracious and crumbling houses backed by the mountains; fish plopping and jumping and kingfishers darting along the water. Girls washing at the water's edge giggled to find themselves suddenly in the proximity of a sahib.

Coming back, the shikara suddenly shot from the river into one of the side waterways.

Pearce asked the boatman where he was going, but they did not perfectly understand each other, though Pearce gathered that the boatman was asserting that one way was as good as another. He left it at that. The waterway was at points closed in by high walls; on all sides were dirty thatched barges, rat-ridden and smelly. The children playing and washing at the water-side steps seemed to have deteriorated. Inside the thatched barges, as he passed alongside, Pearce could see pictures of the squalid domestic life which was the pattern for that of the elegant house-boat. Occasionally a sewer poured itself from above almost upon them.

Pearce began to conjecture: perhaps in broad daylight his throat would not be cut, but he might accidentally be bashed on the head with an oar. No one for a mile or so around would object at all;

126

spectators would merely demand a rupee from his purse for keeping their mouths shut. The boatman punted on, at times only just making his way between the khuchu boats and the rafted timber that lay waiting in the canal. Since leaving the river Pearce had not seen anyone above the bargee class, much less a European or another shikara. His shikara came into the side of the canal, and the boy who was with his boatman got out.

"Possibly the boatman doubts his ability to do me in on his own," thought Pearce. "No doubt the boy will fix a rendezvous with more professional cut-throats, a hundred yards further on."

Mentally Pearce congratulated the boy on being such a help to father.

Pearce thought he had his bearings still, and knew where to make for a more or less main road. Silently he brushed up his unarmed combat, and resolved to hit someone for six at the first sign of any introduction to any of his boatman's friends. He felt no great confidence in the outcome of a brawl; still, it would be an experiment.

Then the shikara shot out into the river. A few yards up the bank, the little boy was waiting. He was panting and smiling, and tied up in an old rag he was holding what was, obviously, daddy's supper.

Going back to his lodgings past a convent school, Pearce found he had the road to himself. Behind him someone was shouting with anxiety in his voice: "Sahib, Sahib!" He thought it must be someone with something to sell, and paid no attention. It was, however, a policeman. The Maharanee had been visiting the school and was just emerging. Very little British girls dressed in red, white and blue were shouting "Hip, hip, hooray" as if they'd read it in a book somewhere, and little Indian girls dressed in red and green were trying to display a not less manly enthusiasm.

That morning, before the visit, the road had been swept and the dust laid with water.

The road had been built, Pearce knew, to enable the Maharajah and the Maharanee to go out to tea. A princess had been living at the time in an upper flat in the house where Pearce was now staying, and this lady had been a friend of the ruling prince and his wife. One day she said to Their Highnesses: "I should like to invite you two to tea, but I can't, because there is no road up to this house."

"Fix the date," said His Highness, "and there will be a road for us."

Thousands of coolies appeared and there was a road. His Highness had never visited a private house in Srinagar before.

The day he was to continue his journey to Gulmarg, Pearce was wakened early and breakfasted in the dusk. It was light, however, when the cooli sent by the house ferryman carried his bedding roll down to the river.

The cooli made unexpected conversation.

"Do you play golf, sahib?"

"No."

The cooli reflected.

"Many sahibs do not," he said.

When Pearce came to the ghat he had to pay off the cooli and fell into the hands of the boatman.

"How much did he give you?" shouted the boatman.

"Four annas."

Pearce had given eight. He concluded that the boatman and cooli might be sharing the proceeds of his departure.

When he reached on the other bank the ghat nearest the bus stop, one of the boatman's familiars was waiting to carry the baggage.

Pearce was annoyed to be regarded as so profitable an object. He paid the boatman somewhat stingily and dismissed the waiting cooli, making signs instead to one of two ragged men who stood near.

The men fought like dogs for his baggage till he shooed one away.

How easy to travel, borne by a numerous and poverty-stricken cooli class! Pearce understood why equality was a revolutionary doctrine.

The bus ride ended at the foot of a pine-clad hill in what had the air of a market place. It was a wide patch of bare earth. There was a café or two, and a shelter where, apparently, one could book tickets for the bus back to Srinagar. One or two cars were parked at the side of the square. What gave the place its character, however, was the dozens of little ponies that stood waiting at one side, saddled ready for hire, and the crowd of coolies that hunted for baggage to carry.

Pearce handed his bedding roll over to a cooli and took the man's work ticket for security. Cooli and baggage disappeared up the path among the pines.

Thus at liberty, Pearce looked inquiringly at all the ponies, ignoring the plentiful advice offered by their attendants, and selected an animal he could ride. Then he set off in pursuit of his cooli.

Above the woods, on a bare sweep of upland, was Gulmarg. The bungalow Pearce was to stay at lay at the far end of the sweep and at the edge of the wilds. When he arrived homely rain was falling and the bearer brought him tea.

He unpacked and went into the lounge.

"But now in wartime," said the old gentleman, "we have people called B.O.R.s, people whose standard of life is *utterly* different."

Pearce's days were spent walking or riding in the woods, except when heavy rain fell and he took a volume of Shakespeare from his bedding-roll and sat reading beside the streaming window panes.

Out in the forest woodmen were throwing timber. One would come suddenly upon the little clearings they had made, or a little camp consisting of a bit of roofing and a fire, with one or two ragged men about it. They might have been woodmen out of mediaeval Europe, or out of the Babes in the Wood.

Once again the country gave Pearce the illusion of being translated in time.

Diogenes had "a blanket, a wallet or bowl to hold his food, and a staff to beat off dogs and bad men". That was something one could see any day in India.

Pearce made the acquaintance of an Englishwoman who had formerly managed an hotel in Gulmarg. One day, when he was present, she received a visit from a babu with a walking-stick, followed by a policeman in uniform. There had obviously been earlier scenes to the play, for the mem sahib opened the discussion brusquely by demanding when her laundry would be returned.

"Have you not paid the dhobi?" enquired the babu, who was a police official.

The mem sahib explained that when she was managing the hotel she had a banderbast with the dhobi: she would recommend him to all the hotel guests and allow no other dhobi on the premises, he in return would do her washing free of charge, and she, at the end of the season, would give him suitable baksheesh. What had actually happened, when the mem sahib left the post of manageress, was that the dhobi did not return her last lot of washing and besides demanded Rs. 58-6 for her laundry for the season.

"But if he doesn't return my laundry, that's theft!"

"Not theft, madam," said the babu. "The dhobi is a very clever man. He has not kept the laundry himself; he has returned it to the hotel office. He says: I do not know where the mem sahib has gone; I return her laundry to the office."

"But he does know where I've gone," objected the mem sahib.

"Yes," replied the babu smiling, but he did not appear to think that anything followed from that.

Meanwhile the hotel, obviously in the racket, refused to give up the laundry.

"But you're the police," said the mem sahib, "Can't you stop this sort of thing?"

"The police are here to deal with crime, madam."

"But this is crime; it's stealing."

"No, not crime, mem sahib."

The babu then enquired how much baksheesh the mem sahib would be prepared to give.

"I will try to make a settlement," he said.

Foolish, thought Pearce, for any European, however hard up, to get involved in this.

A few hours earlier he had been an actor in another scene, somewhat less complex, in which the mem sahib was involved. The lady had come up to him in a fluster.

"Oh, do come and help me out. You speak Urdu don't you?"

Pearce indicated, with truth, that he spoke very little, but he could not refuse the service required.

A few yards away were standing six or seven coolies and horse-wallahs with rebellious looks. The mem sahib had gone out on one pony, swapped on the way for another, and sent a cooli back with the first pony. Now everyone in sight had weighed in in the hope that, in the confusion, a few annas might fall their way. Would Pearce explain the situation and settle everything?

Like Menenius soothing the Roman mob, he approached them, listened to what of the evidence he could understand, gave what explanations his Urdu permitted him to give, and supervised the handing of eight annas to what seemed might be the most appropriate person. The crowd still waited, making noises of protest and the coolies holding out their work tickets. Finally Pearce fixed them with Roman looks and shooed them out of the compound.

"Thank you so much," said the mem sahib, but did not add: "for the injustice."

He rode up the mountainside while mist and cloud blew about him in the pinewoods. As he came over the ridge at a steep part of the track, black woolly sheep and two or three shepherd boys appeared suddenly out of the mist, almost at the level of his eyes.

The mountain flattened; he was on an open stretch over which were scattered grey boulders. Above, with a few trees on its lower slopes, but mostly bare, rocky and green, the mountain towered again.

There were a few huts, and several flocks of sheep that cropped the grass, attended by shepherds wearing skull caps, and with blankets drawn about them.

130

Or he rode on a bright day over paths stony and sodden with rain, or across little streams that bubbled and soggled.

Or across cleared tracks on which were only shrubs, great rocks and grazing cattle, or an occasional hut from which, like pips from a gooseberry, came women in red smocks and little children who sometimes did not even remember to beg.

Or he sat, at the end of a ride, while the pony rested, and ate hard-boiled eggs, the leg of a chicken, bread and butter, cold potatoes, a tomato and the heart of a lettuce.

As he breakfasted alone on the morning of his departure the bearer eyed him from the far end of the room and grew strained and white with expectation. Pearce's slightest movement brought him rushing with unwholesome eagerness to help.

Pearce deferred the payment of baksheesh until the last moment.

He had ordered two coolies; the bearer, on his own initiative, had done likewise. When this dilemma was put to him, Pearce decided judicially to take one of the bearer's coolies and one of his own. Going out on the verandah he saw two coolies squatting.

"Whose coolies are these?" he asked the bearer.

"One of yours, sahib, and one of mine."

At that moment two more men appeared; they were Pearce's coolies.

Pearce cut short the bearer's explanations and went down to make suitable arrangements with the four men.

The bearer complained that his baksheesh was not enough but did not accept Pearce's invitation to return it if he had no use for it.

Once in Srinagar again, Pearce began negotiations for a place on the bus back to the Frontier Province.

The babu who issued the tickets sat at a table on the raised platform of an open-fronted shop. He was a slovenly man in soiled clothes, with a caste mark glowing on his brow and several days' growth of beard that sprinkled his cheeks and chin with grey.

Pearce approached him courteously and enquired whether any bus was likely to leave in the near future. The babu indicated with a gesture that the movement of the buses was very uncertain.

Pearce expressed surprise that the babu did not know anything about the times of departure of his own company's buses.

The babu explained that most companies refused to take passengers at that time of the year, finding it more profitable to carry fruit. His company alone, being exceptionally upright, complied with the terms of the licences and carried passengers.

Pearce expressed his approval of the company's morality and the hope that he might be one of the passengers.

The babu suggested that he should return on the following morning and leave his bedding roll at the bus station. At two in the afternoon, if he returned there, he would find a bus.

Next morning early Pearce arrived with his baggage. He left it, and twelve noon went back to make further enquiries about the bus.

"It is very unfortunate that you have missed it," said the babu. "It went half an hour ago."

"But you said it was going at two o'clock," objected Pearce.

The babu went about imaginary work with a preoccupied air. Then he strolled into the street and talked to one of his acquaintance.

Pearce sat down in the office and awaited the babu's return.

"Will there be a bus tomorrow?" he asked.

The babu indicated that there would be, but declined to sell Pearce a ticket. He said, however, that if Pearce came back on the following day he might find a seat. He added that another passenger was going and that that passenger was paying Rs. 25 for the journey.

The correct fare was Rs. 10-8. Pearce did not insist on that, but said that he thought Rs. 25 excessive.

The babu finally said that it might be possible to give Pearce a place for Rs. 15. Without committing himself to this as a bargain Pearce stood up as if something conclusive had been said and announced that he would return in the morning.

On the following day he was up early and, preceded by a cooli carrying a bedding roll, he arrived at the bus station before business had started.

He sat and smoked and presently the bus appeared. Coolies set to work loading fruit on it.

Presently the babu appeared. He acknowledged Pearce, but would not give him a ticket, though he promised to do so later.

The second passenger appeared. He was a British officer who knew various important people in Srinagar and tried to invoke them on a telephone which did not, however, work.

The babu explained again how exceptional was the virtue of his own company, and seemed to think that he might through the officer's friends find an opportunity, if not of ingratiating himself with the authorities, at least of discrediting his competitors in the authorities' eyes.

Pearce approached the babu cautiously.

"What about my ticket, babu?"

"Do you want a ticket?" he enquired.

"Of course I do," said Pearce, smiling at him.

The babu looked troubled and wrote out the ticket with great care. It was for Rs. 10–8.

"Ah, ten rupees eight, I see," said Pearce smiling still more at the babu, who was now pink beneath his dirty brown and wearing the crestfallen look of the defeated. Pearce paid the amount stated on the ticket.

The babu made out the officer's ticket. It was not for Rs. 25.

Pearce had purposely left a rupee on the table. As he climbed into the bus, the babu came running after him, grinning and shamefaced, and handed it back to him. He was leaving no loophole for accusation.

Next day, Pearce put on the clothes of servitude and was back in his unit.

"Hullo sarge," said a Glasgow voice as he walked into camp, "I thocht you was posted."

"Back to the same bloody dump," said Pearce.

The bitter wind that blows against
The windows of my squalid cell
Re-assures me, if need were,
In all this world nothing is well.

The liar with the microphone
The liar with the printer's ink
The vain with their stupid fantasies
Are shouting what they hope they think.

A rustling pendulum of bones
Parades as the traditional spook
But, hung from an observant skull,
It writes its thoughts down in a book.

A PLAIN five miles long and two broad stretched below the spectator. The moonlight filled it, and emphasized the bodies of the hills slumbrously extended on each side. To the north was a gap, towards which the Plough pointed with a vigorous finger; at the southern exit the ground fell away, so that through it a torrent might have fallen to the presumable plain below. The moon did not illumine that lower darkness: it was the imagination of the spectator that advanced a great hand over the edge of the hills and pointed to the tapering peninsula, the livid pink of a scarcely healed wound. The finger touched; under the tissue stirred, living and shameful, the unformed material of the cosmos, and the flesh of the whole world trembled.

India lay below, the uniform spirit, from which all things that appeared were emanations, ultimately without differentiation. The deceptive multiplicity of her peoples, the sweltering jungles that in places hid them, the tigers that smashed out from the parted bamboo as in a picture book, heavy paw on a million of ants that also started a microcosmos, below which – but one was never there – somewhere, below all that seethed, was the productive nameless matter which was source and end and which could be conceived only as a profound, evasive sea, and which cried out at once that it was not that, but what was beyond that, yet in that too, colourless, suave and trustless – all that the universe represented.

But at the point where the spectator stood some hand exterior to the cosmic matter that lurked under the flat Indian universe had seized and puckered the craven and shapeless world. Hills had stood up; the form matter took was permanent, hard hills against which people struggled and into which they would never melt, against whose greyness the brown figures were distinct, specifically human.

Now the sky lightened till only one star was left, but that a bright one, metallic and embossed on the pale blue silk of the morning. The hills changed: blue, grey, brown and green separated themselves out in the smoothnesses and crevices. A pattern was forming: a terraced and eroded landscape, marked by the patience of peasants and by the impatience of water, and at the northern exit suddenly towered the snow-mountain, a god perhaps, or ice that might crack and melt under the sun till it tumbled irresistibly over the inured hills.

The new light showed a bare spur of the hills advancing from under the feet of the spectator. Streaks of shadow were paths made by the feet of the goats and of the peasants about their business: against the golden surface now small figures in white were busy, brown heads bowed and brown arms plunging where the grass was long: the tick tick of their knives as they cut audible through infinite space to the hilltop. A few kites circled, and below them, not less distinct, their shadows wheeled over the surface of the grass. To the right of the spur, and growing from it, were houses built against the hill: mud walls scarcely darker than the gold of the hillside, and tufts of grass growing on the flat roofs whose eaves only the sharp shadows of morning defined. Before one of the huts a woman in loose trousers stood holding a pitcher: beside her pondered an enormous buffalo, black and massive, and a child sprawled mouthing the dust at their feet. A little below on the hillside stood a group of men, immobile and with dark blankets drawn close around them. Their eyes looked from under reflective brows; deep lines darker than their skins marked their solemn faces, superbly dressed with black beards, or beards fired with consuming henna.

They had one God, which their dark eyes asserted against the multiplicity of India. Was it Mahomet or the poverty that had scoured them to this stony completeness? They drew their blankets more closely about them and stood watching the poor acres, terraced on the hillside, from which they had wrung a livelihood – wretched and stony fields, pitifully shored up with a few stones against the invisible action that had swept soil, riches, all down to the disingenuous plains. Their steady, eager stare was pathetic as the gratitude of the poor; an excess that corresponded to nothing outside lay coiled in the violent passions of their heart.

Beyond the spur the land was more fertile. It fell away on each side and beyond the spur's tip to a few acres of pine and deciduous foliage, not closely planted, and amongst which appeared the shoddy tin roofs of European bungalows. Beyond this lay the bazaar, an island in the foliage, flat and non-committal and from which rose only the tiny white minaret. To lift one's eyes from this nearer prospect was to see, away to the left, the flat sweep of the plain and through it the solitary road that made its way from the southern to the northern exit.

Suddenly, from the nearer hill, bugle notes fell on the town like cannon balls and, echo or repetition, the same metallic calls sang up from all corners of the plain. The day's assault had begun.

When Pearce and his mate awoke in the mornings they swore at one another.

"Good morning."

"What's good about it?"

The conversation continued in a manner which typography cannot render.

The two men occupied a sergeants' bunk at the end of a long low bungalow that served as a barrack room.

"Where's that bearer?"

"Nickled off, as usual."

"Bearer!!!"

There were perhaps twenty-five sentences which could be uttered at that time in the morning. The conversation unfolded on what had become classic lines. There were no *persons* in the dialogue, for the rôles of the two speakers were interchangeable and indistinguishable.

And then there followed a dialogue between master and servant in which either sergeant indifferently, or both in unison, might play the rôle of master.

"Bearer!!!"

"Coming sahib."

"Where's that char wallah?"

"Don't know sahib. Late this morning."

"Well find the..."

On bad mornings when there was an early parade for P.T. the bearer would come in cautiously.

"Parade sahib."

"Who's out there?"

"Two three sergeants sahibs, sahib."

"Is the sergeant major sahib there?"

"No."

The bearer would take another look.

"Sergeant major sahib coming now sahib."

The men would slip out under their mosquito nets and pull on a pair of gym shoes. Their only other garment was a pair of shorts.

A moment later they would be calling the roll in front of a line of men.

"Where's Jones?"

"For Christ's sake answer for him somebody."

Pearce would trot smartly off the parade ground with his line of men.

Once out of sight behind the first barrack-room the file fell from a trot to a walk. Pearce made for his bunk. The men knew what to do.

Within three minutes of leaving his bed Pearce would be on it again, his eyes closed.

"Now where the hell's that char?"

Then he got up at leisure.

137

The dialect of the camp was that of a thousand others between the Khyber Pass and the Arakan. Into the basic English of the army's dozen swear-words was woven a broadening pattern of slang and Urdu.

The Urdu was transmuted by the same assimilative pressure as moulded the word "bifteck" out of its English original. Thus *fikr nahin* for "it doesn't matter" became *figger nay* and dog became *cooter*.

All plurals were made to end in "s" so men became *admis* and horses *goras*. The only known part of the verb was the imperative and other moods and tenses were formed by adding English verb endings or prepositions.

"*Safkaro* that *piala*!" That was the way you said: Clean that mug.

Pialas had to be *safkaroed* when you'd drunk your char so that you could shave out of them.

Verbs could be made out of phrases that had no verbal element in them:

"Either he didn't hear it or else he *figger-nayed* it."

The Urdu buried in the slang Pearce had known in recruit or civilian days came to light and he recognized that he was in the long-established manufactory of language, where bread had first become rooti and tea char.

But if char was chae it was evident that tea was the same word; and no doubt that was why it had once been tay.

Pearce would chase words where he could follow them through a variety of forms, but there were neither books nor people to learn from and anyhow there was neither opportunity nor motive for consecutive reflection.

He paid, however, a number of rupees to Jaman Lal in order to learn a little more of the language, being fascinated by the varied sea of related utterance that found its source in millions of illiterate throats and flowed without check over the plains of northern India.

But discussions with Jaman Lal would often pass beyond the resources of Pearce's Urdu.

"Sex equality is perhaps all right, but you English treat women as if they were *superior* to men."

"Bernard Shaw surely is your greatest writer."

"Perhaps once I was a snake."

In no part of the camp was the military dialect more beautifully spoken than in the sergeants' mess whose members had almost all been in the country several years.

When he dressed Pearce would stroll up to the mess, an ill-lit building where half-a-dozen men might already be at breakfast, their elbows resting on the filthy table cloth.

"Good morning, Bill."

"Morning, Bert."

"Morning."

Or nothing, as the humour of the day dictated.

Pearce would help himself to some of the watery char that poured from the chipped teapot ready mixed with sugar and milk.

"The bergou's ruddy awful this morning."

The porridge was musty. The bearer in soiled white trousers who moved behind the sahibs' chairs made murmurs of excuse and denial.

"Lejao the bloody stuff."

Take it away.

"Sling over the rooti chum."

"Pass the mukkin."

Mukkin was butter.

"Tell the bobajee I'll bash his teeth in if he gives us another breakfast like this."

"Go on, tell him."

The bearer would disappear, ostensibly to convey the message to the cook.

Occasionally an outraged sahib would follow the bearer into the kitchen to enforce the point. But in general, no one cared enough about anything for anger to persist, much less for it to be transmuted into reformatory passion.

"Roll on that boat." The sentence, repeated a hundred times a day, could conclude any argument or discontent by its evocation of the overshadowing myth. One day there would be a return to Blighty and all human ills would end.

"You'll never go home. They'll let you rot in this bleeding country."

"They" were the authorities, irrational, infinitely powerful, and less malevolent than selfish and indifferent; "they" were also the civilians at home, the sovereign people who were behind or under the authorities and who failed to remind them that there was an army in India that would like to go home some time or other; "they" perhaps contained also an element symbolizing the Americans, who in England were burying their seed in willing girls of whom the troops in India were deprived.

The needs of sex, unsatisfied or ill-satisfied, became a fountain of querulousness and suspicion.

One or two found ease in the laps of Anglo-Indian girls, sallow and grinning like corpses. But the girls were few and the officers could generally bid higher.

One might arrange in the bazaar for a girl to be brought up to him,

139

and the bawd sit waiting at the foot of the bed until he had finished.

One might drop annas after him in the street till a boy followed him to his bunk.

One might bugger a dog.

Or one a goat.

But most or many passed their days in lugubrious and unwilling chastity.

"I don't know, I don't fancy it out here."

"You've got to get rid of the stuff somehow."

In the middle of the morning, members of the mess would drop in in ones and twos for char.

"Chae lao!"

"Where's that bloody char?"

One would recount some imbecility of the remote or proximate authorities, or the details of a booze-up.

"I spent forty chips on wallup this weekend."

"That's the shape money is, boy, I don't regret it."

When the Allies landed in Normandy a map appeared on the wall and everyone followed with interest the news of advances.

"Come on, get out the old chalk!"

It was often Pearce who would stand chalk in hand to translate in colour on the map the bulletin read out by the announcer on All-India Radio.

"Can't you make it a bit further today, Pearce?"

Nobody cared about news of the Fourteenth Army, with which most of the members of the mess had served.

Sometimes in the evenings there would be booze and darts and the place became like a friendly pub.

Occasionally a dance would be organized. The problem was to induce enough women to attend.

One or two officers' wives would lend themselves for the occasion. There would be one or two Anglo-Indian girls.

The party would thin till half-a-dozen boozers stood around a girl dancing barefoot in the middle of the floor. And the raw Indian gin would have made thick sore heads for the following day.

At one such dance one of the lady visitors lost her cape. The next afternoon, as Pearce sat chatting in the mess, an Indian police official came in unannounced, followed by a policeman in uniform.

One or two men rose indignantly to question him, but he was less perturbed than was evidently expected of him. He said that he had come to make inquiries about the cape.

"How did you get past the sentry?"

"The police have a right to make enquiries."

"They've no right to get past that – sentry. And anyway, if the sentry let you past, you have no right to be in here."

The police officer explained that he was checking up on the servants.

"And the bearer," he said, "has no right to be here. He is on the police black list."

"So what?"

"He is a bad character. He has been procuring women for officer sahibs at the burra club."

(Pearce wondered what penalty the officer sahibs had incurred.)

The police official smiled with the satisfaction of one who enjoys the unjust exercise of power. The bearer, who stood near, grew pale under his brown skin. It may have been rage but it looked like fear. He was a recent arrival and the only efficient servant the mess had had since Pearce had known it. There was general agreement that the police shouldn't be allowed to remove him.

The police official went off to find the sergeant-major, who wasn't in the mess at the time, and told him the story. The sergeant-major reported it to the C.O.

Meanwhile the bearer, who spoke no English, sought out Pearce as the only member of the mess who knew enough Urdu to understand his story.

"My enemy has done this. There was a case against me, yes, for procuring women, but it was dismissed. The police sahib told me that if I give him forty rupees I can stay here. But I am a poor man. They will let me take no work in the cantonment and I cannot eat."

Pearce had learned to be sceptical but was affected by the earnest manner in which the man told his story. He promised to talk to the sergeant-major sahib.

He found the sergeant-major in company office, anxious as usual to do the behest of all the authorities at once.

"The bearer is dismissed," said the sergeant-major.

"Is this story about him true?" asked Pearce, who supposed it probably was but was convinced that the police official was no less of a crook than the bearer.

"I don't know," said the sergeant-major. "If the police say he's a bad character he's bloody well got to go. That's all there is to it."

"But we don't want to lose a good bearer," said Pearce, knowing better than to ground his arguments on justice. "Why the hell can't we check up about the case? There must be a record somewhere to show whether he was found guilty or not."

The sergeant-major obviously misliked such enterprises and indicated that he couldn't approach the authorities.

"We could ask the Superintendent of Police," suggested Pearce.

The sergeant-major said that enquiries would have to be made officially.

"Can't you get the C.O. to ask about it?" said Pearce.

The enquiries were never made. The C.O. apparently agreed out of hand that the bearer must go. The man never appeared in the mess again.

A job outside Police control was, luckily, found for the bearer. As often as he encountered Pearce he gave by way of greeting a salaam of exceptional quality.

When Pearce was on duty as Orderly Sergeant, he had to go towards evening to the guard-room, where a group of bedraggled sepoys would await him. These were the defaulters. Sometimes there would be two or three British soldiers.

To the British soldiers it was the custom to say:

"All right, bugger off!"

And to the Indians:

"Fall in!"

Pearce would then call the roll of impossible names.

"Into line, right turn!"

The men would be marched off to the parade ground and drilled.

"Sergeant sahib, I have a nail in my boot."

"Don't tell me about it now!"

The man limped as he marked time, and Pearce thought he'd better examine the foot.

"Take off your boots."

"Sahib."

The man stepped forward and took off his boot. Pearce looked at the brown dusty foot and took the boot in his hands.

In the middle of the sole was a somewhat unpleasant nail.

"Put on your boots!"

"Sahib!"

"Jaldi karo! Hurry up, it won't hurt you."

The man fell in scowling, and drill was resumed.

Then Pearce marched the men off to the sergeants' mess to help the bobajee in the kitchen, where the food lay around on imperfectly washed floors and shelves.

Then Pearce returned to the parade ground where the fire picket had meanwhile collected. It was composed half of Indian troops, half of British.

As he went on to the parade ground he was surprised to see half-a-dozen B.O.R.s standing in such soldierly attitudes ("properly at ease everywhere") that it was evident that they had just come from home.

The corporal called the men electrically to attention.

"You don't have to do it like that," said Pearce gently. "This is India."

The men were fresh from a depot at home.

One day a batch of even fresher youths appeared. They had the airs of men of importance and the conversation of gentlemen, and their military duties had hitherto kept them within speaking distance of Nelson in Trafalgar Square.

"– me! Have you seen these new – – ers?"

There were no words left to describe them when, one evening shortly after their arrival, the young gentlemen, who were privates, were suddenly created sergeants. But they were to leave the following day.

The sergeant-major commented on this news in the mess.

"The bastards had the cheek to ask if they could come into the mess. I told them they – couldn't."

There was a murmur of approval.

When would the European war end and reliefs be sent out? Or would they be sent out even when it did end? Wouldn't the troops from Europe simply throw their caps in the air and refuse to embark for the east when they were ordered? Those who were in the East would stay there. The Japanese war might peter out, years later, and the men yield up their ghosts in Siam or in Outer Mongolia.

"Why are the men so discontented?" asked a lady. "I was quite upset the other night to hear the way they were talking at the soldiers' club."

"I thought you'd all be keen to have a crack at the Japs."

"But the men *chose* to come out here, didn't they?"

Rumours from a world that lived cheek by jowl with the camps without having an inkling of their life and mind.

"Oh dear, what has happened? I hear that one of the B.O.R.s has killed one of your servants?"

The ugly proletariat might rise at any moment and break up the petted world of memsahibs.

"Of course there would be nothing for it but to turn the machine guns on them."

And gossip floated down.

"The swimming bath at the burra club was littered with broken bottles. Four of the women bathed naked in the moonlight."

"Who were they?"

"My dear, the four women with the worst figures in the cantonment."

To the south the hills gathered at each side of the entrance to the plain into mountainous knots more portentous than the pillars of Hercules.

Pearce climbed with a companion up the lower slopes of the left-hand mountain. The ground was grey-green like an olive, and where there was no grass loose stones fell away under their feet.

At the first halt they looked back on the little plain with its groups of camps. Bugle calls rose from it and fell back from a sky they could not reach.

At the second halt they saw the kites circling below them.

Then came a stretch of level ground that held a village. Women whose eyes were elusive like a nun's were drawing water from a well in pitchers.

At the third halt a fakir sat with them for a moment as a silent and uninvited third.

Then, suddenly, before them, rose the summit, guarded by cliffs. They followed a little path, then no path, up the west face.

At the top a peasant sat in a tilled field, and around were little houses that grew in the ground like caves.

The sky was vast and yawned above them, on all sides, and below. The travellers hung in the centre of the atmosphere.

Pearce dared at last to peruse the world below him. The cliff they had climbed was the abrupt termination of a gradual slope, but to the south and east the cliff face showed no break for two thousand feet.

One could have walked at a step into the centre of the Punjab plains.

Enormous eagles with wings that whirred like an engine circled and planed a yard above their heads.

"Is there any way to the east?" they inquired of the peasant.

The man picked up a stone and tossed it into the gulf.

Three hours later Pearce was back in the camp. The aery peak had become part of the crenellation of an oppressive sky-line. Pearce was marching round and round. The valley was a prison yard.

Too longing of longing makes me cold
The heart a tight and burning fistful
Hangs like a cold sun in my chest
A hollow kind of firmament.

On the Way Home

ONE OR two men of those more recently arrived from England had gone home from the camp on leave. Pearce and those who had come out with him or before him did not go.

"Those bastards don't know they're born! Going home after a year!"

That which was impossible in a more outlandish spot miraculously became practicable in Delhi, to which Pearce was suddenly posted for no better reason than that he could serve just as uselessly there.

For a few weeks he idled among the corridors of G.H.Q., bestirring himself several times a day to send the chaprassis for tea.

Then he was told he could go home, and a few days later the Bombay express took him to Deolali.

The train arrived in the middle of a perfectly black night. Trucks were waiting, and the men climbed in heaving their baggage after them.

After some delays the truck Pearce was in drove off. It came to a stop in the midst of the darkness without apparently having arrived anywhere in particular. Nobody moved. Then the N.C.O. sitting beside the driver came round to the tail-board.

"You're there," he said.

The men got out and sat on their kitbags. The truck drove off.

"Where the hell are we?"

(After the lapse of a few moments there is always some voice to ask that question where it is needed.)

"This is the Homeward Bound Trooping Depot, men. I hope you like it." The voice was refined in imitation of an officer's.

"– your luck!"

No more questions were asked. Pearce leaned back on his kitbag. Soon all around the darkness was dotted with explosions of matches and the glowing ends of cigarettes.

For hours the men smoked or dozed in the darkness. The dawn began to break, and out of the darkness of the plain a loosely garbed figure became distinguishable.

Suddenly there was the crash and tinkle of a can.

"Char wallah!"

The men unstrapped their mugs and were soon sipping muddy tea sweetened with molasses.

As they finished, two barbers emerged from the ground and began to shave them.

Day had come. There was indeed a camp; one or two huts lay

scattered about the place where the party sat.

Under various directions Pearce and his mates found themselves on a stretch of raw earth bounded by cactus. Here were a dozen tents with the brailing up and charpoys under them.

The men put their baggage and themselves on the beds and lay there, scarcely getting up except for necessary occasions, eating and the formalities of departure. What had been so long desired was enacted in an apathy of unbelief.

After a week the draft moved to Bombay and sailed. Pearce found it difficult to descry in himself movements either of regret or expectation.

"I'll believe it when I get there."

But some were sanguine.

"When I get home I shall tell my wife to sit just like that, with her legs apart, while I have a good look."

"Get up them stairs!"

As they sailed through the Red Sea the men listened to news of the last days of the war they hadn't helped to win. V.E. Day was celebrated by closing all the portholes on the mess-deck as a disciplinary measure.

Pantelleria. Cap Bon. The blue carpet that had spread under the feet of Odysseus.

Beside Gibraltar lay U-Boats that had come in to surrender.

The troops came off ship at Greenock and took train for Glasgow.

"This bush hat ought to be good for a few pints in my home town."

A man from a laundry unit leaned out of the window to wave a Japanese flag he had purchased.

III   To the Beginning

IT WAS in January, 1942 that I swore by Almighty God to defend His Majesty, King George the Sixth, his heirs and successors, and to obey his generals and officers set over me. I vaguely remember that this was somewhere near the Euston Road, and I received two shillings which was then a day's pay for a private soldier – it was the King's shilling. So there I was, technically a volunteer in spite of the immense engineering of conscription which had been designed to reduce to a minimum such disorderly expressions of the individual will. In fact there was no choice. When war was declared, I could not have gone, because I was just over twenty-five and people in my occupation were reserved at that age. But when the age was raised to thirty, so that I would shortly have gone anyway, my employers, affected by a residual recollection of the war of 1914-18, said that I could volunteer at once, if I wished, without waiting to be sent for. That is how I came to swear my oath and get my two shillings.

What I had dimly intended was to go off and join a west country regiment although I knew that the consequence of this romantic gesture would probably be that I found myself in Horfield Barracks, being drilled by the stupid, rather bullying little boy from next door to my home in Bristol who, as I had heard and could well believe, was now a resplendent sergeant on the barrack-square of that establishment. The thought of that little boy put me off; he used to lie down in the horse dung in the street and shout "I be dead". I did not care to start my military life under those auspices. So I thought of the Somersets. But only thought of them. What I did, knowing nothing of the army, was to ask for advice from the civilian authorities responsible for conscription – an extraordinary idea, really. When they discovered I knew some German they were unhesitating. They said I should join the Intelligence Corps and their air of conviction prevailed over my uncertainty. When my call-up papers came they were a surprise. They said that I should report to Omagh, County Tyrone, which was the depot of the Royal Irish Fusiliers, for my infantry training. So I found myself on the boat from Stranraer to Larne with other young men whose civilian lives were drawing to a close, at any rate for the time being.

At Omagh there was a squad of recruits to the Intelligence Corps. They were miscellaneous and came from anywhere from North Africa to South America, included civil servants, commercial travellers, an ex-Indian policeman and an artist in a fishing hat – which he did not keep for long. For the rest the Royal Irish Fusiliers – to judge by the recruits at large – seemed to come from Birmingham. Corporal Minton, who was in charge of the hut I was in, was a grocer's assistant from that town. He bawled orders to perfection and could recite with rapidity the parts of a Bren gun. For our delectation, or his own, he sang – frequently – "I'll be with you in apple-blossom time", in a variation which he thought very humorous. There were still a few of the Irish left among the senior N.C.O.s, and our Sergeant Vaughan was one of these. His song was "The mountains of Mourne", which he sang with great seriousness and had to be prayed to sing, for he regarded it as a treat for us. In a way it was.

The Royal Irish Fusiliers had by no means abandoned their claims to Irishness. When the guard was mounted pipers in kilts played "Believe me if all those endearing young charms" or even "The Wearing of the Green", and we had to sleep on our bayonets in case the I.R.A. should steal them. We also had to keep up an icy and tedious patrol, at nights, lest the I.R.A. should raid the place with some more likely object in mind. The Irishness merely added colour to what was anyway, to an inured civilian, a strange world. Instead of being in an office I was holding a freezing rifle on the barrack-square, stripping a Bren gun or going over an assault course in full kit.

The body will do things one would not imagine it would, as I found. There was a thumb lying on the grass, left by someone in the course of discovering which way you put a shell in a mortar. Exercise made one hungry, and after eating all the army provided it was possible to go out into the town and buy bacon and eggs as well as drink beer at odd hours even though "they" – the Royal Ulster Constabulary – were suspected of being on the road. At the weekend it was sometimes possible to walk in the hills. The people were hospitable beyond belief. They would ask one in to eat egg, and bread and butter, and tea, even if they didn't, to all appearances, have an awful lot of these things themselves. They "would not be beholden to the rations for a bit of butter". While the Protestant townsmen were loyal to the core, the people one met in the countryside asked in a speculative tone: "Do you think you'll win the war?" I imagine it would have been a pleasure to them to think that we might not, though they wouldn't, probably, have cared very much in the end for the consequences of our not winning it. From the Royal Irish Fusiliers the occasional Irishman would go south and desert, but I suppose if one thought about such people at all one thought that they were not very serious.

The Irish, as a race or class, have now almost passed out of the consciousness of the English. It is as if that western island of the once united kingdom, first a gaping wound, then a tetchy area that was apt to itch, has at last been cured or gone numb, nobody knows which, anyway it is no longer noticed. But when one is in Ireland, its unhappy history lives. One says unhappy, because that is what it is supposed to be, being classified, of course, in relation to the history of England. For Ireland was and is a dependency – a notion it hates – if you must look at things politically, as the Irish certainly love to. The Irish history which is not English history is a pathetic affair, but as a province of England, Ireland had her flowering. Dublin is a city of the English ascendency. For English literature, Ireland has been one of those productive frontier areas, something like what the Bohemian marches have been for Germany.

There are reasons why the periphery of a culture may be unusually productive, but this does not mean that such an area can turn in on itself and become a centre. It can only become a provincial centre, with the attendant certainty of exalting the second-rate. Anyway, in Ireland this political nonsense is well advanced and there is nothing for an Englishman to do about it. In the determination to forget the Anglo-Irish, as in most things in Ireland, there is an element of religious politics; Popery has been set historically against the crown of England and it is a sort of revenge for Drogheda that Eire now sends her swarms of priests against the English establishment. It is hard, but just, for an English despiser of Puritans to be held responsible for Oliver Cromwell. Anthony à Wood's brother, after all, saw a soldier "run his sword up the belly or fundament" of a "most hansome virgin" and, "seeing her gasping", himself "took way her money... and flung her downe over the works". The Ireland of the seventeenth century suffered all the violence of the Germany of the Thirty Years' War – so well described by Grimmelshausen. It is not to be wondered at if a residue of violence, more continental than English, remained after the English had taken to Jane Austen. But these antics of a defeated people are not very pretty, and John O'Leary himself said that "all agitating movements, however inevitable and necessary they may be, are at best but a necessary evil, involving all forms of self-seeking and insincerity... opening up the widest field for the exercise of that treachery and cruelty which lies latent in human nature". On the other hand the Irish, because of their late and imperfect involvement in the world of commerce and industry, have carried into our century a vividness of speech and perhaps of perception – along certain lines – not to be found so generally anywhere else in the English-speaking world. These confusions did not concern me analytically when I was in Omagh, but they were in the air.

When at the end of four months training I marched out of the Royal Irish Fusiliers' depôt, it was to the tune of "The minstrel boy to the war has gone", played by the pipers. In fact this minstrel was bound for the Intelligence Corps Depôt in Winchester, where N.C.O.s from the Guards did their best to make soldiers out of a rather sloppy lot. These gentlemen certainly had style. They affected ancient Cockney expressions, rhyming slang and the like, and they bawled as men conscious of the difficulty of their task. One of these men, after I had gone, accidentally shot a recruit with a Bren gun, a live round having got among the dummies during a demonstration, and I am told he lost his head and fled from the depôt. While I was there no such flaw appeared in the character of any of the N.C.O.s, and it would never have occurred to me that it could. They were always right, like the warders in a military prison. If they set you to scrub the floor you would scrub the floor; when you thought it was clean they would say it was dirty, and you said Yes, sergeant. It was understood on all sides, and not least by the N.C.O.s themselves, that they were employed to break your heart. But when I think now of that depôt in Winchester it is usually of the martins dipping over the evening parade. And there was the cathedral, which I then saw for the first time. I have never passed the west front since without thinking of the column of three fell in after church parade.

From Winchester I went off to Beaumanor (or is it manoir?) in Leicestershire – a mansion evidently built to be inhabited by knights out of Lord Tennyson. The inhabitants in my time were not quite up to the architects' specification, and instead of the Lady of Shalott there were hearty members of the A.T.S. whose favourite song (as they wove their magic webs) was "Roll me over", which I suppose is a version – appropriate to a feminist age – of what Fielding calls "the famous old English song of Turnups". I believe that famous song ran:

> Turn up the mistress, turn up the maid
> ...., be not afraid.

Our ladies' song ran:

> Roll me over
> In the clover;
> Roll me over, lay me down and do it again.

Plus ça change.

From Leicestershire I went to a most gentlemanly course in Cambridge. Here I exercised my German and (elementary) Italian on the documents of the enemy armies, and at the end of three weeks laughingly spent a Friday afternoon on the Japanese; it was no doubt this training which qualified me to be sent to India. This was a time of luxury, so far as luxury can be enjoyed by a man in a state of military servitude. I had even the use of a fellow's room in Emmanuel, in the evenings. It is true that the first time I went there I found it occupied by an officer who was entertaining his girl-friend, and he tried a little to make out, as it seemed to me, that I being a private must be the intruder. The position was improved after a weekend when he found me drinking sherry with the rightful tenant of the rooms, and one or two other fellows. In the streets of Cambridge one was struck by the presence of young men who as yet seemed not to know that there was a war. One leaned out of the window of his lodging and asked me the time as I passed; it was as if the whole of Cambridge was a familiar room to him and I one of the handy accessories. In the cafés these young men talked to their young women. One would not have noticed it but for the fact that one felt, after perhaps nine months in the army, all the envy of the dispossessed, even in those unusually fortunate circumstances. Perhaps in my case there was also a touch of envy from an older date, for this was that Oxford-and-Cambridge which I had regarded as a petted race, a sort of Dives to my Lazarus. But if so, that thought was subdued, for I regarded myself then simply as one of the military, enslaved for the public good and living in a world completely uncomprehended by civilians.

From Cambridge I went on attachment to the Signals, and spent winter weeks in a brush factory at Trowbridge, until I moved to the camp above Bradford-on-Avon from which I went overseas, leaving my wife pregnant.

A line of sceptical recruits,
My self among them

I WILL not try to appropriate the declaration of war and the first air-raid sirens. I was part of the general assent to the proposition they announced. There must have been some malice in my attitude, for in October, 1939 I was reminding readers of the *New English Weekly*, *à propos* of the Russo-German pact, that a short time before "any profound doubts of the virtues of Russia" had been "regarded as being in bad taste" and that it had not been "considered proper to mention, for example, the views of the *Action française* or of Mr. Wyndham Lewis on Russia's part in the Spanish war". In November there appeared over my signature a strange little *Dialogue on War and Peace*. The characters were an arrogant A, who had long regarded Europe

155

as the *terre inhabitable* of Sorel and thought of war as a normal part of human conduct, and a confused B, who was a liberal pacifist, much upset because the principles he had held for twenty years had been flouted and the societies of which he had been chairman had all disintegrated. It was an ungentlemanly exchange. B. must have been elder brother to the Tourist whom Eddio later talked down; at any rate he was much cowed by the end of the dialogue. As the months passed, the liberal Anglo-Saxon mind began to entertain itself with new fantasies. In March, 1940 I was displaying *The Argument for Federal Union* in twenty-two stages. The first read: "As Westminster knows what is best for Dorset, New York will know what is best for England". Perhaps I should go on:

II – As we are adequately represented by our Parliament and as the French are adequately represented by their Chamber, we shall both be perfectly represented by the Federal Senate.

III – As every elector understands the government of his country he will still better understand the government of the Federation.

IV – As no one is at present distracted from the affairs of his town by the voices of politicians in London, no one will be distracted from the affairs of his country by the voices of politicians in Moscow.

V – As we have perfected the art of governing a small territory we are proper persons to undertake the government of a larger one.

VI – As the countryside flourishes under the care of the Lords and Commons, it will blossom as never before under the care of the Senate in New York.

VII – As the voter is better able to judge the conduct of his Prime Minister than he is that of his local dustman, he will be better able to judge the conduct of the Federal President than he will that of the Prime Minister.

VIII – As there is no possibility of intrigue in the French Chamber, the example of France may be followed by the whole Federation.

IX – As men care most for ethical ideals, less for their country and least of all for money, there will be no conflict between inclination and duty in the minds of the senators.

X – As there is one philosophy to which all men give assent the senators will easily agree on what principle their policy is to be decided.

XI – As language is merely a vehicle for conveying abstraction, representatives ignorant of one another's tongues will easily understand one another's ideals.

and so on till

XXI – As a foreign army is less ready to oppress a country than a native army, it will be less dangerous for the people of England to support an army of Prussians than to support an army of Englishmen.

and

XXII – As there is little inconvenience in fleeing to another country there can be none at all in fleeing to another continent.

The arrival of the German armies in France no doubt put an end to such reflections. I had been sent with my office to Southport – "evacuated" was the unpleasing but exact expression. People swarmed along the sea-front and took a lunchtime bathe in the pool. It seemed for a moment as if the country might be over-run without ever having been mobilized. Could one admire the passivity of the British while the Germans raced for the channel ports? It had in it a large measure of incomprehension and even of stupidity. I kept watch on a church tower, as a member of the Local Defence Volunteers, in case parachutists should be dropped over the flat surrounding countryside. Having given my country this help, I was recalled to London in time to watch the first daylight raiders and to take part in the more tedious entertainments provided at night. These are vulgar excitements, and it is well that people in need of gross stimuli now get them in comfort on the telly without disturbing the rest of us. The boring diversions went on till just after Christmas, when I found myself in a raging fever, unable to bear my head on the pillow. I had meningitis, and there followed, in an isolation hospital near Bristol, where I happened to be at the time, a series of ochre-coloured dreams of political intrigues in oriental courts – it was the colour of China.

I woke from these dreams to be seriously concerned that I was not at work in the office, where surely I must be needed in a time of such national distress. This was a measure of my sickness and I am bound to say that, as my condition improved, I became less anxious to return. The boy in the next bed had been on a merchantman that had gone down in mid-Atlantic, and he had been adrift for days on a raft. He showed no anxiety, except to please everyone, and in this spirit he one day took communion with an old priest who only afterwards discovered, appalled, that the boy had never been confirmed and had no idea what it was all about. The priest was charity itself and left the room murmuring "I suppose it does not really matter" but he would hardly speak to me for fear that I should want to repeat the sacrilege. The enemy visited us with fire-bombs which were really intended for Avonmouth Docks. One way and another, the place was not free from the confusion of war.

My illness did, however, result in my being sent to the country for a period of convalescence. In the moment of lucidity when I was released from the Chinese I had been visited by a thirst for the green land as if I had been parched; I suppose it was a desire to live. I settled with a cattle transporter at Nether Stowey – which was familiar country – and spent several weeks at first walking, and then riding, among the heather and bracken. It was extraordinary how peace had lingered on there. I even went out with stag-hounds, on a rough pony and at a slight distance. Then I returned to London and my office, and the rest of the year, before I joined the army, was spent in the avocations of the office. I was not very well viewed in those quarters, at that time, and when shortly before I was called up I went to see the official who held the job which is now mine he said he supposed I had come to see whether I could get out of going into the army. He had no doubt heard that I had been offered a job as a scriptwriter for the B.B.C.'s overseas service but not that I had declined it.

War happened like a second birth
Upon an even blinder earth

I HAVE reached the point in my story where I might stop saying "I" and say "he". At any rate this young man, twenty-five years back – half-way to fifty – can be seen, in an illusory way, as another person. Walking down Whitehall in a black hat and with an umbrella, he must have hoped that this protective clothing, highly unfamiliar and against nature as it seemed, would enable him to pass unnoticed in an environment in which he felt as much at home as a stray wild animal among the ruins of Pompeii. Or perhaps by this time – these years after starting work in the office – he might feel as much part of the company as a domestic cat in a house where he was not treated very well – wary, not understanding what was going on, and with an impulse to flee easily aroused. The scenes of this wild or half-tame life were the dilapidated bungalows surrounding the old Montagu House, a building beside Richmond Terrace which has since made way for new constructions, and sometimes in Montagu House itself.

O voi ch'avete intelletto sano,
Mirate la dottrina!

– as I remember having remarked to a colleague on the way into the office one day; it must have seemed rather odd.

However, the trick of seeing oneself in the third person is merely a way of making out that one had a certain savage charm, which I am afraid was not the case. Even one's self can be made to look pleasant by treating it as a thing, but being oneself is a more serious matter. The contrast between the clarity of my utterances, in the *New English Weekly*, and the confusion of my life must have been marked. Domestically I lived with decency enough. I had been married two years, and we inhabited a flat with two large rooms and a kitchen, among the leafier wilds of south-east London. The floor of the sitting room was fitted with coconut matting; there was a table of Finnish birch and two chairs; for guests seats had to be improvised, or we used the armchair and the settee, I cannot remember. A woman whose husband was something respectable in the kitchens of the Army and Navy Club came and cooked our evening meal, as my wife was at work. We rang a bell when she was to clear away the things; it seems incredible. But the escalator was moving rapidly down at the moment when we put our feet on it. I cannot say that I mind.

We had taken *The Times* long enough to be able to give it up after Munich, which was quite the thing to do, and anyway indispensable to health in view of the sickening attempts it made – conscious of its great responsibilities – to assimilate us to a German *Kultur* in the hope, apparently, that this would charm away that bad bogey-man Adolf Hitler and his band of lunatic clowns, Goebbels and Goering, who had only to spit or cough to send a nasty tremor through Europe. It was known that that lot got took particularly bad in the spring and autumn, for we were then near enough to nature for the campaigning weather to matter, strange though that now seems. One also had the impression that it mattered, in those days, what the British Foreign Secretary said, though I am inclined to think that the last moment when that really mattered had already passed by the summer of 1939. So waiting for the war was not quite like waiting for the bomb; there was an element of *wondering* about it; it was not entirely fatal nor equally likely to happen at any moment. I can remember a young lady, born into the most secure liberal traditions of the pre-war middle-middle classes, telling me confidently that, if war came, we – London – should all be destroyed, just like that, but one had to demur at such exaggerations. It was a very dangerous war that was coming up, but it was going to be a war like another; looking back one cannot but think how puny were the resources the human race then still disposed of for blowing one another up. One good laugh in those times was the financiers and economists who had prophesied that Germany could not become very powerful because she hadn't got the resources of the Bank of England but only Dr. Schacht – as if politics and a resolution which seemed to have gone out of western Europe could not direct her forces in a way that would hurt the rich.

In the summer of 1938 we had gone to Savoy, enjoying for the first time the liberty which the sum of our two beginners' salaries could provide. It was extraordinary what it did provide – a pleasant hotel on a terrace overlooking the lake of Annecy, and company of a retired general, or the like, who left the tap running in the bedroom above ours and was found by the maid mopping the floor with his shirt. The *patron* mooched around, as idle as I could have wished to be, and *madame* brooded, full of beauty and sorrows, at the cash desk. In what proved to be the final summer of foreboding we stayed at home in case war came, and with my brother and his wife shared a fisherman's cottage on the coast of North Devon. It was still possible – just – to speak of a fisherman's cottage; such people had not been entirely rooted out, from every nook and cranny of our coast, to make way for urban holiday-makers in their cars. The cottage we lived in had already been "converted" (as it were to believing in the sham ruralities of a technological age) but the other half of the semi-detached twins was still inhabited by Mr. Bagglehole, who thought it natural and not smart to wear a blue jersey and couldn't think of any better way of earning his living than by catching prawns. This art I learned at his skilful hands, though he properly preferred us to practise away from the best bit of shore that he hunted himself. So while Hitler was enjoying the excitement of thinking what fun it would be to unleash his troops on Poland, I was climbing barefoot from rock to rock watching in the pools for a glimpse of the protruding whiskers which indicated the presence of a prawn under an overhanging rock, advancing my stick and net simultaneously and delighting to see the struggling victim jumping when caught, opening and closing like a jack-knife.

On the quay at Bideford one could see the fishing-boats come in and I admired the matter-of-fact way in which the fisherman unloading would quieten any fish that still wriggled too much. This even dealing with life and death, free equally from cruelty and squeamishness, is something absent from the experience of the urbanized populations who eat but have never killed. It is strange to the general hysteria of our times, our lack of contact with reality. Bideford had another wonder. This was a bookshop. I have not been to Bideford since the war and I do not know whether it is still there. I expect not.

Everywhere secondhand bookshops are disappearing in favour of undertakings which can afford to pay better rents. The shop in Bideford was remarkable, even for those days, for its stock of leather bound books of the seventeenth or eighteenth century. I say even for those days because a shop in Charing Cross Road might then put an old folio that was not merely junk among the books on display outside the shop. This is how I bought *The Anatomy of Melancholy* in the same year. At Bideford I was in an agony of doubt, not knowing what to buy with the small amount of money I thought I could afford – though I should have done better to have gone broke and bought up the shop. However I bought a copy of *The Worthy Communicant* of Jeremy Taylor, 1671, and a neat and handy edition of Swift, 1747, in thirteen volumes, a Cowley, 1681 – nothing exotic, but books, for a few shillings, which are now kept for the antiquarian booksellers' special shelves. Or rather I bought the Cowley and the Swift and wrote for the Jeremy Taylor as a Christmas present a little later. Of course the disappearance of old books from the shops is all in the order of nature, one should not complain. The process has just been speeded up, like everything else in this mobile age.

I remember one evening walking down the gully from our fisherman's cottage into a sky red, green and purple with a most lurid sunset. The unreality of the scene increased my slumbering apprehension at the approach of war. I had a definite sense of transience, and was young enough to think it an appropriate reaction to repeat aloud, as I walked, in slow time, the four stanzas of "Sailing to Byzantium", which I knew by heart.

But the observer is observed,
You think. He is not.

IT was on a bookstall at Charing Cross that I first saw a copy of the *New English Weekly*. I must have been looking round for something to write in, for it occurred to me in the first few minutes of the encounter that this was it. It was I suppose the lack of pretension, the lack of commercial gloss, which made the paper seem accessible. I was too ignorant of the commerce in letters to realize my good fortune. No money was paid for contributions to the *New English Weekly* so that, aberration apart, you did not write for it unless about something that interested you. Some established writers must have used it for articles which their usual commercial markets would reject. Other things were no doubt written because the editor asked someone

161

to write them, and Philip Mairet was a good editor who knew how to get the best out of his contributors. I never reached the stage, with the *New English Weekly*, of thinking that I was doing them a favour by writing for them. They were doing me a favour by printing what I wrote.

The columns of this paper were a place of freedom. A certain fairness of tone was expected – certain basic good manners, one might say – but given that, tartness and even acrimony were not excluded and the opinions did not have to be pleasing ones. And though, as a weekly, the paper was naturally concerned with the changing flow of events, and with some current books, it was perfectly allowed to find one's text, instead, in writers who were safely dead – so long as one could demonstrate that what they said had a certain relevance to the times. My first article, which appeared on 22 July 1937, was about "Charles Maurras and the Idea of a Patriot King". It exhibited clear orientations and a certain scorn:

> We have several political poets and too many publicists, yet scarcely any writer since Hulme has formulated a precise political idea. Inevitably, both poetry and political analyses are the worse for the lack of political doctrine. I believe that Charles Maurras is almost the only writer capable of re-directing our political enquiries. He is not, by Englishmen, to be swallowed whole, but he is to be used. What is needed is a transposition of his ideas to fit our own place and prejudices.

It is not a disgraceful first utterance, for the later 1930s. Of course I was dissociating myself from the sentiment which had defaced the poetry of the 1930s and confused its politics. My second article carried an epigraph from Montesquieu which suggested that we lived in a kind of *état despotique* in which education sought to abase the heart and not in a monarchy in which the effort was to elevate it. My third article, towards the end of the year, "Remarks on a Letter of Junius", contended that it was desirable "to limit the public exhibition of virtue, in order that people might escape from the tyrannical consciences and appetites of others". It was the prevalence of democratic *sentiment* which offended me; I imagined the possibility, at this time, of extracting what was called the *individual* from that misty realm.

> The view that the State should provide liberty (and other moral goods) arises from inattention to the individual, where he should be attended to, and from asking his views on questions on which he should have none. Incapable of action in a modern society, the citizen projects a fantasy on the State, which thus acquires the appearance of a person. The State has to appear to be the voice and conscience of the individual.

162

The statesman is regarded less as a man skilled in tricky negotiations than as a voice for popular sentiment. When the State becomes a personal fantasy statesmen become impersonal and responsibility is not properly attributed.

The concluding proposition was that you had to have a clear conception of the State in order to have the possibility of liberty – a poor look-out for the population at large. The fourth article, in the spring of 1938, was called "Prejudice as an Aid to Government", and invoked Machiavelli as well as Montesquieu, and included an aside on the chapter on propaganda in *Mein Kampf*. It looked for the classic exercise of political force amid the bald assurances of democratic politicians.

> Machiavelli recommended the utmost violence. If he were our contemporary he would change nothing in his view of man; he would, however, no doubt see that a subject who can be clubbed into obedience by propaganda is not in need of rougher treatment. Propaganda has made some violence unnecessary. One may, by friendly words, give a despotically-governed people the illusion that it is free. The nobility of the sentiments the new despot governs by makes it hard for people to understand his tyranny. Blows have this advantage, that even the stupidest do not think them signs of good intentions.

Another article was about Vauvenargues and Choderlos de Laclos, and saw Laclos as a type of political mind, as indeed he was. It will be seen how completely, at this time, my mind was taken up by the theory of politics, not for its own sake but because politics had to be got out of the way, placed in the scheme of things, if one was to breathe freely at all. I did not mind the bare mechanics of power; that was what was there, and so irremovable and perhaps intellectually harmless. It was sentiment I viewed with suspicion – democratic sentiment, because it was most in evidence around me, but also the sentiment of nationhood.

> It is undeniable that races, or at any rate nations, have peculiar characters, but these characters are difficult to define. Wherever it is possible, therefore, to explain a change in a society without reference to them one should, I think, in the interests of clarity do so. There is a further reason. Whoever talks of the national character comes near to encouraging it, and I do not think that the national character should be encouraged. It is the fund of vitality from which the conscious life of a nation springs, and if one exploits it one debauches the source of life. To develop a personal life it is perhaps best to fix one's eyes on impersonal values.

The articles in the *New English Weekly* were short, and in the second year of my career as a writer I was already wanting to benefit the public at greater length. In my great innocence of these matters I wrote a longish essay and sent it off to Faber — Faber, thinking that it would fit conveniently into the series of pamphlets which were then appearing under the title of the *Criterion Miscellany*. They declined to be helped out in this way and I remember that the manuscript came back wrapped in a portrait of Miss Prunella Stack, then notable as the promoter of the Women's League of Health and Beauty. I acknowledged the receipt of the manuscript and thanked Faber & Faber for the portrait. The essay was not all wasted, however. There was then a quarterly called *Purpose*, to which a number of the *New English Weekly* writers contributed from time to time. I sent off my essay to them at the very moment when they, having noticed my contributions to the *New English Weekly*, wrote to ask whether I would care to contribute. The auspices were therefore good. The article was returned as being too long, but with an enquiry whether I would prepare a shortened version. This I did cheerfully, and *Order and Anarchy: Extracts from an Essay on Intellectual Liberty*, appeared in the autumn of 1939, in a number which contained contributions by Philip Mairet, Delmore Schwartz, Edwin Muir, Elizabeth Bowen, Rayner Heppenstall and others. I felt that my career as a writer had begun in earnest. But so had the war. It was more than ten years before I again succeeded in publishing anything longer than would fit into the columns of the *New English Weekly*. For five years after I joined the army I published virtually nothing at all.

Pallas Athene, my dear,
Look kindly upon my plain endeavours

IN the years just before the war I must have been a young man of some seriousness of purpose, but it was not at all clear what the purpose was. Indeed I should I think have scorned to define it. I regarded myself as having reached a mature condition of *sans-souci*. I was a sceptic. My scepticism was not, however, directed to what is generally recognized as religion – that was not a serious preoccupation – so much as to the political faith of liberal-socialism which then seemed, to a young man interested in letters, to be almost universally prevalent. No doubt it was the existence of Auden, Spender and Day-Lewis which produced this illusion; at any rate the fact that these three writers, so different from one another, should be lumped together in the minds of those who actually read them, as well as in the minds of the more remote public, indicated the existence of a blanketing confusion which had to be whipped off before one could see what was there. This blanket spread over a lot of things, and a lot of people, in what was regarded by the readers of the weekly press, including myself, as the intellectual world. When I made an excursion into the arcana of Mass-Observation, and went to tea with Charles Madge, I recorded a scornful indignation:

> These people claim to be sceptical! They haven't the energy to be sceptical: they must hold tight to something. Only the active can afford to believe nothing: one must see life as a series of practical problems with NO POINT IN THEM. Magical men and bible classes have an aim.
>
> They are teachers and talkers. They have never seen the intelligence in action, ... They think the intellectual is an observer and a commentator.

I questioned the right of the "revolutionary" to have a philosophy of action, such as Marxism was supposed to be. The idea behind this somewhat obscure position was, I think, that "victory is narrowly conditioned", as Sorel had said, and that political action involved the acceptance of a good deal more that was not acceptable than the revolutionaries pretended. The Marxist-Liberal-littérateurs were soppy, so it seemed to me, because of their detachment from reality. Public schoolboys and the like who called themselves communists really did so because, being remote from the proletariat, the notion of communism gave play to their romantic longings for a world other than their own.

It did not require any great originality on my part to be critical of the Oxford-public school world which seemed, in my particular perspective, to hold the keys alike of politics and letters, for it was not my world. What more natural than to look with suspicion on that from which I felt myself to be excluded? The simple mechanics of envy directed my attention to the contradictions apparent in the young men who enjoyed both the prestige of being revolutionary critics of our society and the comfort of having been coddled by it and offered the freedom of its printing presses. On the other hand I could claim that my critical machine performed something more than a simple recoil from this state of affairs. It was an uneasy device which was searching for a bit of solid ground in a morass. It explored other territories than that of the communist poets. That of scholarship, for example – that too being conceived of in the first place as a social product of the Oxford-and-Cambridge league. The politics of this would be that the young communists would see themselves as bravely rebelling from this milieu, and I saw it as sharing a certain cosiness with them.

While the young communists made a bogus revolution, the scholars fiddled while Rome was burning or being built. The Germans had invented the current brand of scholarship in the nineteenth century when it had been pleasant to their rulers to keep the more active minds off public affairs, so far as might be. I am not now asserting the correctness of this view of the matter but recording that this was how I saw it about 1937. The scholar failed to exhibit the characteristics I had learned from Maurras to regard as the marks of a civilized man – an interest in philosophy and a care for the public good. Specialization went with romanticism and dreaming spires. "Contrast," I exhorted my notebook, "the intelligence of the dog in the street. SMELL, BARK, FORNICATE, BITE." The writers of academic books were remote from the important passions. How could one respect the intelligence of those who did not understand the force of words? My preoccupation with politics was never far from a preoccupation with words, and I can claim that, if I had no definite literary plans for the future, my plans for what was then the present were to write no more than I could say with some precision. The association of good letters with good politics was something I had picked up originally from Pound, and from Paulthier's Confucius which I had read, so to speak, on Pound's instructions. At this time I noted with approval Orage's rendering of the notion: "All government is logocracy. To the extent that the use of words is properly understood, government itself is good". This principle has been obscured in my mind by years of work in Whitehall; at the back of my mind I still hold to it, but I cannot say that its application is easy.

Against the anglicized Marxism then reigning in the literary world I set the socialism of Proudhon and Sorel who wrote and – to judge by the *Propos de Georges Sorel* – talked, with an astringency I did not observe in the *prolétaires bourgeois* who dominated the domestic scene. The *Idée générale de la révolution au XIXe siècle, De la capacité politique des classes ouvrières, La Guerre et la Paix* – these impressively fat volumes were my light reading about this time, and while I should have shrunk in horror from the tedious lucubrations of the Webbs or of G.D.H. Cole the splendidly deductive mind of Proudhon excited sympathy and suggested possibilities even where it did not carry conviction. I suspect that Proudhon is still valuable reading for the right young man at the right point of intellectual *éclosion*. Sorel and Proudhon shared a scorn for those who did not believe in *"droit réel, positif, incontestable de la force"*, and though I was far from having any taste

166

for violence myself, I could not see much sense in any political doctrine which did not give prominent place to it, for we were in the world of Hitler and Mussolini and it could not be said that any of our politicians cut a particularly sprightly figure beside them, however they might lay claim to superior moral virtue as the egg-timer ran out.

The English scene looked sloppy. One could attack the "system" or the "constitution" but not, severely, the people who ran it. That was the kind of liberty of speech we enjoyed. It would have seemed to me more sensible to forbid attacks on the system but to unleash whatever fury might fall on the politicians or officials who played their part incompetently or dishonestly. By attacking the system one merely abetted the work of bad governors by giving people an illusion of free speech while making no one responsible for what went wrong. It was, my notebook says, "collaborating in the trick of impersonality which the wicked now so safely perform".

As was proper, my notebook at that time showed a greater confusion, and a wilder thrashing around among ideas, than the modest exhibits in the *New English Weekly*. I wonder, looking back, what I then thought I would do as a writer, for I was certainly to be that, in some form. I expect the answer is that I did not look beyond my nose, and I dare say that is the best plan, though John Milton thought otherwise. I lived on a threshold.

Every intellectual [to quote my notebook once more] seeks the mode of action in which his mind displays most force (*il ben del intelletto*) and it is difficult to believe that the energy which informs the *Speculations* of Hulme differs in kind from that which informs the *Childermass*. The recognition that different manifestations of energy have one source is a condition of civilization. At certain points, analysis becomes a mode of creation, as in Stendhal or in certain pages of Maurras. The true distinction is not between analytical and creative works (though one may make a distinction between analytical and *imaginative* work, in the proper sense – but that is a distinction of *genres*) but between work in which the writer possesses his subject and work in which he does not.

And a little later: "The depth of the intuition is the test of the writer's 'greatness' (his power to open our eyes) but between good and bad one can judge on grounds of clarity and coherence alone. I am content to distinguish the good from the bad".

Nor have the whimsical humour of pre-war Oxford

WHILE I wrote for the *New English Weekly*, I read also *New Verse*, and it was no doubt to the latter that I owed my acquaintance with the Mass-observers, for the issue of February-March, 1937 announced that "those who wish to co-operate with MASS-OBSERVATION should write to CHARLES MADGE" and gave his address. *New Verse* reflected the intellectual politics of the time in a way that the *New English Weekly* did not. A book review in it might contain this sort of thing:

> Every active maker or sharer of an attitude is now obsessed with the quick arrival of the Doomsday of human culture. Things are all threatened, Mr. Auden and the Archbishop of Canterbury would agree, but the Established Archbishop reads Berdyaev, deplores Communism, dreads a shrinking of Christendom, and puts his hope in God, while Mr. Auden reads Lenin, deplores Fascism, dreads attacks on Communism, and puts his hope in Marx, Freud and, so to speak, Matthias Alexander. Nearly every writer, every thinker, every poet of worth stands (whether Mr. Wyndham Lewis and Mr. Yeats and Mr. E. like it or not) nearer to Mr. Auden than to the Archbishop in this matter... [Aug-Sept. 1936]

This defines pretty accurately the world to which I did not belong. It was not only to a young man who read poetry that this seemed to be "the" intellectual world of the time. Its attitude was the correct one for anyone in his early twenties, and no orthodoxy of the middle-aged could have been more rigorously insisted on. There was a "correct" attitude to the Spanish Civil War. A news item in *New Verse* for February-March 1937 ran:

> Self-exported from Spain: Robert Graves, Laura Riding, Roy Campbell.
> Self-imported to Spain: W.H. Auden.

One had not only to dislike Franco, which was not difficult, but to love the so-called Republicans, for which there seemed to be less reason. One had to denounce Italian and German intervention on behalf of Franco but to decry as a Fascist lie allegations that the Russian Embassy in Madrid was up to any mischief or that the Communist party had any object at heart other than the good of humanity. If one did not read the *Daily Worker* it was respectable to put your trust in the *Manchester Guardian*. As a newly recruited civil servant, I moved among people who – many of them – seemed to do just that. I did not feel that I had much in common with them.

When I first went into the Civil Service my ignorance of it was as complete as it could well be. I was put in a room with a man whose exact status was obscure to me. He was very busy with files about more or less difficult points in the law of unemployment benefit. He gave me some to read and I do not think I have ever encountered any form of reading matter that I found less intelligible. Once or twice I was taken, by an official somewhat more eminent, to listen to appeals before the Umpire, then the supreme court of appeal in these matters. I had very little notion what game they were playing. Once after a hearing I engaged in what I regarded as normal conversation with a Communist who appeared for the appellant, and I was watched with lowered lids and extreme distrust by the official I was accompanying. He could see that I did not know how to behave.

I cannot have been the sort of new entrant that anyone approved of, and I cannot say that this unfavourable view was wrong. My next principal, in the dilapidated bungalows which then surrounded the old Montagu House in Whitehall, was a sympathetic character. I am sure he must have set himself to improve me, in his spare moments. He explained that one should take off one's hat when one passed the Cenotaph. He even conversed about literature, finding that I was interested in it. He had been reading some anthology of verse and could not see why Humbert Wolfe had been excluded from it. There had been later poems of Yeats in the volume, and he quoted one that he could see nothing in:

> "A child found all a child can lack,
> Whether of pleasure or of rest,
> Upon the abundance of my breast":
> *A bone wave-whitened and dried in the wind.*

Both these men were knighted before they died, admittedly at a time when knighthoods were a little easier to come by than they are now in the civil service. Both were, in fact, extremely able men. What I learned in my first years in the office was that what I had thought of as intelligence had little to do with the ordinary management of the world, not because those who managed it were stupid, but because the abilities required for most of the work that had to be done were of a different kind. The discovery had a sobering effect on my view of my own pretensions, for I could see that many people who were not as "intelligent" as myself, in the self-contratulatory way in which I, like most of the literary young, used that term, were much better than I was at most of the operations which went on in the office. At the same time it confirmed my suspicions about "intellectual" politics, which meant the politics of Monsieur Blum as well as those of *New Verse*.

The poet my principal admired, Humbert Wolfe, occupied a

somewhat splendid room in Montagu House itself, for he was then Deputy Secretary of the establishment to which I belonged. He got himself up like a poet, and no mistake. I remember him descending the great marble staircase of Montagu House, his stick in his hand, his broad-brimmed black hat already on his head so that he could raise it dramatically to anyone he met. He was a great raiser of his hat. He raised it to me, insignificant though I was or because I was insignificant. Perhaps he thought I should one day tell my grandchildren that in my youth I had seen the Poet. Perhaps it is unfair to say that Wolfe was "got up" like a poet, for he had a naturally dramatic character and under the black hat there was perfectly natural, plastered, long black hair. He must have thought of his face as hawk-like. I knew this rascal's poems very well, for I had read them when I was sixteen or thereabouts. They claimed modernity by the use of small letters at the beginning of lines. Wolfe had been Umberto Wolff, born in Manchester, and I dare say he saw himself as the Heine of our time.

Somewhere in the office there lurked, in a humbler station, someone who to me was a much more respectable name. This was F.S. Flint. I cannot say that anything he wrote was engraven on my memory, but he belonged, to my way of thinking, to the serious world of letters. He had been an Imagist; his name occurred in Pound; he had for years been entrusted by Eliot with the task of writing a chronicle of current verse in the *Criterion*, and had done this with a lugubriousness which I thought appropriate – at any rate I think I am right in saying that he did not always show enthusiasm for it. He was employed in my Department as, I believe, a translator, no doubt extracting foreign information which proved irrelevant to the concerns of his colleagues and sank without trace to the bottom of their in-trays. I should like to have met him, but it did not occur to me that I could do so. I suppose he would have been not displeased if I had sought him out and showed that I knew who he was. But it would have embarrassed me that he might have been momentarily puzzled as to what I had come for, and I could certainly not have explained. I had a profound sense of being nobody, without any visiting card I could offer to a literary man.

When I came to the office from my flat in south-east London it might have been after twenty minutes with Epictetus, much read by me in those days in the eighteenth century version of Mrs Elizabeth Carter. At home I also played the recorder, or rather taught myself, haltingly, a few songs of Campion and one or two of Henry VIII. I should have liked to draw the human figure, though I never succeeded

170

in this enterprise, which still seems to me as likely as the study of psychology to give one some indication of the nature of the human mind. The abdication of Edward VIII flowed over me and I was accidentally present when the heralds proclaimed the accession of George VI at Charing Cross. One way and another I tried to follow the exhortation of Epictetus: "I do not say you may not groan, but do not groan inwardly". I also got married.

The outward symptoms were ordinary,
Those of a commonplace which fails to please

HOW did I come to enter the Civil Service? By means of an examination. And how did I conceive the idea of sitting for this examination? By elimination. There were so many things I knew I could not do, and passing an examination was a thing I thought I might succeed in. I knew that, if you did well enough in the examination, the Civil Service had to have you, and there was no likelihood that anyone else would take me. That was a possibility which I had tested extensively already. In the two years since I had graduated I had applied for a number of jobs. I had offered myself to the firm of W.D. & H.O. Wills, tobacco manufacturers, of Bristol. I had made some faint effort to attach myself to the *Daily Express*. I had made some enquiries about short-term commissions in the Royal Air Force, but my sight was not good enough. The great crowd of my other potential employers has receded like a crowd of twittering ghosts. The point was, that jobs were hard to come by, and if you had been at a provincial university you did not pick and choose. There was indeed a high probability that, before you settled in a job even in an elementary school, you had to face a period of unemployment. So that theme of the politics of the day was not very remote from us. When I conceived the idea of entering the Civil Service, I sent for the papers about the Administrative Class and about the special competition for inspectors of taxes and Third Class Officers in the Ministry of Labour.

I decided in favour of the Administrative Class, which was the more splendid prospect of the two, because I did not think I should succeed in the other examination; there was something about economics in the syllabus. The translator of the *De Veritate* of Lord Herbert of Cherbury, who was then, – the translator, I mean, and not Lord Herbert himself – one of my instructors, advised me that I had not the right background for the Administrative Class. He advised me to come to London for a few months, to look round. If I had had any money I might have taken this advice. As it was I had difficulty in scraping up enough to pay the examination fee and to stay the two or three weeks in London while I sat for it. A year or two afterwards the examination for the Administrative Class was simplified, but at that time one had to exercise a considerable fantasy in the choice of subjects. Or one had to go to a crammers which, I discovered, was what many of my contemporaries did, though I had never heard of such a thing myself. When I did find out about crammers, from the fact that several of my contemporaries in the service received invitations to a cocktail party given by Davies's, I thought that the system was not a bad one. It seemed to me that anyone who could put up with being crammed with some subject of which he knew nothing, and could answer plausibly about it, was just the man who was needed to ingest and regurgitate the contents of official files. However, through failure to get a job and success in getting scholarships I was then a young man of some education, however non-conformist and uncouth, and besides the compulsory papers in the Use of English, Present Day, Essay, and Supplementary Language (I took German), I was able to do four papers in English Literature, two or three in French Language, two in French Civilization, one in Moral Philosophy and one in Psychology – I think that was it. It gives you some idea of my attainments. There was a further difficulty – an oral examination for which some twenty per cent of the total marks were given.

I have sometimes sat on the successor of this selection board so I view it differently now, but at the time I thought I was being very patient with them. I don't know who sat on that particular board, except Professor Ernest Barker, who was cut out to know what one of the Platonic guardians should look like. When the board put a question to me I answered it, usually with a "Yes" or "No", for I thought they wanted to know the answer. They asked me about Germany, for example, since I had been there and because it was, after all, a Topic, in those days. Did I like the Germans? I said I did not. And so on. They kept me a long time, for then as now the board was composed of very conscientious people. "We had one of your people," Professor Barker told Professor G.C. Field, who had helped to educate me. "But I'm afraid he didn't do very well." It would have been a feather in their caps if they could conscientiously have given good marks to a candidate who did not come from one of the right universities. Reluctantly they marked me down. But the examiners who marked my papers, and did not see me, marked me up, so I was in all the same. There is a moral in this, but whether it tells in favour of written examinations, or against them, it would not be proper for me to say.

There were two other *vivas*. One was the medical examination. A very healthy and rather upper-class sort of doctor, with a bulky, well-covered frame and a military moustache, fingered my skinny thorax with disapproval and said that he thought a bit of arms drill would do me good. The other *viva* was with a nervous and bearded Frenchman who was to test my performance of oral French. With him I had quite interesting conversation about the state of the French press. I was the more plausible because I had just arrived back from Brussels, where I had gone on ten pounds provided by an uncle, one of the few members of the family who had sums of that sort to disburse. I had stayed with a family in Ixelles, who were agreeable themselves and I had as a co-lodger the most beautiful girl I had ever seen. She was a Swede, of rich parents, and I remember that she turned her proud and beautiful face on me at dinner with the most improbable question, as it seemed, that she could have addressed to me: "Est-ce que vous chassez, monsieur?" I did not, and the conversation lapsed. She was not for me. She was born to please, however, and she did please. I last heard of her, a few years after that, working in a store in Paris; rich men in enormous motor cars regularly came to collect her. She certainly had charm.

I suppose I must have spent a couple of months or more before the Civil Service examination reading for it at home. I was certainly at home, having returned from Paris. I had had to calculate the length of my stay in Paris in such a way that I had something left over to give my mother during the time I was at home. When I had been discussing my arrangements with Professor Field he appeared to be rather scandalized that this entered into my calculations. Or perhaps he did not realize that it did, and thought that I wanted to keep a pound a week for pocket money when I got back. The economics of his end of the town were rather different from the economics of mine.

In this city
Other manners prevail

I HAD been standing by the notice board of the Department of Philosophy, in the University of Bristol, one day in the summer of 1935, wondering what I should do for a living, when Professor Field emerged from his room and asked whether I would like to have the Viscount Haldane of Cloane Travelling Scholarship, value £100. This solved all my problems, or at least deferred them for another year, which I regarded as much the same thing. With the £60 I thought I

173

could get out of the City of Bristol, I could see my way to going to Paris which is where I wanted to go. The rate of exchange was unfavourable, so even with £160 – less what I must keep against my return – I could not stay for the whole year. But I could stay for six months.

That is how, in the autumn of the same year I came to be sitting at the end of a long table in a *pension* at 75, rue du cardinal Lemoine, absolutely speechless. I could read French fairly fluently, if it was not too hard, but on arrival in Paris I discovered that I could not speak a word, certainly not a sentence. What was worse, I could not understand anything. At dinner on the first evening my place was set without a knife, and I did not get one till Madame discovered my distress. All the length of the table the conversation poured out. It poured over me for several weeks, at a series of prolonged meal times. Then it began to grow intelligible. It was as if a mist were clearing. I began to discover what made the company so animated. Its members began to separate out more clearly, though I had already studied their appearances. The table was dominated, as it should have been, by Madame, in a large black dress. The dress had to be large, for it had to cover a considerable volume of protuberant flesh, rolling under it like great waves. She had thick lips, small eyes, a face altogether of some animal force. She was by turns sweet to the point of silliness, and choleric when her children got out of hand. Her voice was loud and declamatory, and she supplemented it freely by movements of her great arms and slightly menacing rollings of her whole person. When she was silent her face went slack, and at times she merely trundled in and out, intent on the food. She was a generous person, by her physique, and in her sentiments too so far as she was not restrained by a traditional meanness. She was one of the human race, all right, and on the whole a credit to it. I liked Madame.

Monsieur was by comparison quiet and good. He spoke slowly, which I found an advantage, and with a Norman accent. When Madame or indeed any of the children became particularly exuberant, a worried look came over his grey face and he said "Non, non", in an agonized, barely audible tone, and sometimes "Voyons". His bones seemed a lot smaller than Madame's as he sat opposite her at table, but it may only have been that the flesh on them was looser and sadder, and there was much less of it. He was a schoolmaster. He taught English, but never spoke to me in that language – for which I was grateful – partly I suspect because he did not speak it very well. He had not been out of France for many years.

The youngest of the children was Jacques, fourteen or fifteen, a

174

harmless, spoilt boy, energetic in a pointless sort of way, his mother's darling and scandal, vaguely despaired of by his father, of whom I suppose he took very little notice. Then there was his sister, a little older, like her mother but as yet little more than an embryo of the great French matron she has no doubt since become. The family was completed by the eldest son, who with his wife lived in a separate *appartement* in No. 75 but regularly appeared with her at meal times. Pierre was a wiry young man, who when he was not talking gave the appearance of being disconsolate. His wife was slight, lithe, an olive-skinned beauty with sparkling eyes. She was an actress. Pierre seemed to occupy himself with some subordinate functions about the theatre – lighting and the like – which perhaps accounted for his appearing disconsolate. These two were polite and dutiful children but, as was to be expected, they had visibly broken out of the bands of the family ethos, and occasionally they irrupted in the conversation with talk which made their parents uneasy. They asserted to the accompaniment of "Non, non" and "Voyons", and the blushes of Madame, that it was unreasonable that people should get married until they had made sure that they were physically suited to one another. On one occasion, when the conversation grew animated, Thérèse – I think that was her name – shouted "Merde, alors!" and brought the whole table to an embarrassed standstill, broken after a long interval by a soft, "Oh, pardon, maman, je m'excuse".

Besides the family there were three students and the mother of one of them. The most ardent of the students – I mean in the ardour exhibited by loquacity – was René Chave. He attended courses at the Sorbonne and was the exponent of every kind of political enlightenment. A highly cerebral young man, living among books, eloquent himself like a social democratic treatise. He had long fingers and was I suppose not very healthy. His head shook when he made a point. He felt about politics in great gusts and spoke very quickly. He was good for my French. Then there was Henri Kreitmann, from Lyons but by family an Alsatian, a more solid young man, with a little moustache, moderate, even slightly right wing by the standards prevailing in that house, and likeable, less *foreign*, in his attitudes, than the rest. The student who kept his mother with him was another cerebral, even febrile, character, who said very little and in that little did not contradict his mother. He was long, bony, with head pushed forward. She too was long, bony, with head pushed forward, but where his skin was olive and his hair dark, her skin was dry and baggy and her hair grey. She was an intellectual and the most he could hope to do was to keep up with her. On the whole, however, she was an

175

intellectual of religion, not of politics. She had the complete works of Cardinal Newman, I do not know whether or not in English; and she proclaimed that France was the brain of Europe. She did not expect much of a nation so addicted to sport as she believed the English to be. Her son did not look like disappointing her in that respect.

The conversation at this *pension*, where for months I sat through breakfast and two major meals with great instruction, was political when it was not merely trivial. Monsieur Duchemin soon got to know that I was a reader of the *Action française*, of which he strongly disapproved, and he would come in at dinner time and greet me with: "Et qu'est-ce qu'il dit aujourd'hui, votre Monsieur Maurras?" And I would tell him what Monsieur Maurras had said. He in turn would explain what line had been taken in the *Populaire*, and from this a general conversation was likely to develop. It was lucky we had Jacques to interrupt with his idiotic observations, Madame Duchemin to tell us what had happened during her morning's shopping, Pierre and Thérèse to diversify the scene by their allusions to a world no one else at the table knew much about. The furniture of the establishment was of the simplest. I do not know what luxury there was in Madame's private retiring-room, though I suspect she indulged herself in some comfort. She certainly indulged herself. The dining room contained the necessary elements of such a place, and nothing more. The bathroom, where a cleansing could be got, after great preparations, at not very frequent intervals, was dark and derelict. My own little room contained a bed, a tiny table, a chair. It was freezing cold, though there must have been some heat in the place. But it looked out over the most fascinating street I had ever seen. With its tall houses, shuttered windows, squalor, street traders, policemen, and a population of infinite variety, it was French *au maximum*. There was the street singer whining *"Dans mon pays!"*, the man with his ringing cry of *"Habits!"*, the last syllable of which faded away into the buildings. There were, especially on Sunday mornings, the young men selling newspapers. One would hear them coming up the street: *"Voyez, Humanité, organe centrale du parti communiste"*. Then from another direction: *"Voyez Action Française, organe royaliste et patriote, directeurs politiques Léon Daudet et Charles Maurras!"* Each call was repeated, growing nearer and with a touch of menace or bravado. Then there would be a scuffle. Looking out of the window, I would see the newspapers flying. The police moved in. The news-vendors were bundled into the van waiting in a side street. Then there was quiet again. It was different anyhow from the politics of the Oxford Union, debating in domestic comfort whether they would fight for

King and country. The more so since the police were less respectful of these demonstrators than ours were when they found the young gentlemen of Oxford playing silly games. René Chave had been taken to the police station and punched, not in the face, like the others, but in the back, where it would not show. This kindness he attributed to the fact that his father was a *functionnaire*. His father did not protest, because he too had been at the meeting, and perhaps it was better that that should not be known, in certain quarters.

---

as one
At table, rue du cardinal Lemoine

THE political events of my months in Paris were not of the kind that escape notice. In the summer of 1935 the Italians were advancing on Addis Ababa and there were two ways of thinking about this in Europe. One was that this was a small war like another, and that accommodations might be reached. The other was that it was apocalyptic and should set the whole world by the ears. The latter was the more modern view. Naturally it prevailed. In Geneva, which in those European days was the centre of international panic, fifty countries, members of the League of Nations, decided on economic sanctions against Italy.

It was much more interesting to read the *Action française* on this subject than to read the left-wing papers. The left-wing papers spoke in the same sense as the enlightened masses in England. They saw this affair as an issue of principle. Good men were *for* peace and the League of Nations; bad men thought otherwise. It was very boring. And it prohibited all further analysis. Maurras at least attempted an analysis of interests. I could see even in those days that, although clever, he was not clever enough. He believed that a theoretical spirit should not intrude into the field of politics, but he was an intruder himself and a man with a fatal weakness for saying what he thought and saying it publicly. He would remark that he would have wished to make his more upsetting utterances in the council chamber of the *roi*, but after all there was no *roi* and he would probably not have been admitted to the council chamber if there had been, and meanwhile France had to get on as best she could. Moreover he had little understanding of England, and a Latin weakness for imagining our policies to be much more deeply thought out than is usually the case. None the less his observations did sometimes throw light on the operation of our policies, even when he was wrong in attributing too

177

extensive a consciousness to our government. He saw the demand for sanctions as a crisis of *amour-propre*. The British wanted to see whether they were still a great power; they wanted war if they could succeed in using other powers to advantage. While I had had no sympathy with Cecil and his Peace Ballot, or with the Archbishop of Canterbury saying that we should support the League "on principle", I began to admire the British political mechanisms which, while emitting platitudinous principles for the general good, moved silently into position to defend our own interests. It was the perfection of democratic politics. Mr. Baldwin announced that England would rearm in support of the League. This seemed to me a very good way of putting it. There was a rearguard action by old-fashioned politicians who thought an accommodation could be reached, but all right-minded people thought that the Hoare-Laval pact was an iniquitous affair and Hoare had to resign. Eden became Foreign Secretary and everyone knew that was right, because he was the point of crystallization of all the middle-class sentiment about the League of Nations. Of course, the Italian armies went on, reached Addis Ababa, and drove out the Emperor, who took up his residence near Bath. Sanctions had not prevented the war or saved the victim. They could hardly have been regarded as having given an example to deter future aggressors. After that it was generally held that they had done some other kind of good, but I cannot now remember what it was supposed to have been.

Long before the Abyssinian business reached its conclusion other events occurred which were passionately commented on in the French Press, passionately discussed at 75, rue du cardinal Lemoine and passionately demonstrated about up and down the boulevard St Michel. The movement towards the establishment of the Front populaire began to get underway, in preparation for the elections which took place in April and May, 1936 and brought Blum to power. Blum was a popular subject for abuse or adulation, according to your views. On 13 February he was set upon by a party of Royalists, I believe when his car was somewhere in the neighbourhood of the boulevard St Germain. All democratically minded people believed that he had been seriously injured, and that he bore himself with heroism; the *Action française* not unnaturally spoke of *l'affaire de l'oreille de Blum* more lightly. This did not prevent the government (Laval had resigned by this time and it was not yet Blum, so it must have been Sarraut) uttering a presidential decree dissolving the Royalist leagues. Monsieur Blum must have felt that it's an ill wind that blows nobody any good. A few days after the attack a popular front government came

178

into power in Spain, so he must have felt that his cause was making progress. The new Spanish government was certainly an historic one; five months later the Civil War broke out. The preparations for that, meanwhile, were among the subjects which occupied the attention of the politically minded. There was never a dull moment in European politics in those days. So much the worse for Europe.

The *pièce de résistance*, from the point of view of the English student wandering round the Latin quarter and beyond in search of political instruction, came suddenly in March, 1936. On 7 March Hitler announced that German troops would reoccupy the Rhineland, and offered a non-aggression pact which was to last twenty-five years. Like everyone else in those days, Hitler was always talking about peace – not a very good sign – and through the defective initiative of the western powers he had engineered himself into the position of making more splendid offers than anybody, usually accompanied, as on this occasion, by solid and immediate gains for himself. Sure enough, on 8 March German troops entered Cologne. I have no idea what the real chances of action by the west were. Certainly in Paris, in my circles and far beyond, there was an expectation that we should go in. Of course. It was the last time the French reacted that way. After that they had lost the war. In England the reaction seems most often to have been that, after all, the Rhineland was a part of Germany. Political imbecility could go no further than that. On 12 March the French senate ratified the Franco-Soviet Pact, another piece of paper enthusiastically welcomed by all democratically-minded people at the time, but in the event quite useless. The *Action française* put no trust in it, and that was supposed to show how blind to realities they were. At the end of the month the German people, delirious with success and still unaware of the great democratic future awaiting them after the war, gave a ninety-nine per cent vote for Hitler in the elections for the new Reichstag.

A certain scepticism about political sentiments must be allowed to a young man in the midst of such events. "Duplicity is necessary in democratic politics," I wrote in my notebook, "because the same words don't have the same meaning for all." "Que les pacifistes de dogme et de rêvasserie soient avertis que la question" – the question of peace – "n'est pas" so wrote my favourite journalist at the time of the Abyssinian affair, "idéologique, mais pratique." I do not know whether I grew wiser as a result of my study of these events. I must have had that impression; the young have to console themselves as well as the old. I think on the whole that, so far as people can be educated, it was a bit of education to watch the events of these months

179

from perspectives quite different from those I should have had at home. They were what is called critical months. Europe seemed very anxious to hurry up with her preparation for suicide.

Beyond the Drachenfels
The armies gathered again

JUST before I went to Paris I was reading *Le Rouge et le Noir*, and while I was there I read *La Chartreuse de Parme*. It was not the passions that I admired but the political calculations with which they were managed. I noted with disdain a sentence of Middleton Murry's about Stendhal: "The reality of a man for Stendhal," Murry said, "lay in his faculty of allowing all that is prudential and calculating in him to be dominated by what is instinctive and passionate." That might describe Stendhal's conscious beliefs, but the interesting thing that he achieved was to carry consciousness and deliberation beyond any point to which they had ever been carried before, in the sort of subject matter he dealt with. He was concerned with what distinguishes people, what keeps them apart and demands conscious negotiation between them. Old Sorel spending his life scheming for the satisfaction of his major interest, which happened to be a desire for money, was the prototype of his son, who used his similar talents for other ends. One was in a social world, in which passions ran in their place below the surface. There was a connection between the strength of the underlying passion and the lucidity of consciousness; Smollett had remarked somewhere that lively passions underlie good taste. Stendhal demonstrated the continuity between the world of individual desire and the world of politics. For a young man who had accepted as final the disintegration proposed by D.H. Lawrence, it was a valuable bit of reconstruction.

It would be wrong to suggest that there was any order about my reading in Paris. I had been advised by one of my teachers in Bristol – John Crofts, who in despair at being a Professor of English finally went off and became personnel director of a commercial undertaking, though he told me that the only employee who ever consulted him afterwards committed suicide – to be "a complete rubber-neck" and this bit of instruction at any rate I carried out to the letter. I wandered on the *quais* and in the Luxembourg, I visited museums and art galleries, I attended political demonstrations and watched *défilés* of various kinds. Intermittently I attended lectures at the Sorbonne and at the Collège de France, and at one of these heard for the first time the music

180

of *Aucassin et Nicolette*; I saw plays by Molière at the Odéon. I spent hours in the Bibliothèque Ste Geneviève and in the Mazarine. I was endlessly peripatetic and, mealtimes apart, rather lonely. The arrangement was not a bad one. The mealtimes at No. 75, rue du cardinal Lemoine were prolonged, and I always stayed to the end for the opportunity they gave me to listen and to talk. Then my days were free to the point of emptiness, in spite of my readings in French History – to prepare myself for the Civil Service examination – and my translation of bits of Hardy, Stevenson, and even – at the behest of Monsieur Duchemin – Emerson, which illumined the weaknesses of their style as well as providing an exercise in the language. It was too cold to stay in my room, so when the libraries would hold me no longer I continued my reading in a café on the boulevard St. Michel, one cup of coffee lasting a very long time, as it had to do if my money was not to run out.

While I was reading *Monsieur Teste* with chilled admiration and Laforgue and Corbière because I had, so to speak, been ordered to do so by T.S. Eliot, I do not really count them among the things that were accessible to me, except perhaps the poem of Corbière containing the lines

> J'en ai vu parmi nous, sur la Terre-Patrie,
> Se mourir du mal-du-pays.

My affections hardly went beyond the writers who achieved great lucidity with a small vocabulary – Ronsard, du Bellay, Racine, André Chénier and of course Villon, who is so lucid that you do not have to understand his language, though no doubt it is better if you do. Verlaine had lived only a little distance from the rue du cardinal Lemoine, so I read him; and I read Jean Moréas because he was a classic – a pseudo-classic no doubt – recommended by Maurras. I read bits of surrealists when I found them on the secondhand bookstalls.

Probably the writer who most took possession of my imagination, in a superficial way, was Jules Romains, who was a sort of intellectual guidebook to Paris. It might not be convincing to be told

> Le soleil passe au bout de la rue. On dirait
> Qu'il vient d'avoir vingt ans et qu'il aime la vie.

But at twenty-one one may not be able to avoid seeing oneself as a student in Paris, at the same time that one actually is in that rôle, and this subjectivism Romains fed. There were conversations in *Les Hommes de bonne volonté* which were so much the kind of thing a young man

181

in Paris would have wanted to talk about, if there had been such intellectual characters to talk to, that the books seemed perfect reading for one's idler moments in the boulevard *cafés*. They reinforced one's impression that one understood a little better the Ecole normale and the *milieu* of the intellectual left. That was probably illusory.

The speech that I wanted is not the speech that I have

BEFORE France, Germany. I had gone there in mechanical response to the rate of exchange. In the summer of 1934 I took my degree, failed to find a job, and was offered sixty pounds by the University of Bristol, and a further sixty pounds by the City, if I did post-graduate studies. With a hundred and twenty pounds I could live in Germany, on the 'registered marks' at special rates of exchange which were offered to tourists and students. I could not manage in France. So that decided it. I might have gone to Spain, but did not. There was never any doubt in my mind that I should go abroad.

I knew almost no German and during the summer gave some atten-tion to *der, die, das* and other refinements of the language. Then, one day in the autumn, I set out for Hamburg. The best and cheapest way – for in those days time, of course, did not matter – was by one of Hamburg-Amerika line boats which called at Southampton on their way from New York. My mother conjured up a second cousin, whom I had never seen nor, I think, heard of, in Southampton. So I spent my last night in this country with that respectable relative. He added a bizarre touch to my departure. William lived in a house which I remember as rather empty, though Victorian, and a little chilly. It seems to me that we must have had high tea. Certainly towards the end of the evening we sat round in a circle, in several fusty chairs with high backs, while William read from the Bible. Then, without warning, everyone got up and turned round, rather as if they had been playing some demure parlour game like the Old Family Coach. But they fell suddenly on their knees and buried their faces in their hands on the seats of the chairs. I was only just quick enough in following them to avoid disgrace. Then William prayed, rather loud, as it seemed to me, but that was perhaps only because I felt com-manded to a silence in which you could hear a pin drop. William prayed for our young friend, and our friend's friend – for I was travel-ling with another student – and I could hardly suppress my titters. He said we were going among people who perhaps did not honour God as much as they should, and he asked that we should be protected.

I tried to conduct myself properly among these antics. God was not among the persons whose existence I recognized, so I could only be polite to William. He came with me to the dock on the following day. There is no doubt that he felt he was letting a dove out of the ark, and that it was a very dangerous thing to do. Naturally I was ungrateful and rather relieved when he left me. A tender took my fellow-student and myself out into Southampton Water to the waiting *Amerika*. As we went aboard the band played *God Save the King* and I did not like the looks of the two young German toughs, students no doubt, who stood very rigidly while it was played but caught one another's eyes in what seemed to me a destructive sneer. I resented their insolence. I felt myself already in the Nazi world.

Every moment was miraculous for this was the first time I had been more than a few yards from the shore of my native country. We arrived in Cuxhaven and I was in a foreign land. Certain kinds of autumn weather still evoke the atmosphere of Hamburg with the leaves falling. I am not one of those who find out all about a place before arriving in it. I drifted through the strangenesses to the Schäfer-kampsallee where we were to stay. I stood on the pavement and looked up at the tall houses. They were of formidable respectability. Here and there high up on the housefronts were iron railings, making little verandahs. The street was wide and bare. We went in, climbed up several flights of stairs and found the right flat door. I do not remember who opened it. But almost at once we were welcomed by Tante Else. She was large, I suppose about sixty. I suppose she was grey and had been fair. Her plentiful flesh had begun to retreat a little under the skin. She made positive noises of welcome. She smiled and was boisterous as if she was really glad to see us. We were shown into a large room with two beds furnished with the kind of feather bolster you put on top of yourself. The window looked down on the wide street from which we had come.

When the mealtime came Onkel Willi was revealed. He was shorter than Tante Else, about seventy, bald, fat, white-haired and pink-pated. When he sat down to eat he tucked his napkin in his collar and shouted "Mahlzeit!" Then he took his knife and fork, one in each pink fist, and started to work as an eating-machine. To make sure that everyone else was enjoying the performance as much as he was he looked up from time to time, stuck out his lips, and said "Schmeckt es?" or "Schmeckt gut, was?" I do not remember that he said very much else, but perhaps he did. At any rate it is as an eater that I recall him. He had been a wholesale meat merchant, Tante Else said. I think that she felt that the *wholesale* gave a touch of elegance which might otherwise be lacking. Tante Else was distinctly more *vornehm* than Onkel Willi and I think she feared the English, with their notoriously aristocratic propensities, might not give her full credit for it. But in spite of this touch of anxiety she was a warm-hearted and not insensitive person. One day during the month we spent in Hamburg she went to an exhibition of paintings by Emil Nolde. I had been myself, and could see that there was something in it when she came back saying, with the inevitable touch of German excess, that that man had had sunshine in his heart. She had obviously been impressed.

I went out each day to a German language course at the University where term had not yet begun. For the rest of the time I must have wandered about, sat by the Alster with a single glass of beer or gone on outings arranged for the foreigners taking the course. It was all rather obscure because of my unfamiliarity with German. We visited a local Schloss where the guide talked interminably about der alte Fürst, who turned out to be Bismarck. We went down the Elbe in a boat. One evening we were entertained to supper by a modest family who engaged us in proper talk about the last war and the old Frontkämpfer said it must never happen again. This I rapidly discovered was regulation stuff, but they were friendly and seemed not displeased to entertain young Englishmen. One day we were taken to a labour camp. Here the young men, who would otherwise have been unemployed, did arms drill with shovels and became more soldierly. They did not seem as keen as our guides but they had plentiful meals of coarse food and that, in the Hamburg before Hitler came, had probably not been a thing to be taken for granted. But the reader of the English newspapers knew that the Hamburg dockers had put up a stiff Communist resistance to Hitler, so one was prepared to find drama in the eyes of the young men in the labour camp. All the time one was wondering: How much of what the papers said about the Nazis is true? I looked eagerly for signs of violence and oppression. The signs were masked, and the newspaper violence was not to be seen. But the signs were there. Tante Else was an index. She would have preferred a reaction which left the middle classes their dignity. She was half with the Nazis but felt vaguely threatened. After all she was getting old and the young men had taken over. They did not always speak respectfully to Onkel Willi. And of course her investments had dwindled. There were more obscure and more interesting reactions. When a storm-trooper called with a collecting box Tante Else showed an alarmed alacrity in making her contribution. She knew of a neighbour who had been taken away to a concentration camp for a few weeks, had come back and said nothing about it. It was the silence that was frightening. I went to the window of my room whenever storm-troopers or a squad of boys from the labour camp marched down the street. The *Horst Wessel Lied* floated up:

> *Die Fahne hoch, die Reihe fest geschlossen;*
> *S.A. marschiert mit rühigem, festem, Schritt.*
> *Kameraden, die Rotfront und Reaktion erschossen,*
> *Marschieren noch in unsern Reihen mit!*

Even the "Heil Hitler", with extended arm, as a familiar greeting, had a touch of menace. Of course it was a point of honour to reply to it with a curt "Guten Tag!"

It was not only the politics of the day which made the atmosphere of Hamburg seem strange. Tante Else seemed to think it proper that young men should explore the brothels of the town. Above all she expected them to get drunk. Onkel Willi, no doubt, had been good at that. My fellow student at least came up to scratch by getting drunk. He came home one night after, so he said, spending the evening with a beautiful girl we had met at the students' club, and propped himself against the door jamb of our room. Then he fell. He was beshatten and incapable. I took off his trousers and put them on the iron railing outside the window, then heaved him into his bed. The place stank of vomit. Tante Else regarded the affair with great satisfaction. She was masterly through long practice with this sort of thing. This Engländer at least was a proper one. Next day my roommate talked about the girl. That produced an even more favourable impression. I did not speak. I had thought her adorable but for me nothing, not even conversation, followed from that.

> *Not always in one place,*
> *Yet he is rooted*

I ARRIVED in Berlin from Hamburg, and found my way to the Tiergarten station. From there I walked, with my heavy suitcases, to the Flotowstrasse, just off the Tiergarten, which was to be my headquarters for four months. The houses were tall and yellowish, and nearly opposite the one I was to inhabit was a shop displaying sausage and other delicacies useful for someone who was to fend for himself. The flat to which I was directed was at the top of the house. You entered straight into the room of Herr Bargel, the principal tenant of the establishment, but a low half-partition fenced off a passage along which one went to the other rooms. There were two, besides the

185

kitchen and bathroom. One was inhabited by Herr Dr Mohrhoff and the other I was to share with a young trainee actor called Schmid. It was not a household but a number of square feet shared by the four of us.

Naturally the one I got to know best was Schmid, though in retrospect it seems odd that none the less I knew relatively so little of him. He was red-faced, young, sturdy, a mixture of gravity and ebullience, though the ebullience was chiefly kept, so it seemed to me, for putting expression into bits of the German classics, or of Shakespeare in translation, which he had to learn and recite for the school of Drama he attended. He had recently come to Berlin from Dresden; he knew little of the capital or of the world at large; he had so little money that I felt shamefully rich beside him. Dr Mohrhoff was about thirty, thick-set, unprepossessing, with thick glasses and a cast of face I should have thought Jewish if he had not at all times demonstrated his fervid support of Hitler, Goering and even Goebbels, and been anxious that our black, white and red swastika flag should be hung out of the window promptly whenever there was supposed to be an occasion for it. He worked in an office belonging to a steel firm, so he gave me to understand. His eye lit up whenever the Führer was reported to have said anything supposed to show that Germany was recovering her full dignity. He talked a great deal about the Treaty of Versailles, which I gathered was very shameful. He told me that in their barracks the German army displayed on the walls that one word: Versailles, to remind those young men what had to be done. This was before the reintroduction of conscription, and Mohrhoff told me with glee that he was going off for a "course" with the Reichswehr. That was how they got round the treaty of Versailles. His lips curled in triumph and his eyes shone as well as his spectacles. The joyful implication was that there was nothing we, the Western Allies, could do about it. Schmid seconded these views in a more juvenile – but also less perfervid – manner. One could detect in him occasionally what was perhaps the reflection of reservations his family back in Dresden might have felt about the Nazi delirium; left to himself, his line was rather to assure me that the English press lied, that I could see for myself that there was really no violence against Jews, that the Communists had had to be kept down and that Hitler only just saved the day. Mohrhoff had more money than Schmid, but by all the signs he had very little. However, he saved up enough to go to a brothel from time to time, on which he congratulated himself and purred for the admiration of Schmid.

The most mysterious of the three characters in the flat was Herr

Bargel himself. He was in his middle thirties, but seemed a little older, with the sort of features which might have been called frank if in fact he had ever admitted anything. He slept late every morning and was usually huddled in his blankets when I passed through his room on my way out. He came home very late. I had the impression that his life had been hard, that it didn't amount to much now, but that he was hanging on to what he had got and having an imitation of a good time meanwhile. He was the editor of a Nazi Labour Front journal, so no doubt a man trusted by the party. Such talk as I remember of his was about the past. Like the other two, he was a Saxon, but what he remembered most vividly was the days of 1919-20, or thereabout down on the Silesian-Polish border. All day the villages would be in peace. The men went about the farm work. At night, on Bargel's account of the matter, they got out their guns and stalked one another. The Germans had to kill the Poles because the Poles were out to kill the Germans. Bargel certainly evoked a world of treachery which seemed veridical enough. He did not talk to me much, however, about this or anything else. One night towards the end of my stay he invited me to go out with him and a friend who had come up from Saxony. The friend was a muscular, fair-haired man in a uniform of some kind; I think he may have been in command of a labour camp somewhere. With these two I started on what were obviously, for Bargel, familiar rounds. We looked in at a theatre, then we visited a series of drinking places, including rather posh ones on the Kürfur-stendamm where beauties as Aryan as bleach could make them came to share one's drink and show their sympathy. It was either on this or on some similar occasion when I found myself, at five in the morning at the Friedrichstrasse station, translating Joyce's sentence about "Thought is the thought of thought" in as many German ways as I could think of.

It was curious to find that, with my modest funds, I was compara-tively well off in Berlin. Poverty more or less far-reaching was so common. I do not mean that I lived like a prince, or had any but the simplest ideas of luxury, but that if I sometimes ate as cheaply as one well could at Aschinger – the Lyons tea-shop, so to speak, though soup and Wurst were more in evidence there – I could also go occa-sionally to a restaurant in the Kurfürstendamm and have jugged hare washed down by a glass or two of wine. Sometimes I would do this alone, and sit over my meal with a book, when I wanted a retreat from the world. At other times I would go to the club provided for foreign students not far from the derelict Reichstag building. The German students who were admitted to this establishment were no doubt hand-picked as being not only loyal to the cause but rather genteel. There was a polished and steely-eyed young S.S.-man whose glances were designed to guide the conversation when it threatened to become unsuitable. We could say what we liked, of course, but German students were obviously not intended to share this liberty. One occasionally had glimpses of life, however. I knew a young man who had been a member of Roehm's Storm Troop. When he heard that Hitler had shot Roehm, he fled to the outskirts of Berlin, took a boat and pushed out into one of the lakes and lay on his stomach on a tiny island until he thought the shooting might be over. In the University itself, the students were less carefully chosen. The corridors clattered with the jackboots of storm troopers. If one ate in the canteen one hardly had the impression of being among the most cultivated part of the population. Whatever forces might be supposed to guide it, the Nazi movement was certainly a revolution of the lower orders. To count as a good German in those days you had to respect the popular menace. It was difficult to see what resistance there was, if any. One day a bomb was found in the university cloakroom and there were notices offering rewards for information. But I got no information about the undercurrents, perhaps because they had been deflected from my path, or because they were not there, or because my German was not good enough for me to pick up the clues.

Certainly on public occasions the massing of visible support was impressive. In January 1935 the plebiscite took place in the Saar to decide whether that territory should be transferred to Germany. In Berlin we were bombarded with propaganda as if it had been our votes that were being sought. The air rang not only with the Horst Wessel song but with the song – hymn would be a better word – about the Saar itself. This consisted largely of repetitions of the word: Deutsch.

> Deutsch ist die Saar,
> Deutsch immerdar,
> Und deutsch ist unser Flusses Strand
> Und ewig deutsch das Heimatland
> Und deutsch, deutsch, deutsch, deutsch, deutsch, die deutsche Saar!

The result of the plebiscite was a ninety per cent vote for the transfer of the territory to Germany. This was announced on 15 January. At once posters appeared everywhere saying that there would be a spontaneous demonstration, the same evening, before the old Reichstag building. Goebbels would speak. There would be torchlight processions. I went with Schmid and Mohrhoff. There was torchlight. There were massed bands. There were the Reichswehr, the S.S., the storm troops, Swastika flags everywhere. Deutschland über Alles, the Horst Wessel song, Deutsch ist die Saar. Goebbels appeared on a floodlit daïs and the immense masses waiting below shouted deafening Sieg Heils. I don't know what Goebbels said and no doubt I had difficulty in following him. It did not matter. One could feel what inchoate forces had been released by this devilish movement. When the flags and the torches began to move out one had the impression of being engulfed in some gigantic auto-da-fé or a sabbath of German witches. The crowd was parted to make way for the procession. As the flags came up there were more hysterical Sieg Heils. Arms were flung aloft in salute. I stood to attention. Dr Mohrhoff kept jabbing my elbow, as his excitement grew. Why was I not greeting the flag? I ignored him. The flags went by. The mob loosened gradually and we went home to the Flotowstrasse. "Sir would not greet the flag!" Mohrhoff complained to Schmid. But the atmosphere was relaxed now. He was resigned to the fact that one could expect no better of an Englishman.

Speak to me no more. I have heard only
The marching men

WHILE I was in Berlin I started reading Kafka – with *Beim Bau der Chinesischen Mauer* – and Rilke, and it was Kafka who seemed more like life. But it was impossible not to be bludgeoned and obsessed by politics. There was nothing to help one *think* about these matters; one had merely to take the impact of them. I suppose an occasional thought rose to the surface. One might, for example, wonder what was wrong with the theory sometimes advanced in England, that Germany could not be a real threat because she was economically weak – judged by the criteria then fashionable in the City of London. There are other economic fashions now, but I do not know that they conceal more of permanent truth. The permanent truth, perhaps, is that an enfeebled polity will clutch at any economic or any other theory which will give it an excuse for not directing itself.

When my semester in Berlin came to an end I had six weeks without even the pretence of attending a lecture. I decided to travel and end up at a different university, in the south. My first stop was among the baroque palaces of Dresden; my second was Prague, the most beautiful city I had ever seen. But while one might admire the piles of buildings falling away to the river from the Hradschin, the political obsession was not cured. I had come with introductions to Germans

189

in Prague and, seeing who were my friends in Berlin, it was not unnatural that my acquaintance in Prague should also be Nazis. For all their hatred or distrust of Slavs it is improbable that any of the people I met had any notion of the rapidity with which the German claims would be developed, and certain that none of them foresaw the final *débâcle*. They were merely voicing an historic grievance. I was taken to see a charming old lady who told me that, even in the days of the Austrian Empire, the Germans in Prague had not had a fair deal. Then the anxiety of the government in Vienna had been to do things that would please the Slavs, rather as the disintegrating British Empire later fell over itself to please everyone but the British. There could have been something in that, but when I thought of the menacing armies collecting to the north and west this was not enough to hold my sympathy. The Czechs had their own hostilities but were less certain of having friends beyond the frontier. Their habit seemed to be not to understand a remark addressed to them in German until they had established that the speaker was a foreigner.

When I left Prague my German friends loaded me with Nazi maps and pamphlets. I shoved them just inside my case with the result that, at Eger, the inquisitorial police and customs officials became all smiles at once. They evidently thought that an Englishman who carried such literature into the Reich would not smuggle currency or engage in other hostile acts. The maps showed in red the bits of Bohemia where the German population was thickest. It gave an indication of where the frontier was to be re-drawn three or four years later. Of course nobody yet knew whether Hitler could operate beyond his own frontiers, and the allies were still supposed to be *strong*. I spent a few days in Nuremberg and then went on to Munich, where I met some American friends I had made in Berlin. The Americans were constitutionally even more incapable of understanding the Germans than were the English. I read some more Kafka, looked at baroque churches, and walked in the Englischer Garten. We drank beer or, at appropriate times of day, coffee and *allerlei Kuchen mit Schlagsahne*. Under instruction, I perfected the art of making smoke rings. When we passed the corner where Storm-troopers kept guard in honour of those who were killed in Hitler's *putsch* in 1922, one of the Americans wanted to demonstrate in some facetious manner before those funny men. This I anxiously dissuaded him from. It was not only that the storm trooper might have cut up rough, even with foreigners, but that one did not choose a memorial to the dead, even dead Nazis, for that sort of thing.

I left my Americans in Munich and went off by way of Stuttgart to Freiburg. In Stuttgart I saw the Führer himself, twice, at close quarters. He had just announced that Germany would reintroduce conscription and establish a standing army of four hundred and fifty thousand, and he was touring the country to receive the plaudits of a grateful nation. The tour must have been something of an impromptu affair, for I remember that when I saw him saluting from the low balcony of his hotel there were only a few of us in the road below. He was a disappointing little man, but to understand his power one had to hear him speak. The *Volksgenossen* and *Volksgenossinnen* twanged like the strings of a harp as he worked himself into a frenzy. He had the art of speaking for a people as only one other man I have ever heard, and that other one spoke for a less morbid nation in a more civilized manner and in a better cause.

In Freiburg I settled for as much of the semester as my funds would run to. I lodged with a Frau Bankdirektor, a widow, and went daily to the university and the bookshops. It was in this town that I passed my twenty-first birthday, without speaking to a soul. Despite the benign appearance of the town, the familiar forces were at work in the university. Young men with jackboots clattered about the corridors. There were crude posters on the notice-boards making clear what the German girl was expected to do. This was partly by way of anti-Catholic propaganda, for Freiburg passed for a Catholic centre and that had to be altered. Goering came to the town and broadcast over many loudspeakers a speech the import of which was that priests must be kept in their place, which was somewhere well below that of the storm-trooper. I saw this fat be-uniformed man, said to be genial but with a madman's face, as he drove in an open car preceded by an immense flock of S.S. men on motor cycles.

About the same time there was a more domestic anti-Catholic demonstration in the University itself. Theodor Haecker, whose name was known to me from a mention of him by Eliot, though I had not then read anything of his works, came from Munich to lecture. He took his place at the front of the lecture room. I was several rows back in the auditorium; the first couple of rows were occupied by storm-troopers in uniform. Haecker, whom I remember as a presence of great dignity and absolute calm, began to read. He had read only a few sentences when he came to some words – they were of perfect moderation – which suggested that perhaps the state was not after all the supreme authority. The storm-troopers started to stamp. Haecker turned over a page. They stamped and shouted more. There was no possibility of the lecturer being heard. He showed no sign of surprise, nor of any emotion. He turned over another page; his hand was absolutely steady. He glanced at the storm-troopers but it was clear they were going on stamping till he stopped. He turned over the pages one by one, slowly, but accelerating the pace a little as he got to the end then he folded his papers and went out. The storm-troopers, who were of course themselves students, broke up happily. That had been the kind of entertainment they cared for. When I came a year or two later to read *Christentum und Kultur* and *Vergil, Vater des Abendlandes*, the figure of Haecker seemed to me heavily masked, but I found him again in the *Tag- und Nacht-bücher* published after the war, and written while the allied armies were attacking and the Reich was crumbling from within. It is the best war book I know.

When I left Germany it was by way of Kehl and Strasbourg. As I looked at the lines of poplars in Alsace I hoped that they concealed the guns they were supposed to. For me, as much as for any Frenchman, the Rhine was the frontier of civilization. The railway porters in Strasbourg who looked askance – or so it seemed to me – when I addressed them in German, can hardly have known that they had to do with a passionate Francophil.

Enemy and barbarian.
Inutile, Monsieur, de me saluer

THAT brings me to the University of Bristol from which I had set out. The centre of it was the tall tower which still dominates the top of Park Street and can be seen from various remote points in the city. In certain weathers, too, its bell, Great George, can be heard striking the hours. The tower was the work of a pseudo-goth, Sir George Oakley, and the money for it was provided by the firm of W.D. & H.O. Wills, tobacco and cigarette manufacturers. Its architecture was the subject of derision, by me and other enlightened young men, who thought this imitation of past beauty what one would expect from the impersonal authorities who were supposed, by their very existence, to depress and deprive the young. Now that my contemporaries have had a go, and have added to the university some specimens of light industry, office block architecture, posterity can judge between the generations. The tower and the buildings associated with it has great staircases and much good oak, and the stone is beautiful. It was an attempt to provide us with the decency of ancient buildings, which we could not have, and though we disapproved I am not sure that we did not get some slight benefit from the attempt. After the squalor of most of our classrooms and most of the streets we lived in, it at least made one think of the possibility of dignity.

To this building I came, six days a week during term time, often during the vacations – having little else to do – and read in the excellent library, not ungraciously housed. My home was two and a half miles away, and my pocket money was three shillings a week, so more often than not I walked, to save the fare, which was threepence all the way or twopence part way by tram. By this economy it was possible for me, during term time, most days to go at eleven o'clock to the Berkeley café, just opposite the great tower, and talk with my fellow intellectuals about literature and politics, the two subjects on which intellectuals talked, glancing sideways sometimes at art and psychology. On rare occasions I even took tea at the Berkeley, with yesterday's buns, which were cheaper. A few times I drank half a pint of bitter beer at the University Union. Sometimes – though not too often – I had lunch there, and for this a special allowance of one and sixpence was issued to me; the other days I took sandwiches, which I ate somewhere obscurely, or went home, so that I not infrequently made the journey of two-and-a-half miles four times in the day. In summer one could eat the sandwiches on Brandon Hill, under the Cabot Tower built high above the city to commemorate the venture of John and Sebastian Cabot, who sailed from Bristol in 1493 to discover Newfoundland. It would be wrong to think this a story of abjection. In the first place, many of my fellow students were no better off than I was, so poverty was not a thing I particularly thought about. Secondly, the university, and in particular the library, and the opportunity which I conceived the place offered for an approach to the great world of civilization and the arts, supposed to exist some-where, made it a place to which I came up for air. When I came to the end of my long march through the squalor and drabness of the city I felt I had arrived somewhere.

The university union was well housed in the Victoria Rooms, stand-ing back from the road and fronted by a classic portico. There were common rooms with leather armchairs and the weekly papers, and smaller rooms where meetings of the Literary Society – of which I was chairman in my last year – were held or where the policies of the university magazine, the *Nonesuch*, were debated. The arch intellects of the place, in my day, were communists, one or two of them scien-tists who condescended to the arts as something which could be jus-tified in terms of I. A. Richards and there was thought to be an associ-ation between the arts and sexual freedom, as it is called. There was a good deal of talk about aesthetics, a subject less mysterious to me then than it has since become, and I remember a debate – it must have been in the Literary Society – at which I was puzzled to be encouraged by scientist-communist-art patrons for admitting that there was no other source of poetry than the poet's own experience. I suppose they imagined that anyone not entirely "with" the Marxian dialectic would have to think that beauty came down from heaven in special parcels, or was received by some pure intellectual process from a world of Platonic ideas.

The prevailing intellectual atmosphere – though it must have been among a very small number of people that it prevailed – was that evoked or invented in the poetry of Stephen Spender:

> Oh young men, oh young comrades
> It is too late now to stay in those houses
> Where the money is spent but not made

– or something like that. I did not then know much about the houses Spender had in mind, and on occasion in argument attributed this bourgeois security to my father, who viewed the matter differently and took rather ill the suggestion that he was reposing in comfort while the unemployed starved. I was well aware, however, that Auden, Spender and Day-Lewis inhabited a different world from my own, and it was plain to me that it was a world in which the working class was a fiction rather than a designation for chaps living in the same street and the streets round about. "Wystan, Stephen, Christopher" and the rest were always addressing one another in their poems. They denounced "Majors, Vicars, Lawyers, Doctors, Advertisers, Maiden Aunts", but to my friends and myself they counted as part of those privileged gangs, with which we had little personal acquaintance. The official view of the scientist-communist-art patrons was that these young men were making a laudable effort to identify themselves with the proletariat, shortly to be victorious; their bourgeois origins were a stain on their fine characters but one had to try and forgive them since they were making an effort. They belonged on the side of the pure in heart – for after all the sentiment, though not the language, of those times was very much post-protestant stuff – together with pylons and the "Great nude girls who had no secrets", to which Spender had likened those symptoms of technological advance.

The world of letters was so overlaid with politics in those days that although it could be admitted that Eliot, Yeats and even Pound had talent – even great talent – it was entirely wrong to admit this without reprobating their political attitudes which were all, I am afraid, to be regarded as more or less Fascist. Poor Eliot was to be thought of as more or less diseased, although he was the great innovator of modern poetry. "Classicist in literature, royalist in politics, and anglo-catholic in religion" – he was wrong on every count. I suppose this was ineluctably determined by his bourgeois background so it was no use complaining. One just had to declare him, regretfully because as a poet one acknowledged his existence, as one of the enemies of the working class and leave it at that. Pound and Yeats made more attempt to tie what they said to practical politics, so they were very bad cases of Fascism indeed. Wyndham Lewis was extremely dangerous. It is remarkable, now one comes to think of it, that every one of the writers we admired was supposed to be entirely wrong about politics, indeed about thought in general, for none of them was a Marxist. Herbert Read was the one who came nearest to respectability, I suppose. What he thought wasn't bad for an old man. Nobody considered that this dichotomy between our politics and our literary tastes might be a mark of the superficiality of our politics.

It is difficult for me to reconstruct, at this date, precisely what my own positions were while I was at the university of Bristol. No doubt they changed during the three years. Certainly I shared some of the emotional attitudes of the left. The political scene was dominated by the unemployed and I was acutely conscious of their physical presence. I saw them queueing outside the Labour Exchange and passed them in the street as I walked to and from the university. I was a little afraid of them and thought it quite natural that they should harbour envy and resentment against a person so fortunate as myself. I was with them, collectively, in imagination, against the powers they were supposed to be against – the entrenched bourgeoisie and the government who would do nothing about their condition but would merely assert that nothing could be done. My father said that people would regard me as an extremist and I replied that I was an extremist. I wanted to go to London to demonstrate with the hunger marchers but the Communists gave me to understand that young bourgeois were not expected to go if that would mean a break with their families; obviously the party members were instructed to handle possible converts as Jesuits might. Anyhow the car in which we were to go broke down so this casuistical question did not arise in an acute form. I was not interested in finance or economics; I was against the authorities because I could not believe that they could do nothing about the unemployed, if they wanted to do it. My extremest demonstration of my disjunction from the authorities was once, at the Shakespeare Memorial Theatre in Stratford-on-Avon, to remain seated while "God Save the King" was played. I was with two companions who did the same but it cost me a great moral effort, and I felt acutely the reproach of the Canadian who had accompanied us from the Youth Hostel, and who said regretfully that the people back home would be very sorry if they saw that sort of thing going on here.

And is the noise
I hear from an important quarter?

POLITICS for the young was not so much politics as a substitute for religion – which did not enter the thoughts of any of those I took seriously except as an aberration which T.S. Eliot was known to be lost in. At any rate it was a matter of attitudes to life, or to such elements of life as we happened at that time to notice. In the course of my reading I had encountered a mentor who affected my attitude profoundly, and from whom you may say that I never recovered. This was T.E. Hulme, whose *Speculations* dealt firmly and controversially with all the things which interested me most. It was the perfect antidote to liberalism and romanticism. The first essay in the book, on *Humanism and the Religious Attitude*, begins:

> One of the main achievements of the nineteenth century was the elaboration and universal application of the principle of *continuity*. The destruction of this conception is, on the contrary, an urgent necessity of the present.
> Originally urged only by the few, it has spread – implicit in the popular conception of evolution – till it has attained the status of a category. We now absorb it unconsciously from an environment already completely soaked in it; so that we regard it not as a principle in the light of which certain regions of fact can be conveniently ordered, but as an inevitable constituent of reality itself. When any fact seems to contradict this principle, we are inclined to deny that the fact really exists. We constantly tend to think that the discontinuities in nature are only *apparent*, and that a fuller investigation would reveal the underlying continuity. This shrinking from a *gap* or jump in nature has developed to a degree which paralyses any objective perception, and prejudices our seeing things as they really are. For an objective view of reality we must make use both of the categories of continuity and discontinuity. Our principal concern then at the present moment should be the re-establishment of the temper or disposition of mind which can look at a *gap* or chasm without shuddering.

In terms of politics, this meant that one no longer shared "the righteous indignation which every *real progressive* must feel at the slightest suspicion of anything *reactionary*." Instead of the liberal-democratic background which was, in spite of any theories to the contrary, the real concomitant of English communism at that time, it meant Sorel and the *Réflexions sur la violence*, Hulme's preface to which is the concluding essay in *Speculations*. It meant therefore distinguishing what Hulme still called "the working-class movement" from the ideology which went with it. This was a considerable liberty achieved, in those days. Moreover, in literature, it meant a doctrine which one could take as the foundation of classicism as opposed to romanticism. The line between the two was not drawn in the old place; Shakespeare was a kind of classic and the romantic was Hugo or Swinburne or, more precisely, all those vaguenesses for which one had no further use. The romantic thought "that man is intrinsically good, spoilt by circumstance"; the classic "that he is intrinsically limited, but disciplined by order and tradition to something fairly decent". Unlike most theorists in aesthetics, Hulme had himself a direct perception of the matter he was talking about. He illustrated his notion of classicism by two lines from the song in *Cymbeline*

> Golden lads and girls all must,
> Like chimney sweepers, come to dust.

And his own practice, in *The Complete Poetical Works of T.E. Hulme* appended to the *Speculations*, commanded admiration and respect, and turned one's mind, so far as a young man's can be so turned, away from attempting excessive things beyond one's powers. I do not mean that I stopped dead in my traces on reading those poems, but they were part of the circumstances which made me easier in my mind that my poems did not amount to much and which enabled me, before the end of my student days, to give up the idea of being a poet and to retreat quietly into what I thought I might do properly, as a critic or in some other way. Hulme also professed to provide a doctrine to go with non-naturalistic art, so in his book one had the complete equipment.

The anti-humanism of Hulme provided clues which I followed through a variety of writers. In Gordon Craig's *Art of the Theatre* I noted with satisfaction the formula that "the tendency towards the natural has nothing to do with art". The mask, symbolism, formalization of various kinds were ways of avoiding "the bare passions", which I then, owing to the failure of my own love affair, wanted so much to avoid that I could literally not bear to open a volume of Lawrence's poems for the pain it gave me. I was better off with Wyndham Lewis's *Tarr*, for whom art was "life with all the humbug

197

taken out of it". And I was already reading Benda (*Mon premier testament*) and Maurras (*L'Avenir de l'Intelligence*) as well as Sorel so, though a poor provincial, I could claim to be not quite the complete Anglo-Saxon political simpleton. I imagine that these names came to me through the pages of the *Criterion*, which, I flattered myself, I persuaded the university library to take. It was certainly in those pages that I first became interested in the to me somewhat obscure controversy between Maurras and the Vatican; there was some splendid stuff there about the banning of the *Action française*. I remember one contributor saying something like "that is why, Eminence, I look forward with such calm to the day when we shall both appear before God": it was certainly stylish stuff.

Although I grew in time to dislike *Scrutiny*, I am bound to say that that journal too was useful to me for a time. It was in the pages of *New Bearings in English Poetry* that I first read some lines of "Hugh Selwyn Mauberley", and so had the world of Pound opened to me; and I read *Seven Types of Ambiguity* before it had so entered the atmosphere as to become, itself, almost superfluous. I underwent I.A. Richards, not as something imposed by the English School, which was still on other tacks, but as reading of my own. One way and another I think I was, under that pseudo-gothic tower, exposed to most of the influences which would have rained upon me elsewhere, had I found my way to Oxford or Cambridge rather than to this provincial outpost. But I underwent them in greater isolation, or so it seemed to me, than might have been the case in those establishments, or if I had had more money.

New world, I see you dazzle
Like the sun on a door-knocker

NOT that I lacked friends. Far from it. My most constant companion was an Elizabethan seaman from the Forest of Dean – not that I recognized him in that rôle at the time. But he was – and is – a portion of the *vieille Angleterre*, a man of good timber that had grown with deep roots. I do not mean that he talked about the past, but he was it, though what he talked about was the literature of the day, and more rarely its politics, from which he stood aside in a sort of unpolitical High Toryism. His name was Francis Webb; he became a schoolmaster in the west of England. Then there was Cooper, a short, fair, energetic man, less prudent in his speculations, tempted to an extreme view if only to return from it. Like me he lived in the far recesses of the town, but in a different direction, and I have parted from him more than once, on Bristol Bridge, late at night, reluctant to leave speculation there so that he could walk off his two or three miles towards Bedminster and I towards Eastville. There was Tempest, the son of the librarian of a small Gloucestershire town, very thin, liking to talk of Baudelaire and of his own inexpensive and no doubt infrequent debauches – the nearest thing in our immediate circle to an amused intellectual. I believe he is dead. What a provincial university did not provide was any wide circle of friends who turned up afterwards, as those from Oxford and Cambridge seem to do, in positions of vantage, more or less eminent, in the cultural and other rackets of the times.

There was very little that was not new to me in those days. The members of the university staff shone with a security and affluence of which they were themselves no doubt not conscious. John Crofts, the Professor of English, was gentle and handsome, with dark hair falling over his forehead. The lines of his face were such that one could not be sure that he did not know he was handsome; they were also such as to announce his culture. His charm and singularity were that he seemed anxious to escape from this burden of beauty and cultivation, but never quite succeeded. He had a musical voice and loved oratory; he loved Sir Thomas Browne and was almost shamelessly the victim of that magical prose. Beneath his exterior was a more elusive character who felt a kinship with Wordsworth and liked to hide himself in the depths of Borrowdale. Crofts was generous to a fault – to speak quite exactly. His generosity was so great that he gave too easily before the adolescent iconoclasm of a young man to whom Eliot and Joyce came natural. I suppose he was the type of don who has long ceased to believe in his subject and his teaching. To me he was friendly to the extent of telling me, when I started on my post-graduate travels, to ignore the conditions on which the university had given the money, a piece of advice I took so ingenuously that I never wrote a postgraduate thesis at all, but disported myself as you have heard.

The Professor of Philosophy – my other chief mentor – was a man of different cast. This was Guy Cromwell Field, author of books on Plato and on morals, a character I at first found more forbidding though he proved to be of a profound geniality. He actually was a philosopher. I mean that he did in fact reflect on life as well as write books about philosophy. He had a slightly grey and steely appearance, blinked a little and had the faintest trace of hesitation in his speech. He had been in the 1914–18 war, and had been interested in the play of danger on the mind rather as St. Exupéry was, later. He had lived partly in action and partly in reflection, never one wholly without the other. In a sense I may say that the only real education I received I had at his hands. I sat opposite him reading the *Metaphysic of Morals* and the *Critique of Practical Reason*. He lit match after match from a gigantic box and threw them over his shoulder when he failed to light his pipe. I floundered and he asked definite little questions that one could not evade. There was also Meyrick Carré, who was writing, over what must have been leisurely years, a book on Lord Herbert of Cherbury. He also had been in the war, and had an M.C. He seemed comfortable, and disillusioned so far as a comfortable man needs to be. All three teachers exuded, in different ways, an atmosphere of Oxford and of middle middle-classness. They were kindly foreigners.

A character of a more fashionable kind, whom I knew only very slightly because he pontificated in the Education School, where I never was, was John Pilley. Very Cambridgey, in his mid-thirties, he was the exponent of every sort of enlightenment. I imagine that he was a member of the Communist Party; certainly he was, dogmatically, a figure of the left. He emitted near-Marxism and *The Meaning of Meaning*. He had a beautiful and energetic wife, Angela, who had played hockey for England, and in his flat in Clifton he had a charming nude drawing of her by Eric Gill. More discipular students reported that he had shown them photographs of her getting out of bed and that he would become technical on the subject of sex. All this was recognized as intellectual. Pilley belonged to the future which was supposed certainly to be awaiting us. He was a little beyond the range of my sensibility, but he was a useful exhibit.

There was in existence at this time, in Clifton, a Philosophy Circle which was recruited in part from the university and in part from the odd amateur outside, and this in due course I began to frequent. It met in the houses of members, and it was in this way that I met Alan Jupe, who earned his living by stockbroking and spent his leisures in the pursuit of aesthetic and political hares. In his flat in Royal York Crescent he had what seemed to me a lot of books, and I had an open invitation to visit him and his wife Violet on Sunday evenings. Alan was then in his early thirties – just old enough, that is, to belong to a different world of experience but not so old as not to have connections with my own generation. It astonishes me now that I was always made so welcome when I turned up there, from three long miles or so away, escaping from the sabbath oppression at home. The value of such kindness, combined with so much intelligence, to a young man finding his way, is very great. Proust, Joyce, Lawrence, the lot, you might say, were the repeated subject of our discourses. The flat was a place to exchange enthusiasms – a thing one needs badly, at the age of nineteen or twenty.

My formal studies during my three years as an undergraduate were in the Honours School of Philosophy and English Literature. This meant that for the first year I read the *Republic*, and I dare say some other things and did Anglo-Saxon at the same time so that if one were thrown out of the Philosophy School one could still do what is called English language. After that the time was divided between English Literature and Philosophy, so that one's reading in more luxuriant pastures was accompanied by nibblings at Bacon, Locke, Berkeley and Hume – a not unuseful accompaniment, I think. At least if one had read Berkeley one was not tempted to assert that the best prose was written by Charles Lamb. Roughly speaking, I was taught literature by the light of Bradley and Saintsbury but learned it by the light of Eliot and Pound. I had Eliot's *Poems 1909-25*, at my request, as a prize on leaving school in 1931. In 1932 I acquired Pound's *Selected Poems* and in 1933, when they first appeared in this country, the *Draft of Thirty Cantos*. In 1931 I acquired *The Sacred Wood* and in 1932 *For Lancelot Andrewes*. Some time during my time as an undergraduate I also took to heart Pound's *How to Read*. All these are books from which, taken at that age in a milieu in which they were still not accepted for what they are, one did not recover. The impact of the Communist poets, even of Auden whose original slim volume came my way, was secondary. Yeats dawned on me slowly, starting at the back of the book. The sight of the volume – and even some of the contents – had long been familiar before a day I remember when I took it down from the shelf in the Bristol Central Library and suddenly heard the voice that was speaking. Hopkins became *de rigueur* at some stage; I am not sure that there was not a sense of duty mingled with my enthusiasm. But it was through Eliot that I found my way through the Elizabethan and Jacobean dramatists and the seventeenth century poets, with whom I already had some familiarity. The Muses' Library volumes of Donne, Vaughan, and William Browne of Tavistock had been sought out as birthday presents and I had bought tattered editions of Marvell and Hudibras on a bookstall before I ever laid hands on an Eliot, or he, so to speak, laid hands on me.

The horse looks over the wall

I WAS seventeen when I left school to embark upon the course of learning I have described. It was not a good school, whatever that may mean. It was a county secondary school, ranking somewhat above the worst of these establishments in the city and well below the best. It goes without saying that it was altogether outclassed by Bristol Grammar School and that of Clifton College one had barely heard. The school was for both sexes. That in itself set the *cachet* of mediocrity upon it. At the time I left it, it had never sent anyone directly to Oxford or Cambridge, and the thought of attempting such an *escalade* did not enter my head. But to "go to the university" was an accepted objective, and there was no doubt that I was cut out for that.

My two years in the sixth form – from fifteen to seventeen – were as these years ought to be, a time of rapid development in my tastes. I went in still reading Rupert Brooke, and looking with interest at Edith and Sacheverell Sitwell, in the sixpenny edition of the Augustan Poets. When I came out I had read an extract from *The Waste Land*, in a pamphlet published by the B.B.C. to go with Harold Nicolson's talks on contemporary literature, but I had to wait for my leaving prize to get hold of the book. In between there was a passionate affair with Dante Gabriel Rossetti, a wondering over William Morris, the acquisition of *Hero and Leander* and the poems of Ben Jonson, and so to the seventeenth century poets I have already mentioned. Rossetti was an obsession. There is much to differentiate in the volume of 1870, and for a boy of sixteen the movement from "The Blessed Damozel" to "Jenny" marks a release of sensibility. But the hottest point of the obsession became the *House of Life*, first the sonnets – heavy, dramatic and passionate in the common acceptance of that word – and at last the songs.

> Between the hands, between the brows,
> Between the lips of Love-Lily

This contains I know not exactly what of adolescent mystery; in those days it was beauty to the point of pain. The sonnet became the vehicle of my own hopeless love and I wrote a series, for all the world like Rossetti. It must have been at the emergence from this obsession – the literary one, for from the hopeless love I did not emerge – that my mind began to fix on Song VIII, the "Woodspurge", surely some of the best lines Rossetti ever wrote, with the purest *line*, so to speak:

> From perfect grief there need not be
> Wisdom or even memory:

One thing then learnt remains to me –
The woodspurge has a cup of three.

In the sixth form my subjects were English, French and Latin, and
I could not have chosen better within the available menu. I have
always been glad that I took my Latin so far, even more than I am
sorry that I took it no further. For a man who is to care for letters
this study is beyond price. Even not conducted to the point of high
expertise, it drives piles into the marshes of the mind so that there is
something to build on later. I have much regretted that I have no
Greek, a luxury not provided by Fairfield Secondary School, but
desirable though that is, it is possible that it matters less. It is at least
less involved with our own speech: but perhaps these grapes are sour.
For French one need still make no apology, though there are those
who have the folly to propose some other second language, as more
useful. I assume that anyone who has got so far in this book is not
so drunk with the triumphs of commerce and technology. English is
a more doubtful starter, as a sixth form subject, but I must record
the opportunities it gave me, for which I am grateful.

The special period we had to study was that of the Romantics –
rather *vieux jeu*, no doubt. They gave us *Childe Harold* instead of *Don
Juan*, but otherwise the syllabus was well chosen. There were the
odes of Keats, at a time when those poems could fill the mind, and
Shelley who had long been a star. But the syllabus was centred on
Wordsworth, whom I derided, and while I absorbed a good deal of
it I was driven into the arms of Pope whom I pretended to admire
more than I at that time did, though I sharpened my wits on him.
The poems of Wordsworth, in Matthew Arnold's selection, and the
Prelude, were accompanied by the Preface to the *Lyrical Ballads* and
certain of Coleridge's criticism, so that the whole did amount to some
sort of study. The volume of Coleridge – the *Literary Criticism* in the
Oxford Miscellany – still seems to me to be admirably adapted to the
opening literary mind. There is enough there to bring one to grips
with one of the most remarkable minds of the nineteenth century;
the text is in places difficult and everywhere full of suggestion. The
main sections are on Wordsworth and Shakespeare, and the former
section, from the *Biographia Literaria*, contains the dismemberment
of the *Preface to the Lyrical Ballads*. It is the perfect demonstration of
the critic who tries to understand what he is doing, a thing rare enough
to be worth notice. The snippets drawn from the *Table Talk*, the
Literary Reminiscences and elsewhere, are full of comments on the best
writers of the seventeenth and eighteenth century which stick in the

mind and illuminate their subjects when one comes at last to approach them. They are not a guide to English literature; they are a companion pointing out, with superlative intelligence and great learning, what is to be seen, and though one is too bewildered to notice all these things at the time one finds the hints tucked away, for use later. "Swift was *anima Rabelaisii habitans in sicco*, – the soul of Rabelais dwelling in a dry place." "I know no genuine Saxon English superior to Asgill's. I think his and Defoe's irony often finer than Swift's." "In my judgement Bolingbroke's style is not in any respect equal to that of Cowley or Dryden. Read Algernon Sidney: his style reminds you as little of books as of blackguards. What a gentleman he was!" From such a mind one is prepared to take the merest suggestions, and I found myself following up the suggestions of this book for years: "the wit of Donne!"; "the slang of L'Estrange". The book cost three and six-pence at the time: I have had my money's worth.

Perhaps I should say something of the social arrangements of the sixth form. There was a boys' common room, a dark and rather barbarous place, sometimes used for lessons but otherwise for private study or for mere riot. You ate your sandwiches there at lunch time, if you stayed. There was no one of these boys who shared my interests, or even began to. I suppose I was well trained there for a life in which the things which really interest me have come last, in a social way. The interest of my contemporaries was in rugby. I am not saying that they did not discourse as De Quincey's school-fellows are supposed to have done; there was simply no attempt at communication at all. It was not a thing that mattered to anybody. There was physical movement instead. I do not mean that the terms we lived on were otherwise than friendly. They were not, except perhaps for a rather venomous, dark Welshman who had come to the school at a late age, perhaps from a rougher world than we were used to. He had muscles of iron and liked to use them, but he was the only one from whom, in a scuffle, one would catch a glimpse of murder. Still, it was a savage *milieu*, and I was glad that the privileges of the sixth form included freedom to use the library when one would. The library was the most civilized room in the place, with a long table used for staff meetings, and bookcases which I explored in the lunch hour. They contained no very coherent collection, so far as I remember, but there were odd books that took my fancy – Trelawney's *Last Days of Shelley and Byron*, Peacock's *Memoir of Shelley*, and the three-volume edition of the works of Francis Thompson. There was a time when Thompson's prose seemed magical. Besides, the books were large and splendid; they were *books*. I also found Blake, and was astounded by his naked truthfulness, though I did not think of that particularly, at the time, as poetry.

I need only add that one rarely spoke to a girl, for the school, although for both sexes, was not *mixed*.

Wherever I went I came here first

THIS school, where I spent the years from eleven to seventeen, was a building of brick and stone on two floors, on each of which was a hall surrounded on three sides by classrooms and the like. There was a large wing, mainly of a single storey, where the laboratories and art room were housed, approached by a corridor down which boys used to yell "Oil!" whenever the art mistress rang her bell. In the same region were the gymnasium and the junior classrooms, a wood-work room and a fives court, the latter two in a subterranean world of their own.

The buildings were a tall island surrounded by grey small stone houses on three sides, while the fourth gave on to a railway cutting crossed by a footbridge, with a prospect of more grey houses beyond. I suppose the stone, relatively clean, was pennant grit, edged with Bath stone. Semi-detached houses of this kind, villas you might say, with bay windows, deface many acres in Bristol. They betoken the quiet respectability of the lowest middle classes, for the most part; they are part of the English social plan which has long made transition from the proletariat imperceptible. The school was entered by the boys on one side and by the girls on the other, so that they came in at opposite ends of the hall, and at each side was a playground, separate for the sexes like the other conveniences. The boys' playground had an old gun, or rather a mortar, in it; it is surprising now how pro-minent were the reminders of the First War, in those days. I lived perhaps a mile and three-quarters from school, and though I could and often did come part way on a tram, more often I walked, so I did not lack exercise. The way home was down the hill and then, for the most part, through mean streets. At a certain point I could go left by St. Werbergh's and so out on to a new road which had only just begun to be defaced with houses, or right past Mina Road School and over the footbridge which crossed the shabby urban Frome, by Stapleton Road station and so to the main Eastville junction. The war memorial at the Mina Road School – a squalid elementary school of the usual proletarian type – left in my memory the couplet of Tenny-son.

> Not once or twice, in our rough island's story
> The path of duty was the road to glory.

Across the footbridge there would come, often, little boys with hand-carts full of coal, which they had fetched from the station yard. The whole country was hostile, in spite of its familiarity; its shabbiness I took for granted. I must have gone to and fro in great concentration of spirit, always anxious to get on, never tempted to linger. It was the pattern of my journey through the world.

It seems to me now that I must have been a pupil of unusual passivity, but perhaps it is only from the perspective of age that it seems possible that children should be talked to rather than taught at. My main impression of the school, until my last years, was one of dread, though there was nothing particularly to be afraid of, the discipline was mild; even in the last years, the impression was mitigated rather than removed and I was never at home in the place. In the lower form there was the terror of the subjects I could not do – arithmetic for example and, at first, French, though it was only the appalling teaching which made it seem so difficult. I do not think I was ever led anywhere; I merely found my way. There were of course rare moments of a certain charm. Latin I liked from the first, and we were soon reading a book called *Fabulae Antiquae* which began: "Pygmalion vir Graecus est, et multas, pulchras statuas facit". By the time I was thirteen my poems began to appear in the school magazine; at fourteen I won competitions in *Time and Tide*, put up to it by the English mistress, for I should never have heard of such a journal. A poem about Moses in the wilderness won a guinea; a little later, when I began to be influenced by the Sitwells, it was the second prize of half a guinea. By the time I was in the sixth form, or it may have been even in the fifth, the French master thought fit to ask me to translate a poem, Lamartine I think, into English verse, to show that it could be done. I tried for some time and then reported that it couldn't be done, which he thought rather a poor show.

They are better forgotten, most of my dreary days in that establishment. Sometimes at lunch time – dinner time is what I should call it – I ate my sandwiches quickly and hurried through Stokes Croft to the Upper Arcade, a down-at-heel street of shops roofed with glass. There was just time, before I had to go back, to turn over the books in the outside tray of the secondhand bookshop. I went there often but I cannot often have bought anything, having very little money. Still, some books could be bought for tuppence in those days, and I have a small book of extracts from Malory which I bought at that price and in this place. It was a paper-backed school book, but I took it home and fitted it up with green boards and a spine of white paper, with the title in ink. This was when I was fourteen. I suppose it is a mark of unhappiness that I should have taken so much trouble. Inside the book is marked "17". That will have been the number of the book in my private library. I am not sure now what the first sixteen were. There must have been a good deal of Robert Louis Stevenson, and sixpenny editions of Rider Haggard. An important purchase – costing ninepence at the corner shop by Bristol Bridge – was the *Essays of Elia,* which also became mine when I was fourteen. I must have had the *Selected Poems* of John Drinkwater about the same time, but as a new book, in red buckram, a present, costing three-and-six. Drinkwater soon gave way to a more powerful illusion in the person of Rupert Brooke, in black buckram, the same publisher, price three-and-six. I could hardly have been more remote from the world of Cambridge, country vicarages, beautiful young men recognized as poets by prime ministers. And I should not trust myself, now, to give a critical appraisal of this young man's works. Of course they are of such a kind that, if I came upon them for the first time now, they would not interest me. But at fifteen Rupert Brooke became an outlet for my thwarted ardour.

> When the white flame in us is gone
> And we have lost the world's delight
> Stiffen in darkness, left alone
> To crumble in our separate night.

This was well enough to a boy who had not yet read Donne's *Extasie.* There was an exotic and sensual attraction about

> Mamua, when our laughter ends,
> And hearts and bodies, brown as white,
> Are dust about the doors of friends,
> Or scent a-blowing down the night...

And how was I to know that *The Chilterns* was nothing more than a spoilt-boy cynicism? I had not even read *The Shropshire Lad.*

> And I shall find some girl perhaps,
> And a better one than you,
> With eyes as wise, but kindlier,
> And lips as soft, but true.
> And I dare say she will do.

It is with the sonnets of 1914 that I resign my critical courage completely. I have never been able to regard those sentiments as ridiculous, and when I was thirty tears came into my eyes when I remembered certain of the words, standing beside neglected tombstones in the North-West Frontier Province. That may have nothing to do with poetry. From Brooke I went on to Flecker. One would not miss much if one did not read Flecker, but at the time he seemed to me what he was meant to seem – sweet. If you are young enough you can think that of things like this:

> We shall watch the Sultan's fountains ripple, rumble, splash and rise
> Over terraces of marble, under blue balconies,
> Leaping through the plaster dragon's hollow mouth and empty eyes!
> Waving cypress, waving cypress, let us go to Saadabad.

That stuff was never more than a superficial addiction. I cared more for

> Have I not chased a fluting Pan
> Through Cranham's sober trees?
> Have I not sat on Painswick Hill
> With a nymph upon my knees,
> And she as rosy as the dawn,
> And naked as the breeze?

The attraction of those lines was not less, no doubt, because my own answer to the question had to be a plain negative. If "one outgrows most poetry, as one outgrows most passions", as Eliot says, at a certain point in adolescence, among inchoate emotions, one is sure to admire much of it that is bad, more that is mediocre, and to admire some good verse for the wrong reasons. If there are right reasons, that is. Anyway, I do not think that a schoolboy is any the better for strangling himself with Leavisian scrutinies. Of course it would be an argument for such highbrow teaching that it would produce a violent reaction, something like a vomit, in any boy likely to turn out a poet.

Still with the hope of being understood,
Of understanding myself
Or understanding someone else

THE family home, since I was six years old, had been Heath House, Gadshill Road. This was the last of four semi-detached houses, tall and big-bosomed in comparison with the terrace of hard red brick which disappeared up the street beyond them. The opposite side of the road was blank – a thin strip of allotment separating the street from a railway bank. The road was not in very good repair. It led from Fishponds Road, which had trams and buses and the railway bridge, in a slight rise, as over a sleeping figure, to descend at the other opposite Greenbank Cemetery.

The house consisted of a semi-basement with two storeys above. The front door was at the side, and it was by the basement steps that I usually entered. The basement door, half glass, had the words "Heath House" in white on red glass in the centre pane. Inside was a passage with red, black and yellow tiles, which led straight ahead to the kitchen and scullery and the cool, roof-lit larder. There were two rooms, properly so called, on this floor. At the back, giving on to the yard above which rose the small garden, was what we called the breakfast room, where we ate all meals except on the grandest occasions and lived a good deal of the time. The room at the front was darker – the bedroom of my invalid sister, three years younger than myself and, when I was fourteen, the room she lay dead in; after that we put books there, and called it the library. By this time there were a lot of books, many of them without interest, some of them bound volumes of journals vaguely technical, which had once been instructive, but including a few Mermaid Dramatists and other poets, with the inscription, "W. Sisson" and a date in the nineties. These had belonged to my uncle Wilfred, whom I had never seen, and who had come to an early end, and a bad one, I was given to understand. My father's brothers and sisters were all dead, or rich – by his standards – which came to much the same thing. The survivors were an Uncle Edward and Aunt Bertha, neither of whom had married and who kept house together in Liverpool. Uncle Edward was a bank inspector, whatever that may be; he had investments and, it was somewhat obscurely reported, intermittent intrigues of another kind. Such money as he had he must have made – what is called made – I suppose. Aunt Bertha had been the beneficiary of a will in which a brother of my father's mother had expressed his belief that men, but not women, ought to fend for themselves. He had left the not unuseful sum he had acquired in China and elsewhere to his nieces and nothing to his nephews. We very rarely saw these two from Liverpool and did not like them when we did. Aunt Bertha gave my mother a good deal of help by post, advice about the bringing up of the family – which my mother, I am afraid, received without gratitude. There had been several imprudent but not, perhaps, untalented lives in my father's family. Besides my great-uncle who made his money in China, there was one reputed to have married the daughter of a judge in Ireland, but left her for a simpler way of life, in Canada, where he offered her a home he knew she would not want. There was also one who is supposed to have worked with Marconi, and to have refused a knighthood; I was once shown his portrait in the station at Weston-super-Mare where the Atlantic cable comes up – or where I understood it to come up. He was concerned with the laying of that cable.

The only other place of importance in the semi-basement was "under the stairs", the dump for lumber and important when I was a child. The stairs had a door half-way up, as if the house had been designed to have a Victorian "below stairs" while the no doubt not very grand lady and gentleman reigned above. The first floor had a little hall, a pantry, and two rooms. The back room was the biggest in the house, and the "best"; it had heavy furniture and was called the dining-room. There was a fire here at weekends, in winter, and if we wanted to entertain, which was not very often, this is where it was done. The front room was for years left bare as a play-room, which was an excellent thing. It was on this floor that I set out my model railway, built with bricks, and marshalled the lead soldiers in the rival states of Paphalonia and Gerondia, which I had invented. Paphalonia was a monarchy, and that was the side to be on. Gerondia, I am sorry to say, was a republic; you could not expect much from that. My soldiers included Cameron Highlanders, Bengal Lancers, even Turks (I imagine they were in the service of Gerondia). There were one or two guns, and complicated histories which I no longer remember. This was not altogether a lonely game. Howard Smith, my own age, had soldiers and used to come and play. He once devised a plan for destroying my army without a shot being fired. He was going to put a bath of water out to freeze, get me to put my men on the ice, and then put the bath in front of the fire. When I was a little older and my armies had retired the room was let at rent for several years to an old lady, I suppose to help balance a precarious budget. Then in slightly better days it was furnished as a drawing-room, but not very well.

On the way up to the bedroom floor, where the staircase turned and the ceiling was lofty, there stood an old grandfather clock, with horsemen visible through the dark varnish of the case. My brother and I would both have liked to keep this relic, but finally neither of us did. There were three bedrooms. The front bedroom, which had a small dressing room, was my parents'; my elder sister had the small back bedroom. The larger back bedroom contained the iron beds of my brother and myself. From the window one could see the university tower, when it came to be built. More close at hand one could see the back gardens of Berkeley Street, which was parallel with Gadshill Road. The people there were rougher; beer was supposed to be drunk rather freely, the women wore men's caps and the children were dirty. I really must go and see who lives there now.

Naturally we were of quite a different class from the people who lived in the terraced houses in Gadshill Road as well as from those who lived in Berkeley Street. I am afraid that Mrs Fry – not old Mrs Fry, who lived next door, and was very respectable, but fat Mrs Fry, who lived next door but one – used to pass down the road with a cloth cap on her head, a jug in her half-extended hand, on her way to the Bottle and Jug Department or may be to the Live and Let Live off licence. Fishponds Road had every amenity in the way of shops. Just opposite the bottom of Gadshill Road was Batten's Dairy, where I was sometimes sent for a quarter of clotted cream (it was the genuine article): there was a fish and chip shop, more frequented by working class people than by us. There was the fat woman's grocer's store where I was sent for corned beef; this groceress puzzled by me at first, showed her discrimination by saying, when enlightened as to who my parents were: "I thought he was not an ordinary boy". Further down the road was Mr Williamson's seed shop, where I was sent for seven pounds of rolled oats, for porridge, and where I bought bran and crushed oats for my rabbits. My rabbits – only one at a time, a black-and-white Dutch, and then a long-haired albino of some kind, lived in a hutch in the garden and I tended them with punctilio. They had to die, and my tortoise died in his straw in the winter. Then I kept white mice; they died too, but that did not matter so much.

This is the house that I was brought up in. My mother never wanted to live in it; it was a stubborn man's notion of a suitable house for a family. It meant a lot of work, my mother said, and well she might; for years we carried the bath-water up two flights of stairs in buckets, though we had an electric hot-water-tank in the end. The outlook on both sides was squalid. When I was at the university I was not proud to bring people there; hardly anyone came anyway; it was too far and there was nothing to come for. But when I was a boy, and more among even poorer people, at chapel or at my elementary school, it was rather superior. I understand how the layers of society go right into the ground.

The child in setting out is innocent,
Or is he?

211

THE streets around had each its special ambiance and social tone. If the people of Berkeley Street were wilder and rougher than those of Gadshill Road, Freemantle Road had the advantage in decorum and politeness over Gadshill Road. In Freemantle Road all the houses were identical, as near as makes no matter. The same pattern filled both side of the road, and nothing disturbed the quiet except the milkman. That fiery passions could none the less live inside such houses I knew, for in one of them lived Howard Smith with his choleric and sadistic parents. But Freemantle Road was on the opposite side of Fishponds Road from us, a territory more benign than ours, even where it was dowdy, perhaps because the dowdiest quarters in it were associated in my mind not with violent boys but with the hunchback lady who used to come sometimes to sit with my invalid sister. On our side of the road, beyond Berkeley Street, lay Freeland Buildings. There it seems the tone was lower than in Berkeley Street, for Pooch Horseman lived there, whose father was a drunk, and the children ran in the road without shoes or socks; it was difficult sometimes for Pooch to find the clothes to come to school in. Below that one came to the spacious grounds of the Eastville Workhouse – no doubt it is called a hospital now. The walls of its estate ran far over towards Greenbank, where my elementary school was, and I knew a shy, charming boy whose mother, it was whispered, had been sent to prison for climbing over that wall and stealing firewood. One did not care for the workhouse.

If, instead of turning left as you came down Gadshill Road you turned right, you could see through the railway bridge to Eastville Park beyond. That was really the way out. But opposite it, and on our side of the road, was the tall gable end of Eastville United Methodist Chapel, or may be it already called itself, *church* – a habit which such establishments have certainly acquired now. The caretakers were the Mills, Mr & Mrs – the "dark satanic Mills" was the title I applied to them when I learned the expression. They were small and dark, with some ingrained dirt, glad enough, I dare say, to have found this way of saving themselves from the gulf of unemployment. The chapel itself was of somewhat pretentious appearance. You went *up* to it; that was the fault of the ground. But inside, there was the pale varnish of the pews, the pulpit in the central position backed by the choir and the organ; that was the fault of the theology.

Nothing demonstrates more egregiously the vices of the Reformation than this putting the preacher where the altar should be; it was when I saw how this is done – with much greater pomp, of course – in Edinburgh that I understood certain weaknesses in the Scotch character. The jack-in-the-box most often seen in the pulpit of the Eastville United Methodist Chapel, in my day, was a little, pale, bald man with bunches of brown hair above each ear, a weak, pseudo-ecstatic character for whom one could have no respect. It was a sign of my mother's submissiveness that we went to this establishment instead of to St. Thomas's Church, where certainly the language of the Prayer Book would have touched me, for in the Methodist Hymn Book I came to look for the odd hymn by George Herbert and the "Ancient Hymns of the Church" at the end of the hymnal which included the *Te Deum*. Behind the chapel, in Gloucester Street (socially above Berkeley Street but not, I should think quite up to the level of Gadshill Road), were rooms adapted for Sunday Schools and other social purposes; the wig-haired pastor put the chapel into debt for a handsome amount in order to extend them – a not unuseful creation of credit, at the time, I suppose. Here I went to Sunday School and was taught by a pair of superior young men from Thingwall Park – further towards Fishponds and quite distinctly beyond our social reach. They had been to the Bristol Grammar School, and I remember being put to an appalled shame when they asked me, at what seemed an advanced age (I have no idea now what it was) whether I had *done* Milton at school and I had to admit that I had not. But my chief mentor, in the social activities of the chapel, was Fred Crocker, who came from Freemantle Road. While the grammar school boys were in a bank, he was with the Customs and Excise. He was fair and thin and dapper; he made a great impression in one of the chapel concerts by his rendering of "Burlington Bertie", an action song for which he must have been felt to be well equipped, dressed in a borrowed topper and all. But his main influence on me was as captain of the Boys' Life Brigade (later amalgamated with the Boys' Brigade, on which occasion he said, I remember, "That word 'life' is very dear to me".) Fred Crocker had fought in the war, it must have been as a very young man, at the end of it; he curdled my blood by imitating the sound of a bayonet as it went in and twisted. He knew, I suppose; he had been left with a heap of dead in a ditch and the German had gone round prodding those they suspected of being alive, and finishing off those who were. Under Fred Crocker's instruction, or more exactly under his presiding presence, I drilled and did gym on winter evenings, even boxed – I can remember being put to toe a line with a boy half as heavy again and with huge muscles; one's toe had not to leave that line. And with the same martial body I went camping in the Mendips; infinitely miserable, I remember when, at the end of one week, I was given the special treat of staying on for another weekend, while my father came down to join a few of the organisers after the boys had gone home. With the Boys' Life Brigade and Boys Brigade I must have served a number of years; I was still at it when I was old enough to be helping to run the Life Boys, who were the junior échelon, the Wolf Cubs as it were. So when I joined the army I knew the elements of foot drill, though in my boyhood we formed fours, like the soldiers of the first war, not threes, in the manner of the King's later army.

Eastville Park was an expanse I had known, from different approaches, from the beginning of my life. It was defaced by footballers, whom I sought to avoid, but it had trees and grass, a lake in a hollow, the muddy Frome beyond it. And it was the way to a wilder land beyond. Past the bandstand, down the hill by the lake, and then along the bank of the Frome, you could reach Snowdon, a wild steep place, and the Black Rocks, which overhung the Frome from stupendous heights and were crossed by a dangerous path. The opposite end of the Frome at this point was meadow, so you were in the country. Beyond the Black Rocks you crossed a lane and descended into a low-lying meadow, still by the Frome; there were water-skaters and sticklebacks in plenty, and cows among the buttercups. The real fishing-ground was beyond that still, and it was there that I hurried with my jam-jar. The Snuff Hills, since tarted up into a sort of park with made walks, was a ruin in a wild valley. The river spread out, there were stepping-stones from which minnows and sticklebacks could be netted. Among the trees at the side lizards were to be found, and grass snakes; there was a dangerous quarry pond, nearly stagnant, where newts could be captured. This was the land of my discovery, but there were other places only second to it in wonder. If you crossed Eastville Park at the lower instead of the upper end you crossed the Frome and went up Bell Hill to Stapleton, still a village. Here was a dilapidated, small Georgian house that my mother had wanted when my father bought Heath House. A little further on, the red sandstone obtruded. To the left was the Duchess's park, an old dower house of the Beaufort estate, then used as a home for boys whom one later learned to classify as retarded but were then merely wonderful and rather fearsome. There was a sweep of landscaped country, edged with woods; an old tower, said to be unsafe; stiles which led to still remoter lands where I often went because I had aunts living at Hambrook and Frenchay.

The aunt at Hambrook was married, and lived at the lodge of The Conifers, a house belonging to a director of a local brewery who finally made an end of himself by lying in wait for a train and kneeling submissively on the line. Aunt Julia was the youngest and sweetest of all my aunts. She had a thoughtful, rather melancholy, long face, and plentiful soft hair. Her voice was charming and musical, a very feminine voice, a little husky with Gloucestershire resonances. The house was tiny – two bedrooms, a kitchen, a sitting room. There were Daisy and May, my cousins, and Uncle George when he came in from the garden. Uncle George was short, bald, with a large scraggy moustache and exceedingly bright, twinkling eyes. He leaned on his stick and looked at me by way of a humorous greeting. He was always in his shirt sleeves, with a clean shirt, but never with a collar or tie. He had driven one of the brewer's drays until he fell off and shortened his leg, when he became the gardener. He practically grew in that garden, and when he was not tending his master's he was at work on his own vegetable patch. He had more than any man I can think of the air of being deeply contented. I was a little afraid of his strength but I felt the atmosphere of the place to be a happy one; I do not know whether it seemed like that to its inhabitants. Uncle George regarded his employer's family with an irony which was not unaffectionate. The young gentleman – a boy just a little older than I was – seemed particularly to take his fancy; I remember him reporting kindly, but without mercy, the boy's dictum: "When I catch a ball I close my eyes, for some unknown reason". Uncle George saw such reasons with great clarity, but did not let on.

At Frenchay there was Auntie Kate, who kept a little, old-fashioned shop with Miss Good. Auntie Kate was grey and short, Miss Good a little taller, thin, dark-haired. The shop was adjacent to the cottage where they lived with an old man I understood to be Miss Good's uncle. He was massive and silent, and busied himself in the yard and outbuildings, where there was a saw-pit as well as an upstairs where I one day found him and another man hammering down a coffin. He was the village joiner, I suppose, who did a bit of undertaking as well. The shop was fascinating and had bins of grain which it was pleasant to run through the hands. Later Aunt Kate and Miss Good moved to a new house at the far end of the village. Tea there was served with a certain elegance; they were a whole field from the road, and one could go out with them collecting the eggs which the hens left occasionally in the hedges – they seemed undisciplined. I last remember Aunt Kate after she had had a stroke, and could not speak, unless a few strange noises are speech; though it worried her friends, she would come on the bus to Bristol to see us, and sit there, rather frightening, unable to communicate, her face awry. I could tell you also of Aunt Bessie at Tormarton, silver-haired and grand, with a band of velvet round her neck, who lived in a splendid farmhouse with people who must have been second cousins. Or of Aunt Lizzie at Yate, a widow, with Betty and Freda and Fitz.

Story and fable now are all there is
And so I tell it now

THE other way Gadshill Road led to the cemetery. By the time my sister was buried there I had ceased to go that way, for it led nowhere else except to my elementary school at Greenbank, unless it were (turning left instead of right) to the coalpit in whose ponds there were so many tadpoles, and at fifteen I preferred other forms of poetry. For the most part the cemetery was a long wall, topped with railings. There was a faint whiff of the dead sometimes, but no more. The side of the road not lined by these railings was a high stone wall, one of the frontiers of the workhouse, I suppose. It was along this road I ran, from the age of six to the age of eleven, to go to school. At the end of the road was a hill. One was then in an area of small silent houses, respectable *à la mode de* Freemantle Road. Embedded in it was Greenbank Elementary School, Boys', Girls' and Infants', three separate establishments in one ghastly heap. It was a building of grey stone, with asphalt playgrounds, one for girls and infants and one for the big boys, as they were rather misleadingly called.

Of course it was with the Infants that I started my career in the place. The occasion was not without scandal. I was already six years old and had never set foot in a school. This made a poor impression on the headmistress who was sitting on a dais in the hall when she received the appalling news. In these grave circumstances I should start the next day. I did. It then emerged that I could not read. I had been put in a class suitable to my age, but all my new associates were more learned than I. All I had done was to copy out, at home, "The tiger lives in the long grass", without any clear notion of the relationship between those marks and that tiger, who impressed me none the less. So I was taken out of the class, a figure of shame, and put in an empty classroom, I suppose while they thought about me. Then one or two other children were introduced. I expect we were all backward. A thin woman with dark hair, jerky movements and a rasping voice pointed at pictures on a blackboard with a stick. I cannot imagine how this led to my learning to read. I do not think it did, for I recall standing by the playroom window at home, with a book, and a brother or sister, I cannot remember which, and suddenly receiving

216

illumination. I don't suppose the illumination was as sudden as that, but after that I could read. I was a nice little boy. That is not a particularly good thing to be, in cruder circles. I also made lassoos and tried to catch children in the playground. Before I reached the age of eight, and was separated from girls for ever, so to speak, I became acquainted with love. The object of my wonder was Noreen Jacobs, slim and fair. I held her hand in the playground and was bewildered at the derision of the bystanders. It was certainly love. Then I went up to the big boys and never saw her again.

In the Infants' School they screamed and hit children with rulers. In the Big Boys there were canes everywhere, which ensured a certain order. My punctuality was ensured by the fact that the headmaster lined up in the hall everyone who was late, and gave him the cane. The learning of tables – which I found difficult – was guaranteed by the fact that those who failed to learn them were caned in the classroom. When the whistle blew in the yard there was silence, for the same reason. My later preceptor Guy Cromwell Field thought it reasonable to use a stick in training dogs and boys. The headmaster was short, fat, bald, pink and silver, with thick lips. If he had merits, I never saw them, but I did not seek them out, or him. The senior master was Mr Arthur, short, important, grey, with waxed moustache ends. I expect being just and upright was his line. His bearing was military; I expect he had been too old to be in the forces in the First War. Mr Yendall had been in it, and told us frequently. He explained that, had we not won the war, we should not have had him standing there, but a German with a horsewhip. Mr Yendall had only an exceptionally long cane. I do not think any master at this school ever spoke to me, as expecting a reply – I mean as distinct from asking a question, the answer to which would be right or wrong, they knew which. This method of schooling must have been beneficent, for I did well in the City Junior Scholarship – the eleven plus of those days. My essay on the history of a piece of paper, from the time it was growing in a Scandinavian forest, must have been excellent, for I cannot imagine that the arithmetic was more than moderate, even though I did know my tables.

This was the only time of my life when I produced a magazine. I produced two in succession – *The Pyramid* and *The Sphinx*. The technical peculiarity of these journals was that there was only one copy, and more than one subscriber was surprised to learn that, having paid your tuppence (the price on the cover) you had none the less to give the magazine back to the editor when you had read it. The covers of these journals were painted in watercolours. They showed the Egyptian monuments from which the names of the periodicals derived. My brother and elder sister made some contributions. There were stories and jokes. There was a correspondence corner. I imagine these magazines were well worth tuppence a look, but the subscribers were not numerous. Outside the family I can remember only the Miss Jellies, and I do not know how they came to subscribe. They were, very properly, like jelly, rather wobbly. One of them taught in the Infants' School at this time, though not when I was there, I think. They lived between the railway bridge and the United Methodist Chapel, in a house which had to be approached by steep steps.

Was no day happy then? Is any now?

NOW that I am approaching my birth pangs, I must introduce another scene. This is the shop where my father was established in 1908. During my schooldays, at Greenbank and at Fairfield, I was often employed there – not in the sense of being hired and paid, of course, but in the sense that on Saturday mornings I was expected to help. Helping began usually with sweeping off the front – the pavement in front of the shop – carrying out the rather sumptuous brass sign which said SISSON, polishing it, sweeping the shop inside, dusting, in particular the case of test lenses, and minding the shop in a vague way while my father was messing about in the workshop. The scene of these endeavours changed somewhat during the time I was connected with it. First of all R.P. Sisson was a watchmaker and jeweller, and the sign said "From Coventry", because this extraction was understood to be a recommendation – people should know that it was the centre of the clock trade. During the clock-making period – watch-and clock-repairing was what it meant – there were successively one or two apprentices, but they did not have the application those boys in Coventry had formerly had, and I don't think they got on very well with my father or he with them. Finally they were thought to be more trouble than they were worth. And there was no money in the jewellery trade – I can well imagine it – in the middle 1920s and later. My mother would enquire, at the end of the day, whether my father had had many people in. So my father took to optics, as they were called. I could give a good imitation of a man testing your eyes and, with a suitable consulting room, probably fit you up with a pair of glasses which would suit you tolerably well. I know all about "How far down can you see?" "What about this small print?" "Where is the light in relation to the line?" and so on. I am not sure what you have to look for at the point when you say "Will you look over my left shoulder?" and shine a light in the patient's eye, but I gather that this does not matter unless the patient's eye is diseased. So with luck it would not matter. My father soon found that to get the people on health insurance he had to have qualifications, so he set about getting them. He must have been over fifty when he took his examination and became F.B.O.A. – Fellow of the British Optical Association, no less – because he was forty when I was born. This saved the family from ruin, I suppose; things were pretty bad before that, with everything mortgaged.

I was not enthusiastic about my association with the shop and did not like to be seen sweeping off the front. The best moment of the Saturday morning was when my father decided that I should go to town for him. The fare was usually paid one way; the other I walked. There were two or three places to call at, in the centre of the city. One was the bank, for my father did not want his affairs known to a local branch. So I paid money in and took money out, on a system I did not understand, at a branch of the Midland Bank in Corn Street. And I went to Chard & Gay's, where an old witch swept the wooden stairs. Her head shook and she nodded over her broom. Chard & Gay's were on the first floor of a building in Bridge Street, by Bristol Bridge; they were watch wholesalers and also did repairs for the trade. I could walk to town down Stapleton Road, into Old Market, where the old Pie Powder Court was, or through Newfoundland Road and Milk Street to the Horsefair. Milk Street was the birthplace of Christopher Homm; at least that was the street which came into my mind as I wrote the final chapters.

There was a time when we not only lived from the shop, but over it, in the rooms behind and above it. It was 468, Stapleton Road, the numbering starting from the town end. At this point the main roads form a Y, the leg coming from the town, one arm continuing Stapleton Road till it petered out into the country near Stapleton, the other being Fishponds Road from which the suburbs had made a new spurt, so to speak. At this junction were the main gates of the workhouse, a Primitive Methodist Chapel in the centre of the Y, a bank, the White Swan, the butcher's, the draper's, the grocer's. 468 itself had a newsagent's on one side and on the other a doctor we did not trust. Outside the door was the Eastville tram terminus. In my day it was Mr Hardwell the butcher, with a military moustache; Mr Moxham the draper, in whose shop I learned religious respect; Mr Coneybeare the newsagent, a sluggish man whose wife was older than he was, and wobbly, while he was like a sack of flour. As well as the White Swan, a modern brick building, there was the Black Swan, perhaps a seventeenth century inn. We had nothing to do with the pubs but our fellow tradespeople were consulted on such matters as, When are you going to close for the holiday? In those days my father fetched the right time from the station.

What was 468 like inside? There was a living room and a kitchen behind, a tiny back yard which supplied mud for pies. Upstairs were the bedrooms, and the back window was barred. The place underwent so many metamorphoses in time that it is difficult to remember exactly how it was arranged, when I last slept there, in 1920. But I remember clearly one morning awaking, it cannot have been long before then, and singing, we all three older children sang: "Katie! K-k-k-Katie! You're the only g-g-g-girl that I adore. When the m-m-moon shines, Over the cow-shed, I'll be waiting at the k-k-k-kitchen door." It was because we were going on holiday. We went by train to Blagdon, at the foot of the Mendips, or it may be to Burrington Station, and we were met by the pony and trap from Ellick Farm. It must have been Burrington Station for we went up the Combe, between the bracken and heather-covered moors of Blackdown and the Ham. The gate is at the top of the combe. I saw it a few years ago, it had not changed. A rutted track led below a steep bank to the farmhouse, far back off the road and approached through the farmyard. Pigs wallowed in the mud. There were ducks. In the farmhouse – the date 1689 is chipped above the door – was an old-style kitchen, through which one entered, and a best room, with a red squirrel stuffed in a glass case. At one end of the house was the dairy, at the other the hay-loft. Foxgloves were massed in the hedge that could be seen from the window. It was a beautiful land. I made bows and arrows among the woods and rocks of the demesne. We wandered abroad and picnicked by the Twin Brooks of Blackdown, while my mother made cowslip balls. Or we picnicked on the Ham, and climbed the perilous Long Rock. Or we went further afield to the rabbit warrens and lead mines of Charterhouse, and beyond that to Cheddar. This is a conflation of impressions, for we went to Ellick Farm several times, some of them after we had moved to Heath House. My mother had been born on a farm, at West Kington in Wiltshire; the middle years of her childhood were spent on another farm at Stoke, near Filton; her later years, perhaps from twelve or thirteen, at an old farm called Codrington Court near Mangotsfield, where she was sent because the family at Stoke were too many to feed.

It was at 468, Stapleton Road that I spent the years of the First War, and the two that followed. I remember a Scotch soldier coming to tea, in uniform and bandages. I remember, after the war, the tram conductresses throwing sand at men rioting, ineffectively, at the terminus, returned soldiers wanting their jobs back. It was above this shop that, on the twenty-second of April, nineteen hundred and fourteen, I was born. The place is now the Bristol Rovers Supporters Club.

The child can grow
Only by being blind

IV A Letter from the Present

So, if anything can be concluded from this book, it is that I was born. There remains a gap in the evidence connecting 468 Stapleton Road with the figure shivering on the banks of the Parrett while the television team parleyed with swans who were as wise as they were. How did the author last seen speculating on identity in 1964 arrive at this ambiguous situation?

By living another twenty to twenty-five years. Nobody's years, after the age of fifty, are exactly formative; they cannot help being, one way or another, years of reaping as one has sown. That is no great claim to make, and in one's eighth decade it may be hard to remember when one ever did anything sensible. This is partly a trick of memory, partly no more than facing the sober truth.

However that may be, it is certainly the case that my last years in the Civil Service were hardly creditable, by the standards obtaining in those circles. The relative exhilaration which has left traces on the opening sections of this narrative was without precedent, so far as my career was concerned, and it was also without suite. The world of Whitehall is a world of fashion – inevitably, since governments can move only in a current of opinion – and I am by temperament resistant to fashion. So, instead of being given the promotion I had been promised, I was swept away from my post, where I had too much say in the organization of the Department's business, to one where I could do less harm. There was, after an interval, a modest nominal improvement of status and even of pay, but that would not have been accorded to me had the change not been so designed as to leave me out of sight. Such affronts are rarely agreeable, even to people of more benign temperament than I, and even though they may leave one – as was the case with me – with considerably more leisure than before. The devil finds work for idle hands to do and I set the seal on my disgrace by publishing in the *Spectator* three knowledgeable articles about the management of the Civil Service, which was then reaching a high pitch of folly under the late Sir William (afterwards Lord) Armstrong.

However, I also looked around for literary work more time-consuming than the poems which still popped up from time to time. For the first time in my life I had a contract for a book before it was written. This was *English Poetry 1900-1950*, a subject which had been suggested by David Wright, who had thoughtfully designed it as a task for my eventual retirement. Then, having come across a complete set of the works of Walter Bagehot, I conceived the idea of putting that great Victorian publicist, whose ghost then still stalked in university departments of government, in leading articles, and in the minds of politicians who had perhaps in their time done P.P.E. at Oxford. This project was not unconnected with my by now somewhat jaundiced view of the gentlemen who ran the Civil Service, where Bagehot's type of cleverness was always welcome. But it was, much more, an exercise in a subject which has not left me since my first article in the *New English Weekly*, the theme of "government and polity" which one critic has gone so far as to say has always been my subject, "whether it be couched in verse, literary criticism or discursive prose" – adding, justly, as it seems to me, that "there is no more classical subject than that".

If the acquisition of the collected works was the original stimulus for *The Case of Walter Bagehot*, a further impulsion was given by the chance that, about this time, I bought a house only a few yards from his grave and not many more from his birthplace in the main street of Langport, Somerset. The association with Bagehot had had nothing to do with the purchase of the house, though I discovered, when the book came out and proved to be something other than laudatory, that at least one person suspected that it had. The wife of a neighbour assumed that I had come to Langport with hostile intent. When her husband, a retired general, took her a copy of the book to the hospital where she was temporarily undergoing treatment, she wrote me an indignant, I might say denunciatory letter, drawing my attention to St Paul's injunction to think on whatsoever things are good. These neighbours were a friendly pair and when I next saw the general I apologised for having caused his wife distress at so unsuitable a time. He replied that apologies were unnecessary; his wife's indignation had "brought her to life" and she was quite herself again. There is apparently no end to the usefulness of literature.

The book aroused hostility elsewhere than in Taunton hospital. The *Economist*, which Bagehot edited from 1861, and which might have been expected to give some attention to a critical study of its *grand ancêtre*, declined even to mention the existence of the volume. Alastair Burnet, who was the editor when the book appeared, maintained that the paper "had fulfilled its responsibility in sending the book to a knowledgeable reviewer, and in accepting the reviewer's opinion of it". The reviewer was not named. Norman St John Stevas, the editor of the *Economist*'s own edition of Bagehot (then incomplete) had announced before he saw my book that he did not see why anyone should write a book about Bagehot if he did not admire him. My book was certainly not for hero-worshippers. Not only did it contain damaging material from the *Report of the Bridgwater Bribery Commission*, 1869, but it questioned elements in Bagehot's underlying philosophy which had been accepted with complacency for nearly a hundred years, and which were still echoed.

The book appeared in 1972, which was my last year in the Civil Service. I had made myself so unpopular with my superiors that my post had become untenable. At least, I did not care to hold it, in spite of the income and the comparative leisure it gave me. So I withdrew to Langport as De Gaulle had done to Colombey-les-Deux-Eglises, but with the difference that for me there was no possibility of staging a come-back. My wife and I had some time before left the house in Sevenoaks for a flat in Paddington, and we already spent our weekends in Langport. So the move to Somerset was merely a matter of going home for good. For the first time since my student days my time was my own. In the first few weeks I could not altogether escape from that sense of entering a gulf of vacuity which is often felt by people who leave great organizations after long years. Then we went to Provence. The legendary world sighted for a moment at Avignon, fifteen years before, was there to wander in. We had not brought a car – that destroyer of distances which, as of its own volition, flashes past so much one would wish to see. I have often been back to Provence since, usually in one of those destructive but indispensable vehicles, but nothing can equal the pleasure of arrivals on foot or in long-awaited local buses. We were mercifully out of season. The amphi-theatre at Arles, on my first sight of it, was coloured only by the red or blue plastic macs of small local children climbing down from the upper tiers to join in a *farandole*, while a man in old Provençal costume played the pipe and drum. Conventional old hat, no doubt, to the familiars, but for the moment I felt as Sir Philip Sidney did when he heard the ballad of Chevy-Chase.

We went to Martigues, and there when I least expected it there were before my eyes the words "Chemin de Paradis". They invoked overpoweringly the presence of Charles Maurras, whose works I had not opened for many years, and whose name, I am sometimes told, is not to be mentioned in polite society because of the implication of the Vichy government in Nazi excesses. Such thoughts did not enter my mind then. For me Maurras was a pre-war figure, warning as he had done for half a century of the dangers of a German onslaught. I thought of him, at that moment, as he was in his old age during the Second World War, a frail figure on the terrace of the Chemin de Paradis, refusing even to see the German officer who saluted him. As I leaned over the gate, the old gardener beckoned to me: my sleep in Marseilles that night was interrupted by the poem in which I recounted this meeting. But the poem was, as is usually the case, less the celebration of an incident than the establishment of a new perspective. I was seeing the past, and my new situation in Somerset, in the almost blinding light of the classical south.

"Martigues" was published in the first volume of mine which appeared from the Carcanet Press. My association with that institution had begun when I had collected enough material to be thinking of another slim volume to follow *Metamorphoses*. Several years before – in fact about the time when *On the Lookout* begins – there had been an extraordinary interlude with Methuens. Walter Michel, the author of an authoritative book on the paintings of Wyndham Lewis, had mentioned my name to Alan White, who was then the Chairman. Walter and Peg had been my first American readers, put on to my work by C.J. Fox, the Canadian critic and journalist. The Michels had "happened to tell him", White said when he wrote to me out of the blue, that I had more than one unpublished manuscript; Methuens "would be very happy to consider these books". And so it was that in 1965 the dam burst, so to speak, and three volumes poured out of the presses – the novel *Christopher Homm*, a volume of poems, *Numbers*, and a volume of critical essays, *Art & Action*. It cannot be said that this major publishing event attracted the attention it might have done; still, it set me up as never before. *Metamorphoses* was my second volume of poems from Methuen; it appeared in 1968. Soon afterwards, White retired and Methuens for the time being more or less gave up poetry. They also gave up me – temporarily, it must be said, for one of my books has since been published by them in paperback. So, being at this time in touch with Faber & Faber, who were publishing *The Case of Walter Bagehot*, I asked Peter du Sautoy, without sending him a TS, whether he would be interested in a volume of poems. I cannot recall ever having sent a volume of poems to that establishment, but when the reply came it said, with a touch of *hubris*, I thought, from Eliot's old firm, that "if they had been wrong about me in the first place, it was too late now". While I was reflecting on the next step a letter arrived from Robert Nye, whom I had never met, but who had done an excellent review of the Bagehot book in *The Scotsman*. He suggested that, if I wanted to publish another volume of poems, I should get in touch with Carcanet Press which was beginning to stretch its muscles. So I sent the typescript. They replied that they would do a collection which would print the new poems and at the same time reprint the volumes previously published. This is how *In the Trojan Ditch: Collected Poems and Selected Translations*, came into being.

By the time I got back from my first visit to Provence I began to see the possibility of using my new-found leisure for the kind of writing which interested me most – which was really no more than a continuation, more at large and in more sybaritic circumstances, of the discipline which had been forced on me all my life by the necessity of earning my living by other means. I had not written what any publisher dictated then and I was not going to start now.

I certainly had no programme, nor the beginnings of one. I should like to have written a book about Swift, an observer of politics and society beside whom Bagehot looks merely silly, but after some messing about with the subject I decided that it was one which only someone who knew much more than I did about the history of the period could treat at any length. And anyway, having escaped the *corvées* of the office, with all that they involved in the way of provisional material, did I want to go haring after a mass of names and dates and all the detritus of affairs? I did not. It may be that, if I had had a natural taste for such material, I should have been a better civil servant than I was; certainly I should have been a more enthusiastic one. The odd thing was to be able to follow my natural turn of mind at last. I relaxed and did so. A few years before I had done my translations of Catullus in half-hours, typically reading some lines before going to sleep at night and turning these into English verse next day as I drank my early morning tea. Apart from a few hours at weekends, that is all the time there was for such things. I had originally translated a poem here and there, for diversion and out of a vague feeling that my own poems needed a fresh technical direction: to get as close as one can to a foreign original one has to attempt an English version. I showed my first exercises to David Wright – as I have explained, my diagnostic machine, so far as verse is concerned. He properly registered some uneasinesses, which helped as usual, but to my astonishment he suggested that I should translate the whole of my author. Such work is addictive and when I got over my surprise I had no difficulty in complying. If the direct results are to be found in *Catullus* (1966), indirect results are to be found in my 1968 volume and beyond. So by natural sequence, in Langport, with more time to myself, I turned back to the Latin poets.

Translation is the perfect non-theoretical activity. It is as practical as gardening or as writing a poem. Most of my versions have been of poets with whom I had an old acquaintance, going back fifty years or more, so I have been at once making something new and drawing on something old. One cannot translate any poem one likes: the possibilities are defined by one's own development as a poet. An incautious reviewer asserted recently that I believed myself to have *composed* three plays of Racine, "together with the works of Virgil and Dante". Well, no. What the modest translator will find, however, is that he may wilfully attempt some work he has been reading with pleasure, only to find that the tones and rhythms which are available to him are not such as to enable him to re-tell the matter of the original in an unforced and natural manner. The poet-translator has a different objective from someone who aims merely at assisting the reader with a foreign language. His own sense of his own language and of its rhythms is an impediment. This is the final point of control, once the meaning has become as clear as it is going to be in the translator's mind, and he is on the point of finding his own English words. As I have put it elsewhere, one tries to give way before the text, but acknowledges that one can never do so completely. The translator's drive is towards this extinction. When I did my *Reading of Virgil's Eclogues*, in the early 1960s, I recognized that the elaboration of the Latin text was far beyond what I could euphoniously render; my solution was boldly to leave aside words I could not digest into my own verse. The result is something which might be said to take account of the shape of each eclogue, even of each sentence – a version which is clearly less than the full matter of the original but translated as much as I could of my delight in it. In my version of the *Aeneid*, some twenty years later, little or nothing is left unaccounted for. Between the two comes the huge exercise on Dante, a master of lucidity in the formative style of the Italian language. It is not that the translator imagines that he has composed all these originals, as my rather bumptious reviewer alleged, but that he has learned from them something about the handling of his own language.

This on the whole rather little understood subject is explored further in "The Poet & the Translator", which is the title I gave in 1984 to the Sixteenth Jackson Knight Memorial Lecture at the University of Exeter – one of my rare intrusions into the academic world. My engagement with Virgil is not the only one which has involved more than one attempt. I had tried my hand at some lines of Lucretius in the 1960s, only to give them up as hopeless. Then one day when I was enjoying my new-found liberty in Provence, I found myself at Avignon with nothing to read. I searched hopelessly in the bookshops, as one does, and finally dug out of a dark corner a copy of the *De Rerum Natura* with a French prose version *en face*. Going back in the bus to Tarascon, where I was staying, the first lines of the poem rose to the surface in English, and from that moment I knew that I could go on. A good part of the poem was, as it happened, done a few months later further east in Provence, in the Var, where we were staying in a house lent by friends, looking after their cats while they were in England. So the moment of decision to undertake a version comes, not when it is sought but when it does come, by some confluence of old memories of the original with the development of one's own writing of verse. The case of Dante was not dissimilar. In this case it was not a bookshop and a bus but my editor who provided the occasion. Sitting in the back of my car, as I drove him away from Taunton station in the direction of Langport, he leaned forward and said: "I've thought of something for you to do. Translate *The Divine Comedy*." My reply, over my shoulder, was rude and peremptory. But he knew he was stirring an old pot. I had been approaching my subject, intermittently, for forty-five years at least.

Moreover, one or two of my poems then fairly recent had contained lines which could not have been written by someone who had forgotten Dante. Most significantly, in *In Insula Avalonia*, I had found myself using an unrhymed tercet which, at a great distance, reproduced some of the characteristics of Dante's form. Whatever my weaknesses, I can boast that I am not the man to be bullied by a publisher, even the most *sympathique*, and I put the idea out of my mind. But it came back. I found myself opening my volume of the *Inferno* – the same I had carried around in my kitbag – and reading again words which this time transformed themselves into English verse.

If the finding of something one can translate is an incontrovertible moment one cannot freely choose, the translation of a long poem is *work*, of a rather voluptuous kind. One lives for days and weeks, months and even years, with an author one has never properly had time for before, however long the acquaintance. And work, of course, was what I needed, having contracted that vicious habit so profoundly that it had become incurable. For the same reason there was some reviewing, which is more closely related to the office work to which I had been accustomed. It can naturally give one none of the stimulus which comes from labouring with other people, and finding solutions to practical problems through a maze of personal relationships, usually more or less friendly and occasionally more or less hostile. In the kind of reviewing I did there was little pressure of time-tables – none certainly by the standards of day-to-day and hour-to-hour urgency which are to be encountered in ordinary affairs. But at least I had thrown at me books I should never have read but for the promise of payment – a slight burden compared with the stream of files my secretary had for years dumped on my desk. Still, the occupation reminded me of the existence of a world in which one could not always choose one's reading matter, and sent me back with fresh pleasure to the poet who was so to speak flowing through me. For a few years I became a church-warden again – a diminutive world of affairs which has its own complications. I had other local dealings which gave me some fleeting *aperçus* of the economic life of the countryside, which was in my blood rather than in my experience, and so enabled me to continue my lifelong study of my own ineptitude.

What I did not pursue, except in the most off-hand way, was the world of the poetry trade, now open to me as a "writer" and you might say "an established poet" instead of a mere civil servant. In what was almost my initiation, I arrived in Leicester with a group of well-briefed poets, myself not having given a thought to what I should read. Naturally it did not take me long to correct this slackness, and to manufacture the bits of nonchalant chat expected of a creative writer: no one wants to listen to poems all the time, and who can blame an audience for that? I quickly learned to distinguish between those audiences, largely middle-aged, or geriatric cases like myself, who stoically go to "poetry readings" whatever the fare, and those which contain a kernel of people who have read something of the author and, understandably, want to know what he sounds like. It must be said that the business of poetry readings is overdone.

Suppose there are not two or three hundred poets whose work is worth reading? Suppose that, as in all previous generations, there is only a handful of real poets? The real objection to the system is that it rests on the assumption that a new age has dawned – I suppose about 1950 – and that the standard of human equipment now includes a mechanism which will produce poems at the drop of a hat. It is probably a human right. The process begins at a very early age. A child has only to scratch out a few words supposed to embody some "experience" for the claim to be made on his behalf that he has written a poem; the only condition is that the lines must not all reach the right-hand margin. The idea that he should first learn to construct a simple grammatical sentence is repugnant to all decent people; that he should learn to count syllables or to rhyme, let alone try his hand at some difficult form such as the sonnet, is probably a reactionary demand. Are only educated people to write poems? The answer, alas, is Yes, though that leaves a wide range of possibilities as to the education required. But the art of verse has to be learned, as it always has been, by ear of course, and the subject has been rendered more rather than less difficult in a world for ever noisy with millions of approximate words uttered for commercial purposes and rated according to the number of people who listen to them.

For the author of this book, however, the English language has been important, from whenever in or after 1914 it first became of interest to him to the moment when he is approaching more or less closely to the time when it will be of interest only to others. The civil servant's words are carefully chosen, so that the resultant meanings can be shown to correspond to something socially recognized as a fact, according to the canons of truth and falsity obtaining in his time and place. That is a discipline and it is one of the uses of language which no one is entitled to make light of in the name of art or on any other pretext. If that use fails, great corruptions follow. The poet, on the other hand, does not choose his meanings: they are given, as something involuntarily collected in himself. My meanings are those of the life you have now read a little about; they represent that little and all the rest besides, some of it clear to the author but most, no doubt, not. Yet the part in the words that is his own is small in relation to that of the language to which he has made his tiny modification. The primary duty of us all is clarity, so far as the subject-matter allows, and in this we all have a common interest. The notion, now so often promulgated, that one way of saying things is as good as another, is a help on the way to chaos and to nowhere else. The proprieties are not those of a social class, and they operate among the residual traces of dialect as elsewhere, as anyone will know who has listened to the gradual deterioration of country speech over half a century.

My mother, born in 1875 in what was then a remote Wiltshire village, must have been brought up among a language far less flawed than what can be heard anywhere in this country now. The language she spoke when I knew her was certainly nothing which could be called dialect. There was the occasional local word or an old phrase you would not hear now, the faint intonation and marked rhythms of west country speech, and what, looking back, I recognize as an organic structure not of her making but made by those centuries of the spoken word which preceded the intrusion of the omnipresent printed word and, finally, of radio and television. Those who now talk of "an aural culture" are referring, usually, to these last two sources, the language of which derives less from speech than from modes of the written word debased for commercial and institutional purposes of which the aims are not clarity but popularity. It is the end at once of art and of common sense.

I am glad that the bulk of this book was written long ago, for I should not want to write it now. A septuagenarian may be allowed regrets, but they are no more to the point than the hopes of earlier years. One can hardly do better than to turn to the visible world, and there I am fortunate. Before my window the fields stretch away to the Dorset hills; the willows, no longer pollarded, have not all been removed. The river flows or overflows among them, according to the season. What it all means, God knows.

The minutes have gone by, the hours, the days,
The years have counted themselves up, and now
That little piece of time, a life, is proud
To show itself complete: "fini", it says.
Yet I who speak for it so many ways
Cannot say this: the when, the where, the how
Must be determined first, and who knows
Less well than I what may be the delays?
To be on the outside and yet to speak
Is not a thing the mind of man can compass,
Yet inside I am inside something else
Than the completed life and cannot break
The circle of it to see it as it is
Even now, at the end even less.